THERE'S ONLY ONE STEVIE BACON

MY LIFE WATCHING WEST HAM THROUGH A CAMERA LENS

STEVE BACON WITH KIRK BLOWS

Biteback Publishing

First published in Great Britain in 2012 by
Biteback Publishing Ltd
Westminster Tower
3 Albert Embankment
London SE1 7SP

ISBN 978-1-84954-331-6

10 9 8 7 6 5 4 3 2 1

A CIP catalogue record for this book is available from the
British Library.

Set in Chronicle and Franchise

Printed and bound in Great Britain by
CPI Group (UK) Ltd, Croydon CR0 4YY

This book is dedicated to my family. To my late parents, Thomas and Eileen, my sister Diane, brothers Rod and Martin, plus the Bacon, Burton and Duchars families.

ACKNOWLEDGEMENTS

I would like to acknowledge the people who have helped me throughout my photographic career, from those very early days to the present.

To Arthur Edwards, for giving me my first real break in the business, and to Bill Storey, his partner in Tower Hamlets Studios. To the fellow snappers on the touchline way back then, such as the Frescos – Monty, Monte and Michael – Lawrence Lustig, Peter Jay, Kent Gavin, Mike Maloney, Norman Quick, Jack Kay, Bob Stiggins, Reg Lancaster, Frank Haggis and Tony Furby.

In more recent years, to 'Arfa' Griffiths and Avril Husband who stepped in when I was taken ill. Also Richard Pelham, Steve Lindsell, Alan Walter, Stuart Robinson, Nicky Hayes, Tom Hevezi and Rob Newell – with apologies to anyone I may have overlooked.

Several journalists have provided great company on my travels: Trevor Smith, Ken Dyer, Michael Hart, Kevin Moseley, Peter Lorenzo, Vic Railton, Ken Montgomery, Colin Benson, Jack and John Helliar, Tony McDonald, Steve Blowers, Peter Stewart and, of course, my collaborator Kirk Blows.

To the many West Ham people who have helped me in my

career, starting with John Lyall, of course, who was instru-
mental in my becoming club photographer back in 1980.

To the managers who have allowed me my continued close
connection with the club: Billy Bonds, Harry Redknapp,
Lou Macari, Glenn Roeder, Sir Trevor Brooking and Alan
Curbishley. Not to mention the former chairmen and direc-
tors, including Martin Cearns, Peter Storrie and Terry
Brown, plus former secretaries Eddie Chapman, Peter
Barnes and Tom Finn.

To my many friends on the backroom staff: Ronnie Boyce,
Mick McGiven, Tony Carr, Mervyn Day, Rob Jenkins, Dave
Gladstone, Allan Young, Jimmy Frith, Roger Morgan, Tim
De'Ath, Pete Williams, Shirley Austin, Anita Taylor and
Sean Howlett. And of course my great buddies Eddie Gillam,
John Green and Ges Steinbergs, who with me make up the
Four Amigos.

I must also mention some of the great friends I have made
among the players over the years: Paul Brush, Ray Stewart,
Alvin Martin, Phil Parkes, Alan Devonshire, Geoff Pike,
Paul Allen, David Cross, Alan Taylor, Keith Robson, Frank
Lampard Sr, Bryan 'Pop' Robson, Brian Dear, Pat Holland,
Tony Gale, Tony Cottee, Frank McAvennie ... the list is really
too long to mention everyone by name, but they have all
become firm friends.

Talking of which, some special friendships have been
formed with club employees such as Caron Pettit, who has
worked on match days at Upton Park for almost as many
years as me (but not quite!), Brian Blower, Sue Page, Kim
Montague, Adrienne and Gary Williams, Tony Bellchambers,
Debbie Laver and many more members of the commercial
department.

I've met thousands of great Hammers fans during my

time with the club, but I'd like to mention just a few who have become good friends. I'll start by name-dropping Ray Winstone, who I have known since his boxing days at Repton Boxing Club, but also Dan Jarvis, who is about as fanatical about our team as it's possible to be, and Steve Roof – just as fanatical but perhaps a little less scary than 'Jarvo'.

Finally, at this very late stage of my life, I have found myself a good, West Ham-supporting girlfriend, Natasha Weldon, so I think she deserves a special mention for taking me on!

CONTENTS

FOREWORD
SIR TREVOR BROOKING CBE

The West Ham United supporters used to chant 'There's only one Stevie Bacon', and I can certainly endorse the view that he is indeed a unique individual, one whose many qualities as a person and photographer have ensured a longevity that has established his face as an integral part of the club over the last thirty-five years or so.

The popularity of football, as England's national game, has mushroomed incredibly since the mid-1970s, but even in those days it was important for somebody in Steve's position to win the trust of a club's management and players. Footballers didn't quite enjoy the celebrity and financial status that they do now, but there could still be a slight suspicion of outsiders who were allowed access behind the scenes. However, that was never the case with Steve Bacon.

There was a great spirit and sense of camaraderie in the West Ham camp under manager John Lyall when I was playing, and Steve was welcomed into the fold without any concerns because he was a friendly, affable character who immediately won our confidence. He joined us on the team bus to away games, stayed overnight with us in hotels, flew with us on our trips abroad and was always considered part of our small entourage. And when new players arrived at Upton Park in later years they immediately had faith in Steve because he was such an established figure at the club.

As the official club photographer, Steve had a way of working with players, encouraging and cajoling them rather than being pushy or dictatorial. He always seemed sensitive to the wishes of individuals and made them feel comfortable in his presence.

It's true to say that Steve was a larger-than-life character and the fact that he was a big lad certainly gave some of the players – who enjoyed a bit of friendly mickey-taking if given half a chance – the opportunity to wind him up. But Steve took all the banter very well and it all helped to cement his unique status. He was a one-off figure and, as he lumped his equipment around at games, you couldn't help but notice him. Once you'd met Steve you couldn't fail to recognise or remember him, and he became a face that everybody associated with West Ham United.

The club enjoyed a reputation for having a friendly, family-orientated atmosphere and even fans of other clubs seemed to look upon us as their second-favourite team because of the entertaining style in which we played, something developed under the management of Ron Greenwood and John Lyall. The Hammers are renowned for cultivating their own players through their youth academy, but there's also a great unpredictability about the club. It's incredible how its fortunes seem to fluctuate and you simply couldn't make up some of the things that have happened over the years.

However, the fans remain as ardent and loyal as any you will find and they have stuck with the club throughout the highs and lows over the past few decades. The fact that West Ham continued to attract gates in excess of 30,000 in the

2011/12 season while in the Championship is evidence of the faith of their supporters. Once the club is in your blood it remains there forever and that's the case for both Steve and me, who will always be associated with the Hammers come what may.

There has been a lot of change at Upton Park over the years – as there has been in football as a whole – but Steve has remained a constant feature, even though he is a much 'trimmer' figure nowadays than he was originally! People such as him have played a role in what has made West Ham so strong, and whenever former players returned to Upton Park in some capacity they would always make sure they said hello to Steve because he was part of the club's infrastructure.

The quality of his work is first and foremost, but for Steve to have remained in a potentially sensitive position within the media at one club for such an extensive period of time is the greatest testimony to how well he has conducted himself throughout the years. I think it's an incredible story.

INTRODUCTION

West Ham are preparing to play an away game at Queens Park Rangers and I'm in one of the dressing rooms at Loftus Road helping my good friend Eddie Gillam lay out the kit for the players, when Billy Bonds MBE – the man who made a club-record 793 appearances for the Hammers over a 21-year period, captained them in two magical FA Cup triumphs and later guided the club to two promotions as manager – just happens to spot me from the corridor outside. Bonzo, at this particular point in time, has a coaching role at QPR and is showing some youngsters around the west London club. 'Boys,' he says, as he begins to do the honours, 'this man is a legend at West Ham.'

It was, of course, an outrageous thing for him to say, especially as Billy is a true hero for Hammers supporters and the player I idolised most during the 1970s and 1980s. I couldn't help but laugh, although I must admit his words did leave me feeling a little chuffed. And hey, if that's how Billy (or anybody else, for that matter) wants to think of me, I'm certainly not going to argue. He's taller than me, for a start.

I mention this story not to blow my own trumpet – I haven't got enough energy to blow anything at my age. In all seriousness, I think what Bonzo was trying to convey to those kids was that I'm West Ham through and through. I've been around for quite a while and so enjoy a reasonably high profile at Upton Park – the crowd have even sung my name. While the chant of 'There's only one Stevie Bacon' might have caused me some embarrassment from time to time, it has also – if I'm honest – secretly given me a little bit of pleasure. And if that constitutes a 'legend' in Billy Bonds's eyes, then so be it.

It's often been said that West Ham United represents a real-life East End soap opera, and when I reflect on my experiences with the club over the past thirty-five years or so I certainly agree. In fact, it's not an overstatement to suggest that fiction writers would struggle to invent some of the things I've seen – the events with which the supporters are already familiar as well as some of the more personal stories that I can tell having developed relationships with so many managers and players since becoming the club's official photographer in 1980.

Indeed, friends have been telling me for many years that I should write a book about the special insight I've enjoyed behind the scenes at Upton Park, both as a photographer and unofficial assistant to kit manager Eddie. I consider this to be my unique story, based on the people I've known – mostly good but some not so – and the things I've done, seen and heard. It also reflects the turbulent adventures of the Hammers during the several dramatic decades I have spent working as a part of the backroom team. West Ham through my eyes rather than my camera lens, if you like.

I have worked for the club under ten permanent managers – John Lyall, Lou Macari, Billy Bonds, Harry Redknapp, Glenn Roeder, Alan Pardew, Alan Curbishley, Gianfranco Zola, Avram Grant and Sam Allardyce (which isn't bad when you consider the club has only employed fourteen in their entire history). Among these were managers who commanded respect in the dressing room and others who struggled to make their mark; men I liked and men I didn't. They include the man who played a key role in influencing the direction of my life and, conversely, the one who failed to mutter a single word in my direction during his entire tenure at Upton Park; the many who took me into their confidence and the one who tried to shut me out.

Similarly, I've established close relationships and highly valued friendships with many players over the years, as well as encountering others who would never make my Christmas card list. There have been players who encouraged team spirit and others who stirred up trouble; some I considered to be good signings and some I felt were rather dodgy; those with great intelligence and those with very little; players who integrated with each other and players who kept themselves to themselves; some who made me laugh and others who nearly reduced me to tears.

And meanwhile, upstairs in the corridors of power, there were directors I trusted and ones I didn't, appointments I questioned and men who I believe exerted either positive or negative influences on the club over the years.

Together, they represent an unforgettable group of contrasting characters that has shaped my time at the club. The identities of all will be revealed...

They say that a picture is worth a thousand words – and as a photographer I'm hardly likely to dispute that – but the many thousands of words contained in this book represent what could never be photographed: my personal views on the events of the last four decades.

There has been triumph and trauma, comedy and chaos,

but while football has provided a dramatic backdrop, I like to think that this story is really about the people, and I consider myself extremely fortunate to have shared this journey with them.

Come on you Irons!

Steve Bacon, May 2012

CHAPTER 1

'YOU AND I HAVE SEEN THE BEST OF FOOTBALL'

I t's not the worst way to kick off your career as West Ham
United's official club photographer: making sure that the
FA Cup – in all its gleaming glory – is perfectly positioned
as the squad proudly smiles for the camera. It's August 1980
and the Hammers have just won the prestigious trophy for
the second time in five years. For manager John Lyall and
senior players such as Trevor Brooking, Billy Bonds, Frank
Lampard and Pat Holland, I guess it's like welcoming back an
old friend to the training ground in Chadwell Heath. Little
did I realise then that this would be the last time that West
Ham would get their hands on the cup for the next thirty
years or so.

If I'm honest, I was a little nervous at that first team photo-
shoot – though I had already formed good relationships with
most of the players through covering West Ham games for
the local *Recorder* group of newspapers for the previous four
years – and even invited my brother Martin along for moral
support. I wasn't using my own equipment and instead
borrowed a large-format camera for the day as programme
editor and club historian Jack Helliar had insisted on me
producing five-inch by four-inch colour transparencies

from the session. But thankfully I produced the goods. Taking the annual team photo at the start of every season is a responsibility I've felt privileged to enjoy right up to the current day, even if I haven't had to worry about the centralisation of silverware on many occasions!

It was John Lyall who approached me at the close of the season in 1980, following that famous victory against Arsenal at Wembley, and asked if I would be interested in taking the official team photograph. In recent years the club had been employing a freelancer, brought in after an open press day went horribly wrong when some photographers got the players to hurdle the benches – or something equally silly – and one of them suffered an injury. Unsurprisingly, Ron Greenwood, the manager at that time, decided to put a stop to that and insisted on a single photographer taking the shot. John asked me if there was any particular reason why I couldn't do it. He said it seemed a bit pointless getting somebody else to come in when I knew all the lads and got on really well with them. '*Of course* I can do it,' I insisted, wondering why he would have any doubts. 'I'd love to.' And that's how I became the West Ham United club photographer.

Actually, there's a little more to it than that, if you take into account the story of my life up until that point. It was the culmination of a 28-year journey that began when I was born in Plaistow, east London, at the same hospital as West Ham defender Paul Brush (who by coincidence would become one of my closest friends in the late 1970s and early 1980s). I grew up in Manor Park and went to Essex Road infants and junior schools, passed my eleven-plus and moved up to East Ham Grammar School for Boys.

It was while I was there that I started taking an interest in photography. The school had a photographic society, which was attended by about four members and had a reputation for being a bit geeky, but my enthusiasm for the subject began there. Fortunately we had a cellar at home, which I was able to make into a darkroom. We had no running water in there so I had to take down trays of water and that's where I started developing my own pictures in my early teenage years.

My family, including my father Tom, who was a Billingsgate fish porter, and mother Eileen, were West Ham fans, but as a youngster I was more interested in speedway than football, which might be considered a sinful confession to some people. In 1964, at the age of twelve, I'd started to visit West Ham Speedway when it was re-launched at Custom House. Having said that, I did go to the Boleyn Ground once as a five-year-old when the parents of my friend next door, whose name was Martin Waple, took us to a game. I've got no idea who the opposition was, but West Ham were in the old Second Division and the only thing I remember from the day is that we had lemonade and crisps, which obviously made some kind of impression on me. In fact, it still irritates my brother Martin, who is a huge West Ham fan, that I saw them play before he did.

I left school with three O-levels and the hope of landing a job in photography, but I couldn't find anything so instead I went into the civil service. I worked in telephone accounts for the General Post Office in Oxford Street but I only lasted about four months because it was just the same old routine every day and it drove me barmy. I bought the *Evening Standard* every night and eventually found a full-time position in the photographic department of a company called Fuller & Watts, which was associated with the registration of trademarks and copyright.

I was a mere junior but it gave me a good grounding in darkroom and studio work, even though it wasn't necessarily the sort of photography I wanted to do. One of the products we worked on was the new Vosene shampoo bottle – they called it the drip bottle because of its shape – which we had to photograph from every possible angle to reveal its full perspective. Another memorable project was the modern-style shop mannequins, which were complete, life-like bodies rather than the faceless torsos of old. So yes, I have taken pictures of a few dummies in my time!

The first of several useful coincidences occurred when I discovered that there was a guy in another department at Fuller & Watts who also worked on the starting gate at West Ham Speedway. And again, by pure coincidence, he had a friend who ran a small speedway magazine, a real one-man-band kind of thing. I expressed an interest and was asked if I'd like to take some photographs for him; of course, I said I'd love to, especially if it got me onto the centre circle and close to the action. I thought it was a great opportunity.

And so I started working at West Ham Speedway on Tuesday evenings, where I happened to meet a couple of photographers who were running an agency under the name of Tower Hamlets Studios. One of them was a guy called Bill Storey and his colleague was Arthur Edwards. Ironically, they both hated speedway with a passion, and one day Arthur asked me if I covered every meeting there. I told him I loved the sport. 'Could you do it for us?' he said. 'We'll pay you a few quid because we hate coming here and that would be great for us.' Not quite believing my luck, I started covering the speedway for their agency, which supplied pictures to a lot of the local papers, such as the *East London Advertiser*, the *Stratford Express* and the *Recorder* titles. It was great fun, all about getting that first shot as the four bikes came out of the grid equally spaced and vied for position on the first turn.

It was around this time that I became friends with Len Herbert, who was working as a mechanic for a young up-and-coming speedway rider called Roger Johns. Roger was only sixteen or seventeen years of age and didn't have a driving licence so Len was driving Roger to races, but he was finding the routine a bit of a struggle and I was happy to suggest that I take over. I therefore found myself teamed up with Roger, with a rack on the back of my old Ford Consul Classic that we could hang the bike on when we drove to meetings. Roger rode for Eastbourne and their home fixtures were on Sunday, so I'd stay at his place in Worcester Park on Saturday and we'd drive down to Eastbourne the following day. And it was while I was driving for Roger that yet another happy coincidence occurred – I met a wannabe rider called Shane Hearty, who wasn't having much success.

Shane was starting a new venture importing Bell Helmets from California to sell in the United Kingdom, as well as supplying various speedway spares and accessories. As I was travelling the country with Roger I was in an ideal position to help him. It was a chance to get more involved in speedway and I was a little frustrated at Fuller & Watts, so I went to work for Shane, first with his mail-order business at his home in Sydenham in south-east London and then behind the counter when he opened a shop in Shortlands near Bromley in Kent.

The year was 1973, glam rock was all the rage and my ties and flares were getting wider. In fact, it was the year of Paul McCartney's *Red Rose Speedway* album and I was soon sprouting Wings myself (I know, a terrible line) when a good friend called George Barclay – a former West Ham speedway rider – offered me an opportunity I couldn't resist. George owned a grocery shop in Plaistow and also had a garage out the back. He told me that his wife Sheila could use some help in the shop in the mornings and then I could work in the garage in the afternoons. But I'd also have the freedom to accept any photographic work that came my way, which was fantastic news because it was getting to the point where Arthur Edwards was asking if I'd be interested in covering a few non-speedway activities for him. So that became the routine; I'd spend a few hours operating the bacon slicer and serving the old dears, before going into the garage and helping George on the cars. I would also drive his oldest son Terry to Sunderland for Friday night speedway meetings – and yes, that was a heck of a drive to undertake on a weekly basis.

Now that I had greater freedom to take on extra photographic jobs, Arthur asked me if I was interested in working at football matches. I said I'd give it a go and started shooting games at East Ham United, Clapton, Ilford and other local non-league clubs, before moving up a level to cover the likes of Orient and Millwall. I never got anywhere near West Ham in those days because Arthur was a big fan and would always try to cover their games himself. But it quickly got to the stage where I could earn a living purely from the photographic jobs that Arthur was giving me. He was doing a lot of shifts for *The Sun* at that time and was fairly keen to secure a staff job on the newspaper, so he was putting all his efforts into that and I was getting more and more local work.

In the early part of 1975 Arthur finally succeeded in landing himself a full-time position with *The Sun* – where he would eventually become their royal photographer – and since Bill Storey had already left the partnership to work for the *Newham Recorder*, I inherited all of their agency work.

And so I started visiting West Ham on a fortnightly basis, while also covering Orient's home games, and the seeds of what would be a lifetime commitment were sown.

As a mere freelancer, I was unable to obtain a photographer's pass for the 1975 FA Cup final, although I did succeed in buying a regular ticket – in the Fulham end, of all places. I kept my West Ham scarf in my pocket until just before kick-off but put it on when the match started and, needless to say, got some very funny looks. I enjoyed some 'friendly' banter with the Fulham fans that day – not least when Alan Taylor scored twice in five minutes during the second half and ensured the trophy returned to the Boleyn Ground for the first time since 1964. Believe it or not, it was the last time that an all-English side won the FA Cup, a record that is likely to live on forever.

The following season West Ham reached the final of the European Cup Winners' Cup and thankfully this time I managed to secure accreditation for the big game against Anderlecht at the Heysel Stadium in Brussels. I was doing a lot of freelance work on *Ford News* at the time for a guy called Dave Pringle and they were running a staff trip to the final, so I was invited to join them on the basis that I supplied the title with photos. It was a great experience to work at that game, even though we were beaten 4-2 (with future West Ham midfielder François Van Der Elst scoring twice).

Not long afterwards the *Recorder* group parted company with their freelance sports photographer, Keith Gilbert, and they asked me if I'd like to cover West Ham every week, home and away. I initially said no because I was very busy at that time and thought it might be detrimental to my other work. However, I put some further thought into the matter and eventually changed my mind – and it's probably the best

decision I've ever made, because that's when my association with West Ham really began in earnest. If I'd not taken
the *Recorder* position I would not have developed – if you'll
excuse the photographic pun – the relationship with manager
John Lyall and the players that resulted in my appointment
as the club photographer. In short, my life from that point
onwards would have been very different.

Trevor Smith was the group sports editor at the *Recorder*
at that time and I started to accompany him down to the
West Ham training ground on Fridays for lunch. We would
sit and eat with John and his coaching staff – namely Ronnie
Boyce and Mick McGiven – and gradually I started to get to
know them all. Trevor also used to get invited up to John's
office in the old West Stand after home games along with a
bunch of other journalists, and I slowly became accepted as
part of the group.

John would generally be busy for a while after games,
but we used to go upstairs and wait for him in his tight little
office. You had to be quick to get a seat. There'd be about half
a dozen people – established writers such as Peter Lorenzo,
Reg Drury, Vic Railton, Ken Montgomery, Kevin Moseley
and Ken Dyer – but it was a fairly select group. John would
eventually turn up and inevitably we'd chat about the game, if
there'd been any major incidents or anything controversial.
It was all very informal and it was accepted that everything
said was off the record. Totally.

Much of the talk would be about football, obviously, but
we'd regularly get on to other subjects and we discussed all
sorts of things. For example, John had two very good friends
in the Flying Squad of the Metropolitan Police, so quite often
we'd chat about a case or a story that had been in the papers
where John might have a little bit of inside knowledge. But

in general we'd talk about anything and just put the world to rights.

There was one particular bloke – an FA coach or something – who used to hang around at these chats and just wanted to ingratiate himself to everybody. John being John, however, would put up with him. The guy would always be saying, 'Can I get anything for you, John? Does anyone want another drink?' John had a drinks cabinet in his office and his tipple was Harveys Bristol Cream, of which I tended to have a drop as well, so I used to go home with a red face. Not that I was alone. One of the group used to occasionally drink a bit too much and John would confiscate his car keys and arrange for someone to take him home to make sure he didn't drive while under the influence.

At some point in the evening, the FA man would generally offer to go and get the late papers. That would often be the signal for Vic Railton to say, 'I'm off now, boys.' That's because he knew John wouldn't appreciate his report. Sometimes you'd see Vic in the tunnel after the final whistle and he'd say, 'I'm not coming up tonight, not after what I've written!'

I was still relatively young and in the honeymoon period of getting to know these people, so I tended to just sit and listen more than anything. If the conversation moved on to a topic about which I felt I had something to say I'd obviously contribute, but generally I was just so captivated by being there. John Lyall was always fascinating company.

There was an awards lunch at the club in the early 1980s and former Tottenham Hotspur manager Bill Nicholson was a guest. I was sitting with John, chief scout Eddie Baily and Mr Nicholson, of whom I was in total awe even though he was a Spurs man. And it was amazing listening to these people who had so much knowledge about football – a sport

I knew little about in a technical sense and still don't, if I'm honest. I've never played the game apart from at school and if you asked me about the formation of a team, I wouldn't really be able to tell you. Because of this I'd often just keep my head down at these meetings, although I'd always stay to the bitter end. The game would be finished before five o'clock but it wasn't unknown for us to leave the ground at 11 p.m.

So that's how I got to develop a relationship with John. He was very easy to get on with. A lot easier than Ron Greenwood, his predecessor, who became the general manager of West Ham for three years before taking charge of the England team in 1977. Ron could be an awkward bugger at times and I had a run-in with him during my early days at the club. Trevor Smith had arranged for me to take some pictures in the dressing room after one particular game and when I got there, John said, 'Yes, just give us five minutes and we'll tell you to come in.' Once I had been allowed in I encountered Greenwood and he looked at me and said, 'You can't just walk in here like that. It would have been nice if you'd asked someone.' So I said, 'I did, I asked the manager – and he said it was okay.' And Ron just moaned, 'Oh all right, then.'

I told Trevor Smith about what had happened and I was in the office the next day when he was speaking to Greenwood on the phone. He gave him a right rollocking. 'Why would you say that to my mate?' he demanded. 'He was in there working with John; you're out of order.' He really laid into him. Apparently, Greenwood just replied meekly, 'Oh sorry, Trev.' Later that week there was a youth game at Chadwell Heath and Greenwood was there, wearing his usual old mac. He came over, put his arm around me and apologised. When I told Trevor, he said, 'I wish I'd had your camera. What a picture that would have made!'

I didn't know Ron for very long, but from my limited experience he didn't display the man-management skills that John Lyall did. I don't think I was the only one to have had a run-in with Ron. Trevor Smith told me that he used to go to games in the early 1970s and visit Ron in his office later in the week to discuss things. Ron would give his view of the game and Trevor would say, 'That's not how I saw it.' 'Did you not *see* the game?' Ron would exclaim, and Trevor would reply, 'Of course I did.' Ron would then insist that he mustn't write such a thing in the paper and Trevor would say, 'Why not? It's the truth!'

I think Ron was a bit of a moaner. John Lyall was a very different character, but he owed a hell of a lot to Ron in terms of his footballing education and for having been given a chance to move into coaching after his playing career was ended prematurely through injury. Had it not been for Ron, he could easily have drifted away from the game. Both men were deep thinkers when it came to football and wanted their teams to play the game in the right way, but they had different management styles.

John was very straight with people and everybody knew where they stood with him. Nobody had a bad word to say about him because he was such a nice guy. I know people always say those kinds of things but it's the truth. For example, when we reached the FA Cup final in 1980, I was down at Chadwell Heath a few weeks before the big day and John gave Trevor Smith, Ken Dyer and me an envelope each containing two tickets for the game with a little thank you note. People would pay anything to get cup final tickets, so you don't often see managers and players giving them away, but that was John. He was so genuine.

By that time John had already illustrated his generous

spirit by inviting me to travel on the team bus to away games. I think it was a match at Wrexham in the middle of the 1978/79 season – our first in the Second Division following relegation – when there was a rail strike on and it seemed like a hellish effort to drive, so John just said, 'Why don't you come up to the game with us on the coach?' It was a nice offer and I duly accepted. West Ham lost the game 4-3 and from that day on this became standard practice – being allowed to travel with the management and players that is, not the team losing seven-goal thrillers.

I was naturally delighted to be invited onto the team coach and I considered it a real privilege. It was also good fun and made life much easier for me on match days. 'It's no problem,' said John. 'We're going anyway; you just pay for your hotel room.' If our destination was no further than Birmingham, we'd just travel on the day of the game, but the team would generally travel on Friday and stay in a hotel if the game was beyond the Midlands. I spoke to the *Recorder* about John's offer and they said that if I wanted to use my travelling expenses to pay for overnight accommodation then that was entirely up to me.

In those days, there was plenty of room on the coach because we didn't have the ancillary staff that teams now take with them when they play away. When I first started travelling with the club, we had kit man Albert Walker, the former West Ham player from the 1930s who had returned to the club as a coach, physiotherapist Rob Jenkins and either Ronnie Boyce or Mick McGiven, who used to take turns assisting John Lyall on the bench. And that was it.

The players tended to gravitate towards the back of the coach and the management would sit at the front. Once I become more confident I would get involved in a bit of conversation with John and Ron and some banter with Rob Jenkins; however, to begin with it was just a case of keeping my head down and joining in when invited. But I started to get to know the players a lot better in time and began to develop some really good friendships.

The first player I got to know well was Paul Brush. He was another local boy, originating from just across the Boleyn Ground towards Central Park, and I think that's why I got on so well with him. We seemed to have a few things in common. I also became good friends with Ray Stewart when he arrived at the club at the start of the 1979/80 season. Back then, we didn't have press conferences when players joined the club. John Lyall would just ring Trevor Smith and say, 'We've got a new signing, tell Steve to come down this afternoon to take a few photographs.' So I was frequently one of the first points of contact for players when they arrived at West Ham.

Ray was just nineteen when John Lyall splashed out £430,000 to bring the defender down from Dundee United and make him Britain's most expensive teenager at that time. I met him on Saturday morning to take some shots of him and then we went to Watford that afternoon for a league game. At that time, the benches at Vicarage Road were literally on the touchline and Ray was sitting there as a spectator while I was working just a few yards away. It was a bit of a tasty match and the tackles were flying in when Ray turned to me and said, 'Fucking hell! What have I let myself in for?'

That helped the pair of us to build an immediate rapport and I quickly got to know his girlfriend Carolyn, who came down from Scotland to join him. I think the club called in a few favours to get them a council flat just around the corner from me, so I'd go round to visit them and see how they were settling in. Ray was a good lad. He's a bubbly character and we've maintained a friendship that has lasted through to today. Not that I can understand what he's saying half the time with that strong Scottish accent of his. I'm all right when we're face to face, but when he's on a dodgy mobile line it's impossible to know what he's talking about. I just agree with him most of the time.

Of course, back in those days there were no mobile phones, no iPods and no personal DVD players, so in terms of the players entertaining themselves on trips it was a case of either joining the card school or having a good chat (an old-fashioned concept, I know). The card sharps tended to be at the back of the coach while the rest of us would sit in the middle. And that's where Paul Brush and Ray Stewart used to be because they didn't get into the card school. Brushy would generally sit behind me, so we'd talk over the top of the seat.

However, all the lads, regardless of their place on the coach, were fine with me because they saw me down at the training ground regularly and so they knew I was okay. I remember Lou Macari, John Lyall's successor, saying he'd had no idea who I was when he first saw me at the training ground and had asked Mick McGiven, 'Who the fuck is that?' Mick told him I was Stevie Bacon, the club photographer, and that I was as good as gold – and that was good enough for him. If you were in with them then you were trusted.

This attitude seemed to be totally unique to West Ham. I used to meet other photographers around the country and they would say they couldn't believe I was allowed to travel with the players – especially as I was still only working for the local paper at that stage. They would say, 'You travel with the team? Bloody hell!' When we went to the FA Cup semi-final replay at Elland Road, a couple of journalists asked

Everton manager Gordon Lee if there was any chance of a lift back to Merseyside after the game. He asked how they had got there and when they said by train, he suggested that's how they should return. That's how it generally was.

I think managers distrusted the media even in those days. But John was a different kettle of fish and knew instinctively that he could trust me. He was a special sort of bloke and his warmth reflected the family feeling of the club. Everyone was very friendly. In those early days, our coach had no toilet or anything, so we'd pull up under a bridge and you would find yourself having a pee behind the vehicle alongside chairman Reg Pratt. He'd nod and say, 'All right, big boy?'

The first full season for me on the coach was a very memorable one because West Ham reached the FA Cup final that year. We travelled up to the semi-final game at Villa Park on Friday and the following morning John Lyall suggested that since the hotel had some nice grounds we all go for a wander after breakfast. John was chatting, but not about the semi-final. I think he wanted to play down the occasion and treat it like a normal game.

It was anything but, of course, and the traffic to Villa Park was so heavy that we needed a police escort with all the lights and sirens to carve a passage for us on the Aston Expressway, which was absolutely chock-a-block. When we turned towards the ground all you could see were West Ham fans. It was unbelievable. I remember looking down the aisle of the coach and thinking that defender Alvin Martin looked particularly nervous. We later discovered he had tonsillitis, but I assumed that he was bricking himself about the game.

In the end, we drew 1-1 after Everton's Brian Kidd was sent off for having a scuffle with Ray Stewart. I thought Kidd was a horrible little shit, trying to plead his innocence, but the fact is that Ray would have gone as well nowadays for his part in the incident. It was Ray we had to thank for getting us to the semi-final in the first place after he'd scored a last-gasp penalty against Aston Villa in the previous round. It was a strike that resulted in one of my favourite photographs. My old mentor Arthur Edwards, who was still shooting news and sport for *The Sun*, said to me, 'Ray Stewart's the story; can you get him after the game?' John Lyall was fine about it, so we told Ray we'd like to get a shot of him sitting on the ball on the penalty spot. The Boleyn pitch was a complete quagmire, but Ray was happy to wander out across the mud in his nice suit and shiny polished shoes to pose for the picture. He certainly doesn't mind a bit of publicity, does Ray.

I also took a lovely photo of Ray with his dad Archie after the semi-final replay victory at Elland Road. Yet the picture that everybody talks about from that game is obviously the diving header by Frank Lampard – who was only in the side because of Alvin's illness – that secured the 2-1 extra-time win and took West Ham back to Wembley. The problem at Elland Road was that you had to lie down at one end of the ground to work. Initially, I wasn't sure if I'd got the actual header but thankfully I did, even though I thought the picture was a bit muzzy. I must admit that I didn't even see Frank's comical corner-flag dance because I was on the other side of the goal, but the crucial thing was that I'd captured his header. Of course, the big question was what the full-back was doing up there in attack in the first place.

I've got to be honest and say that as a photographer you don't really appreciate the emotional aspects of a game while you're working. You're concentrating so intensely that the impact of the result doesn't really hit you until after the match. If you've won an important game, there are obviously different sorts of pictures you might want after the final whistle. But it's difficult to assess how things have really gone when all you see of a game is through an eyepiece.

Of course, spirits were extremely high on the return journey from Elland Road and I'd be lying if I said there wasn't a bit of bubbly involved. Everybody was buzzing because we had an FA Cup final and a visit to the famous old Twin Towers to look forward to, although we had to spare a thought for Alvin whose tonsillitis had now been diagnosed and was consequently laid up in considerable pain. In fact, the next day I went round to his house to take a picture of him tucked up in bed reading all about West Ham's semi-final success on the back page of the *Evening Standard*, the poor lad.

Come the big day, I made my own way to the final as I was taking members of my family to the game. It was the first time I'd had the chance to work at Wembley Stadium, so it was a new experience for me. I know West Ham deserve all the credit for upsetting the odds and beating cup holders Arsenal, given they were a Second Division side at the time, but I don't remember the game as being a classic. Those with good memories talk about John Lyall's tactical masterstroke of deploying David Cross as a lone striker, which apparently confused the Arsenal defence, but these things tend to go over my head.

Thankfully, little went over the head of Trevor Brooking, who nodded in the thirteenth-minute goal that proved to be the winner. I was behind the Arsenal goal and looking to my left when Trevor scored and fortunately I managed to get the shot. It's always my intention to capture every goal – and I'm certainly happy that I got that one, for obvious reasons – but I always say that the best goals don't necessarily make the best pictures. A thirty-yard screamer doesn't make a picture, whereas a tap-in on the goal-line does. When people talk about 'a goal for the cameras', they generally mean the television ones because otherwise it's just a case of man kicks ball. Simple goals make for much better pictures than stunning goals – not that I'm complaining about Trevor's wonderful piece of instinctive finishing. But I do tend to prefer celebration pictures because of the motion and emotion they illustrate.

There was plenty to rejoice about after the final whistle at Wembley and it felt brilliant to see skipper Billy Bonds holding up the trophy during the presentation. The players were on a massive high as they paraded the trophy around the pitch and, although I was concentrating on getting all the celebration shots, there was still time to embrace the moment and enjoy the fact that West Ham had achieved something very special. You have to make the most of these occasions because you never know when they might come around again.

Later that evening, the club held their celebration dinner at Quaglino's restaurant just off Piccadilly in London's West End. I took my family home, quickly got myself suited and booted and caught the train back into town. When I walked into Quaglino's there was the FA Cup, in all its splendour, sitting on a table in front of me. I had my camera with me, of course, and the first man I saw was David Cross. 'Come here,' he said. 'You've been taking pictures of everyone else with the cup today; now it's your turn.' He grabbed my camera, told me to pick up the FA Cup and took a picture of me, which turned out to be rather good, as it happens. And then, it was a case of enjoying the evening. The party had been booked regardless of the result, and I think most of us had assumed before the game that it might be a rather sombre affair given that Arsenal were expected to beat us, but the fact that we won made all the difference and the players were able to let their hair down.

The team had been escorted to and from Wembley and, John Lyall being the man he was, one of the police outriders had been invited to the bash. John had even told the guy to bring his wife, although as it turned out, she couldn't get a babysitter at such short notice. But the outrider still joined us and I felt it was such a lovely gesture, so typical of John. We all sat down for a meal and there were some speeches and announcements. It was a happy, lively affair. I seem to remember that Brian Blower, the club's commercial manager, had another function to attend at the Royal Lancaster that evening and wanted some of the players to go there afterwards. That was no problem for them because they were staying in town that night, whereas I had to return home by train and make my way back up to the hotel the following morning to meet the coach for the trophy parade.

I returned to the hotel by 10.30 a.m. and was standing outside, waiting, when Paul Allen, who at the age of seventeen years and 256 days had just become the youngest player to appear in an FA Cup final at Wembley at that time, suddenly appeared from the foyer and sat down on the kerb outside with the trophy. I took a wonderful shot of him sitting on the pavement with one of the motorcycle cops watching over him, keeping an eye on the cup.

Nowadays the club would arrange for a special open-top bus to take the players back to Newham for their parade, but in those days all travel arrangements at West Ham went through a company called Lacey's (who also carried the supporters around the country) and they simply took some skylights out of the roof of a regular coach. The players could only pop their heads out of the skylights, and from my point of view it was pretty useless as there were no pictures in it for me. I couldn't get up there to take any shots, so I simply enjoyed the drive through the streets while waving at people as if I'd just won the FA Cup myself. You mean you didn't spot me supplying that wonderful cross for Trevor to score?

My work didn't really start until we got to East Ham Town Hall. There we met Marjorie Helps, the Newham mayor, who spoke to all the players before the civic reception. David Cross had picked up a huge plastic hammer so I got a shot of him inside the town hall with this bloody great thing. Before the reception, the players went upstairs to greet the fans and TV commentator Martin Tyler said he was a bit worried because he thought the area in which the team was congregated was 'less a balcony and more a balustrade'. He said something about hoping it could take the weight – and that was before I got anywhere near it!

I went up to try and get a shot of the players on the balcony with the crowd in the background but that didn't really work so I went downstairs and did a few shots looking up at John Lyall as he addressed the crowd with a microphone. There was a huge mob of people outside the town hall and it was great to be involved in such a fantastic occasion – it's a memory that people still cherish to this day. It was just a few months later that John invited me to become the club's official photographer as the team prepared to pose with the FA Cup ahead of the following season. I'd been taking pictures of West Ham for four years, but now I really felt like a member of the family.

The Estadio Santiago Bernabéu could be seen from my hotel balcony and it was a wonderful view. We ventured down to the venue of the opening match of West Ham's 1980/81 European campaign – my first with the club – for a training session the evening before the big game. Sadly, the Hammers weren't playing the mighty Real Madrid, who at that time had been crowned league champions on twenty occasions (including five of the previous six seasons), but their nursery team, Castilla, who had qualified for the Cup Winners' Cup as losing finalists of the Copa del Rey after being thrashed 6-1 by their senior side. Nevertheless, it was a hugely impressive stadium and I noticed that the trophy cabinet was marginally bigger than ours at Upton Park.

The prospects of sticking another piece of silverware on the Boleyn sideboard hardly looked promising after West Ham crashed to a 3-1 first-leg defeat by the Spaniards. The result wasn't the only disappointment of the night, however – there had been some aggravation in one section of the ground during the game and we later heard whispers that there were further problems outside after the final whistle. We weren't aware of the exact nature of the trouble at that time and so we went back to the hotel to have something to eat before going out for a late drink.

What we hadn't intended to do was end up surrounded by a load of Spanish men with a twinkle in their eye. We found a bar that seemed very nice and noticed that it had a sailing theme – it was only after we were all safely inside that we realised the emphasis was more naughty than nautical. Talk about hello sailor! It slowly dawned on us that the bar was full of over-friendly blokes and I think it was Frank Lampard who, with as much subtlety as he could muster, suddenly blurted out, 'Here, this is a fucking gay bar!'

Our club surgeon had come out with us and had obviously had a few drinks. His wife then mentioned that he was operating in London the next day, at which point I said I'd love to be in the hospital theatre just before his next patient went under the knife, warning them that his surgeon was in a Spanish gay bar at 2 a.m. that morning. 'Don't worry about him,' she said. 'He carves better when he's had a few!' Anyway, the bar turned out to be a decent enough place, despite Frank's concerns, so we ended up staying there for the evening.

By the time we flew out of the country the next day, however, the good humour of the night before was firmly behind us. We'd heard stories that a fan had been tragically killed after being crushed by a coach outside the stadium and Eddie Chapman, the club secretary, was left to establish exactly what had happened. When we got back to Heathrow, the press were waiting for us and Billy Bonds was quoted describing some of the fans as 'scum' and 'animals', which he subsequently got a bit of stick for when we played at home to Watford a few days later. Personally, I blame the journalist, who was probably still pissed from the previous night, for that story because, knowing Bonzo, he'd have thought the chat was off the record.

There were big fears that West Ham could be thrown out of the Cup Winners' Cup or forced to play the second leg in Sunderland, so it was something of a relief when we learned the extent of the repercussions was that the game at Upton Park would be played behind closed doors. I suddenly had far more friends than I'd ever realised, as lots of people I'd not heard from for ages made contact with generous offers of carrying my equipment boxes in order to try and get into the game.

The match itself was rather surreal. It was like watching a training game in that we could hear everything that was said by anybody. David Cross scored the world's quietest, least-celebrated hat-trick as West Ham won 5-1 after extra time to go through 6-4 on aggregate. But the two things I remember most was hearing Eddie Baily foul-mouthing from the dug-out, which, in normal circumstances, would have been lost in the noise of the crowd, plus Bryon Butler's radio commentary. It was so eerie that night. There were only 262 of us there, so it was nice to be included in the official statistics for the game.

In the second round of the competition we played Poli Timişoara and, being as diplomatic as my education allows, I thought Romania was the arsehole of the universe. What a dismal place. And the food was absolutely awful! We had chicken and chips in the hotel – well, we thought it might have been a chicken at some stage in its long life – but the only thing that was edible was the ice-cream, and there wasn't much of that. Obviously I wasn't very happy, what with me being a growing lad and all that, but programme editor Jack Helliar, who was a larger-than-life character, told me, 'Come up to my room, boy, you'll be all right.' I had no idea what he was offering, but I thought I'd take a chance. I got to his room and he opened up a huge case crammed full of confectionary – Mars Bars, Dairy Milk, Crunchies, you name it. 'Help yourself, son,' he said, 'but don't tell anyone else.' He was a good old boy and knew what these trips were like, but I can't say it did much for my diet!

On the night before the game, John Lyall suggested that a few us go for a walk, as he often did. We were strolling past all these hovels and shacks that people lived in when John pointed out that virtually all of them had beautiful chandeliers on display. We could only assume it was a status thing. It was the same in the hotel – plenty of grandiose lighting arrangements that contained fourteen light sockets ... and one bulb. Like I said, dismal.

Whenever we went outside the hotel we had the distinct impression that we were being followed. There was a gaggle of shady characters hanging around and even if you wandered out just to stretch your legs for a few minutes there would be someone behind you. Needless to say, the West Ham players weren't happy and just wondered what they were doing in this dung-heap. But it was probably all that Timişoara had to offer; it was possibly their best hotel. At one stage it had obviously been a splendid place to stay but it was now incredibly run down. I remember I had to ask the staff for a bath plug. On each landing there was a very stern-looking woman sitting at a desk and you'd have to ask her for a plug if you wanted a bath. Maybe they only had the one.

We were located close to a big department store and when we went inside it was like going back in time. For a start, there was virtually nothing on the shelves. We walked through the electrical department and there was just one big black-and-white television on display with a grainy picture of the test card. That was the height of technology out there.

Everything was just so dark, dank and drizzly and everybody looked so miserable. They all seemed to have the same anoraks on. So from the point of view of the trip it was a case of getting in and getting out, especially as West Ham were 4-0 up from the first leg and the 1-0 defeat out there proved irrelevant. The only consolation was that *The Sun* wanted some pictures from the game, so I sent them a shot of Paul Allen getting scythed down by one of Timişoara's hard men.

I got a bit of extra cash out of the trip, but it was an awful place – just in case you hadn't realised by now.

Incredibly, there was a four-month wait before West Ham returned to European action in March 1981. We were drawn against Dinamo Tbilisi in the third round, so once again we headed behind the Iron Curtain to Georgia, but this time, in stark contrast to our previous experience, we had a very interesting trip. Everybody needed special visas, so the first thing I had to do was to get the players' mug shots. 'Don't smile, for Christ's sake,' I'd say to them. 'They'll never let you in.'

Because of the huge distance to Tbilisi – around 2,200 miles – we had to fly via Moscow and so we left London on Monday evening. The club had decided it made sense to charter an Aeroflot plane, which they hoped would ease the passage into Russia. The aircraft might have once been an impressive sight, but it looked a bit tatty around the edges by the time it fell into our hands. We assumed it was legal to fly but I wasn't so sure, to be honest.

By the time we reached Russia, the weather was absolutely atrocious. In fact, we were caught in the heaviest blizzard I'd ever encountered. We circled around above the airport in Moscow for a while and started to crap ourselves a bit, thinking of the Munich air disaster and all that malarkey. All of sudden, it was apparent from the sound of the engines that we were making our approach. There was snow everywhere and we bounced and skidded on the tarmac, but they somehow got the plane down. We had a Russian-speaking crew but the pilot managed to tell us it was the worst conditions he'd ever flown and landed in – not that we found that information particularly reassuring.

We entered the terminal, only to hear one of the officials say, 'Thank you very much, goodnight, the airport is

now closed.' He said they had decided to close the airport
the moment we landed because it was apparently now
too dangerous. I thought, 'Tell us about it, we're the ones
who were on the plane!' We were told we'd have to spend
the night at the airport, but John Lyall wasn't prepared to
accept that. John insisted that we needed a hotel. We had a
guy with us called George Scanlan, a lecturer at Liverpool
University who was acting as our interpreter. He'd made
a lot of trips into Europe with Liverpool and wasn't at his
best after drinking for a few hours, but at least he could
speak Russian. Mind you, after a few whiskies, you'd think I
was speaking Russian as well.

The negotiations continued and we asked about the players having something to eat, but were told the airport was
closed, the restaurant was closed, the kitchen was closed.
Closed, closed, closed. In other words, Закрытый. In case
you haven't guessed, that's Russian for closed. At this point,
we suggested that we would retrieve the food that we had
brought with us on the flight. After the dreadful food in
Romania, the club had decided to provide their own catering
this time around and so we just needed to get the skips off the
plane and be allowed access to the kitchens for us to enjoy
a good meal. However, we were told this wasn't possible.
Thankfully, a guy called Brad, who represented travel agents
Thomas Cook who organised the trip, was able to sweeten
the way with a load of gifts and stuff he'd brought with him
and eventually a woman in a white coat – somebody from the
Ministry of Health, we were led to believe – arrived to cook
the food for us. We didn't care if she worked for KFC or the
KGB, as long as she could switch the ovens on.

This meant that we were at least able to have a decent
meal while John Lyall was elsewhere trying to sort out some

accommodation. If we were going to be stuck there for the night, at least we'd had our dinner. I remember sitting with the press pack, including some bloke I didn't like from the *Daily Express* who they called 'the banker', because he was renowned for purloining dozens of blank receipts for the reporters to ramp up their expenses. Suddenly one of the more respectable journalists got up and started to walk away. The rest of the guys were saying, 'What's he up to? Where's he going? Maybe somebody should follow him.' And I'm thinking, 'We're locked in Moscow airport, the place is closed down, there's no means of communication available to us, but they think this guy is going to somehow put a story through.' And they say the Russians are paranoid!

Of course, the bloke was only heading to the toilet. Where else was he going to go? But even that turned out to be a song and dance because the authorities would only let you visit the toilets under armed guard. It's difficult enough to take a leak at certain times but it's almost impossible when you've got a big weapon being waved at you – if you know what I mean.

As for the players, most of them were killing time by playing cards, which they would do wherever they were. They could be in the middle of a nuclear war zone but as long as they could sit there and play cards it didn't really matter what else was going on. I think a lot of them just considered it a novel experience, being trapped in an airport and surrounded by armed guards. Some of them may even have quite enjoyed it.

Eventually, John Lyall reappeared and told everybody to get ready because he'd somehow managed to find a place that could accommodate us. When you consider there were about twenty-five or thirty people in our party, you have to say the boy done good. The hotel was a modern place that had been used by officials during the previous year's Olympic Games, but again it was a bit tatty around the edges. John asked if Ken Dyer and I would be happy to share a room and I insisted that wasn't a problem. 'Don't worry,' I said to Ken reassuringly, 'I can never really sleep in hotels.' However, he was quick to tell me the next morning that the only thing he could hear all night was the sound of my heavy snoring, because I'd gone out like a light. So much for not being able to sleep in hotels.

For breakfast we again tucked into our own food and some of the locals looked a little bemused as we scoffed smoked salmon, scrambled eggs and bacon. We were in Moscow, it was minus ten degrees outside and there was thick snow everywhere, but I was eating better than I had anywhere in the world. It all seemed rather surreal. Thankfully, the airport was now operational again and we were able to complete the final leg of our journey to Tbilisi without any further delays.

By this stage, word had got out back home that the West Ham squad had been delayed in Moscow and all sorts of stories began to emerge about us being victims of a Communist conspiracy. I don't know if there was any games-manship afoot in terms of the authorities trying to keep us at the airport, but the fact that John Lyall secured us a hotel for the night foiled any such plans – and, when you think about it, nobody could have envisaged the weather being as bad as it was.

When we finally arrived in Georgia it was a completely different story from Moscow; everyone was so friendly and apologetic for what we'd been put through. The people were so nice and all they kept saying was, 'They're Russians, but we're *Georgians.*'

This might be an appropriate time to remind you that West Ham had been handsomely beaten 4-1 in the home leg a fortnight earlier, so this second game was something of a formality. West Ham were effectively out of the competition. Dinamo Tbilisi had been absolutely superb in that first game at Upton Park and our fans, who appreciate great football perhaps more than most, were so magnanimous in defeat that they applauded the opposition off the pitch. Stuart Pearson scored the only goal of a second leg watched by 80,000 people and I made a point of taking a picture of the scoreboard showing the 1-0 win to West Ham, even though it was written in Russian. But Tbilisi were such a good side it was no surprise to me that they went on to win the competition.

After the problems we'd had getting out to Georgia, it was probably asking a bit too much for the return journey to pass without incident. We'd been handing out various bits of West Ham memorabilia to ease our passage through Moscow airport and thought things were going well, when we suddenly realised that the officials had apprehended the real 'bad boy' among the first-team squad – Trevor Brooking. The Russians clearly recognise a man who has a licence to thrill, but while Trevor has all the class and sophistication of the James Bond character, he's the last person who would deliberately break any laws and so it was a big shock to discover that he was being held for having mysteriously acquired more currency than he'd entered the country with. Of course, the simple explanation was that he'd had a successful time at cards and all the other lads, who had lost their money, were naturally wetting themselves as they saw Trevor being interrogated by the customs officials.

But once things had been properly explained to the

authorities, they were fine, even though we needed a few
sweeteners to speed up the process. A short while later, we
saw the security guards leafing their way through West Ham
programmes and various bits and pieces, so clearly we'd
done the best we could to extract our star player from their
clutches without exacerbating the Cold War. Even Trevor
looked a bit sweaty above the lip for a while, though; it's
impossible to know what's going to happen in those situations. What the Russians did somehow overlook, however,
was the fact that our skips were nearly as full as they had
been on the outbound journey, with one member of our party
fulfilling a cunning plan to bring back a ton of Beluga caviar.

It was a hectic period for West Ham, with the journey to
Georgia commencing just two days after the players had
held mighty Liverpool to a dramatic 1-1 draw in extra time
in the League Cup final at Wembley. The Reds were the
existing league champions and would lift the European
Cup just a couple of months later, so it was a remarkable
effort by the Hammers – especially after Alan Kennedy had
controversially put his side ahead with just two minutes
of extra time remaining, despite the fact that teammate
Sammy Lee was miles offside. Against all the odds, however,
West Ham managed to stage a stunning comeback and won
a last-second penalty when Liverpool midfielder Terry
McDermott punched Alvin Martin's goal-bound header over
the bar. Ray Stewart duly thumped home the equaliser and
I later complimented him on how cool he had been to beat
England keeper Ray Clemence under such intense pressure.
'It's nae bother,' said the Scotsman, as if it was all in a normal
day's work.

My work for the day wasn't over, though, and I made sure
to take pictures of John Lyall having a go at referee Clive

Thomas after the final whistle. I fully sympathised with John; there was no way that Liverpool's goal should have been allowed to stand because Lee was clearly interfering with play – especially given the general interpretation of the offside rules in those days. The referee never even consulted his flagging linesman, but that's Clive Thomas for you.

As for the replay at Villa Park, I thought it was the worst thing we could have done when Paul Goddard headed us in front after just ten minutes because Liverpool simply turned up the heat and quickly scored twice. A strike by Kenny Dalglish and an Alan Hansen effort that deflected off Billy Bonds saw the Reds go on to claim the trophy.

The 1980/81 season was an amazing one to be involved in because, rather than seeing West Ham get beaten away from home, as was traditionally the norm, we were going to places just knowing that we were going to win as we barnstormed our way to promotion. We set a post-war Second Division record of sixty-six points (when it was two for a win) and clinched the title at Grimsby Town in April. It was funny because we saw their local paper when we got up there on the Friday and the back-page story warned us that West Ham wouldn't know what had hit them because of the red-hot atmosphere. I wouldn't mind, but this was Blundell Park, not the Bernabéu. And, of course, David Cross scored four times as we stuffed them 5-1. The other comical incident was that when we took the kit down to the ground in the morning, everything was locked up. We sat outside in the street and suddenly a cleaning lady turned up, threw us a set of keys and told us to let ourselves in. Like I say, this was Blundell Park, not the Bernabéu.

We had arranged with John Lyall that if we did the business, I could take a celebratory picture of the boys in the dressing room after the game. I had two cameras with me – one for regular match action and another that accommodated a flash. I was sitting on the touchline during the game when winger Jimmy Neighbour came crashing into me. 'Bloody hell!' he moaned. 'That hurt!' He ran off, rubbing his backside and I picked up my second camera to discover the front had been ripped off, meaning I couldn't use it in the dressing room after the game.

As the boys posed for the title-winning picture, I ended up having to use my other camera, the one without the flash, while Nicky Morgan, one of our reserve strikers (whose mum, incidentally, worked as a receptionist at the *Recorder*), tried to synchronise the flashgun as I fired the shutter. It was a ridiculous scenario and I managed to get just one decent shot. Or maybe I should say one *indecent* shot, because David Cross had decided to drop his towel at the key moment – obviously thinking he could supply his own idea of a flash. So I was left with just one potentially usable picture – and even that had Crossy's bollocks hanging out! Sadly, Photoshop wasn't available in those days, instead I simply produced a print and blacked out the offending area – not that there was much to cover – and that's how the shot appeared in the papers.

Crossy – or 'Psycho', as the fans preferred to call him – was a classic centre-forward, complete with broken nose and a talent for going in where it hurts. He scored thirty-three goals that season, was as popular with the players as he was with the fans and I think it was Alvin Martin who recently described him as the funniest man he's ever met. He was just full of gags and clubs always need somebody like that in their squad.

We'd be on the coach and Crossy would point out the window and say, 'Can you see over there? They're building the country's biggest ophthalmic hospital.' Everyone would say, 'Really?' And he'd say, 'Yeah, it's a real sight for sore eyes.' He was absolutely terrible. You'd go and have a cup of tea somewhere and he'd pull out of his pocket a big piece of paper that would unfold into a huge five-pound note. 'Sorry, love,' he'd say to the girl behind the counter, 'but I've got nothing smaller.'

Most of the time he'd just get silence from people. He used to embarrass his girlfriend Hillary dreadfully. They went out to buy a hi-fi system in Romford once and, while the shop assistant had his back turned to switch the equipment on, Crossy put on a big pair of rubber ears. 'I'm deaf,' he said. 'Can you turn it up a bit?' On another occasion, he went to the theatre with Hillary to see a Shakespeare play and at the interval stood up and started applauding. 'Brilliant! Brilliant!' The bloke in front of him turned round and said, 'It's not over yet, it's only half-time.' Everybody was walking off to get a drink and Crossy was shouting, 'Come back! It's not over! Come back!' He was just so embarrassing, but a nice guy as well.

West Ham vice-chairman Will Cearns was in the legal profession and Crossy once turned to him and said, 'Will, you're a lawyer, aren't you?' Will replied, 'Yes, I am.' And Crossy said, 'That's funny, because my girlfriend is a lawyer.' 'Really?' asked Will. 'Yeah,' Crossy laughed, 'but she won't let me see her briefs.' The joke went completely over the head of poor old Will, who just said, 'Well, they're very confidential, old boy.' Crossy's humour was wasted on Will Cearns, to be honest. I must admit I don't think I'd have wanted him representing me. He was a bumbling sort of character. He took Ray Stewart for lunch at a very expensive restaurant once before disappearing and leaving him with the bill. 'I wouldn't have minded,' said Ray, 'but he invited me!'

Another bloke who used to make me laugh at times was Rob Jenkins, the club physiotherapist. He'd taken over from his father Bill and it wasn't exactly a high-tech job in those days. Rob has still got his clinic in Green Street and it wouldn't surprise me if he's still got half the same equipment he used to have then. I remember going to see him when I hurt my knee a long time ago and he applied a bandage with two metal plates and said before disappearing, 'When it gets too hot, just press the buzzer.' After a while it started getting very hot and so I pressed the buzzer only to get no answer. I kept buzzing and it was getting hotter and hotter until it was almost unbearable. Rob eventually returned with a smile on his face and said, 'Oh sorry, I didn't hear you buzzing...'

In the early 1980s, the club acquired a new team bus with kitchen and toilet facilities and we hired a guy called Allan Young, a former defender who had played for Arsenal and Chelsea, to be in charge of the catering for away games. Rob got very friendly with him and they became a sort of double-act. At the hotel they would disappear, saying they were 'going for a walk', but everyone knew they were heading for the pub. Rob took on the role of waiter on the coach and would serve food to the players. He'd bring round the prawn cocktails and say, 'Do you want some shit on that?' I'd say, 'What?' And he'd say, 'Do you want some shit on that?' 'Do you mean the sauce?' I'd ask. And he'd repeat, 'Yeah, do you want the shit?'

The spirit among the players was sky high at that time, as you would expect with results going so well. There were different factions within the squad but everyone got on really well together. The divisions were mostly geographical. There were the Romford boys, such as Ray Stewart, Alvin Martin and Geoff Pike. There were the west London boys like Phil Parkes, Alan Devonshire and Paul Goddard, who all travelled across town together for training and games. And then there were good friends such as Trevor Brooking and Billy Bonds, who were part of the card school. It's a mystery how a team containing so many quality players managed to spend three years in the old Second Division. It's inexplicable really, but as a group of lads they were just superb and it was fantastic to feel a part of the team – in a non-playing sense, that is.

The Hammer of the Year in 1981 was Phil Parkes – and deservedly so. Like a lot of goalkeepers we've had at Upton Park over the years, Phil was a gentle giant. We signed him from QPR in February 1979 and it was big news at the time because, as unbelievable as it might sound, West Ham set a world record fee for a goalkeeper when they agreed to pay £565,000 for his services. I can't think what we set world records for nowadays, apart from perhaps fines and compensation figures.

John Lyall told me that Reg Pratt, the chairman at the time, had backed him to the hilt over the deal and said to the board, 'If you don't agree to sign Phil Parkes, I'm quitting the club.' The other directors were against spending that kind of money and were dragging their heels, but when Reg issued that ultimatum they were forced to back down. I know John was immensely grateful to the chairman for that and couldn't have asked for better support.

John invited me to Chadwell Heath to take some pictures of Phil on the day of his arrival at the club and, not surprisingly, there was a bit of a media circus down there. I was having something to eat at the training ground afterwards when John came over and asked where I was heading off to next. I said I'd be going back to the *Recorder* offices, then asked why and he said, 'Phil needs to get to Barking station.' I said that wouldn't be a problem and so John brought Phil over and told him I'd be giving him a lift.

While I was driving Parkes to the station in my Austin Princess, I thought to myself, 'I wonder what my insurance company would think if they knew I had the world's most expensive goalkeeper in my car?' It seemed a bit surreal. We then hit some heavy traffic in Longbridge Road and suddenly the car was surrounded by people wanting autographs – Phil's, not mine! But it just goes to show how much the game has changed. To John at that time, it just seemed totally natural to ask me to give Phil a ride. Personally, I'd have thought that if you'd just signed the world's most expensive goalkeeper, the least you could do was book a taxi cab for him. But no, it was a case of, 'Let's get Steve to drop him off.' Crazy! That's the way that things were done in those days.

I came to like Phil very much during his time with the Hammers. And even to this day I get on very well with him. Phil owned a windows firm and had John Lyall's son, Murray, working for him at one stage. He was just such a good guy and a big favourite with the ladies. In fact, my current girlfriend Tash used to have a huge crush on him. I told her I'd tell him but she did insist that she was only thirteen at the time. Phil still talks about the Cossack hairspray advertisement that he did in the 1970s. People ask him if it was worth it, given the stick he's been given for that over the years, and he tells them it covered the price of a small house, so of course it was. Not that he ever used the stuff – or so he claimed.

The west London boys, who also included Tony Gale after he arrived in 1984, had their own little clique and I used to feel sorry for one of its members, Paul Goddard – or Sarge, as he was known. We set another club record in 1980 when we signed Paul from QPR for £800,000. Sarge was so straight-laced. They used to call him 'goody two-shoes', knowing he'd been in the Boys' Brigade and all that. The lads would come back from an evening game and want to go for a beer, so they would stop Goddard from going home because it would look strange if he got in at one in the morning and the rest of them crawled in much later. Poor old Sarge got dragged everywhere. The others would just pretend that's how long their journey back had taken.

Parkesy was a great goalkeeper and he should have won more than just one England cap, but it was obviously diffi-cult for him with the likes of Peter Shilton and Ray Clemence also playing for the country at that time. I never picked up on any bitterness on his part, however; he's just not that sort of character. Phil still hosts the lounges at West Ham these days and the fans just love him for how he played throughout the 1980s.

The arrival of Parkes signalled the end of the road for Bobby Ferguson and Mervyn Day, our other keepers at Upton Park. Ferguson always sounded so threatening when he spoke to you because he had such a broad Scottish accent. When we got to the FA Cup final in 1980, Bobby ran the play-ers' pool and, to be fair to the *Recorder*, they were always the first with their cheque. Yet Bobby came up to me once and said, 'What are *you* gonna chip in?' I told him firmly, 'I'm not gonna chip in anything. Why should I?' And he said, 'Well, all these pictures you're taking and everything.' I said, 'I'm taking them for the paper, not for myself.' Cheeky bastard.

As for 'Merv the Swerve', I think half my shots were of him sitting on his backside with the ball in the back of the net. He'd always end up sitting on the ground in disbelief. I was asked to take the photographs at his wedding in Great Baddow in Essex and it was a big event for everyone in the village, which coincidentally was where my sister Diane lived. Mervyn was a quiet character anyway, but I'm sure his confidence was shot to pieces by the late 1970s. He had great talent but his position in the team had become untenable by then because of the mistakes he made.

As I stated earlier, my big playing idol from that era was Billy Bonds. I think it was Paper Lace who had a number one hit in the 1970s with a song called 'Billy, Don't Be a Hero', but he was certainly mine – and many others'. He was simply the best as far as I was concerned. He had that swashbuckling swagger on the field. The term 'hard but fair' was made for Bonzo.

One of my favourite pictures is of Billy with a bloodied bandage above his left eye following a clash of heads with Alvin Martin during a home game. I struggled to get him afterwards as his dad would always be waiting for him in the car park – the joke used to be that Bonzo would be halfway through the Blackwall Tunnel before anyone else had even got changed. He'd jump out the shower, grab four little tins of Heineken and be off through the pipe – presumably after putting some clothes on. On this particular occasion, I asked Bill if I could take his picture but he said no, he wanted to get off home. I pleaded with him to let me take just one shot and chased him down the corridor before he relented and allowed me a few seconds to get the picture. He even took the trouble to smile. Of course, what I didn't realise until I printed the picture was there was a trickle of blood running down his nose. It was totally compatible with his reputation for being Captain Courageous.

The irony is that Billy is such a totally different character off the pitch. That's what I find so fascinating about

him. For example, he's a birdwatcher; a twitcher. He loves
Thomas Hardy novels, so much so that he's bought a place in
Dorchester, which is where the author resided. *Far from the
Madding Crowd* indeed. In fact, his initial plan was to buy a
post office down there, but he then decided against it. He's
just not the sort of bloke you'd imagine him to be if you judged
him on his playing persona. He's very kind and caring. When
he became manager of West Ham in the early 1990s, we were
playing away somewhere when an old dear was allowed to
walk down the touchline to make an early exit. Billy went
over to her, asked if she was all right and escorted her down
the tunnel. The game was still in full fury, but that was Bill.

On another occasion, we were in a hotel restaurant and
one of the lads was a bit rude to a waitress. Bill pulled him
up on it and said, 'Hang on a minute – that could be your
mum or your sister doing a little part-time job. Don't speak
to her like that.' And we were eating somewhere else when
midfielder Martin Allen was being a bit loud. He could be
near the knuckle at times. It was Valentine's Day and a
couple was having a meal. Martin was coming out with some
naughty stuff, so Bonzo sent over a bottle of champagne as
an apology. He was that sort of bloke; he was old school.

I tried to do Bill a favour once, when he was still a player,
but things didn't quite go as planned. We were in Shrewsbury
and he wanted to buy a camera for his wife Lynne. There
was a little camera shop opposite the hotel and Bill asked if
I could help sort something out for him. It didn't help the
situation that David Cross had decided to join us and kept
telling the shop assistant that I was a famous photographer,
but I offered my advice and helped negotiate a deal for one
particular camera, so Bill was very grateful. 'Thanks very
much, Steve, I'm very happy with that,' he said. When we got

back to the hotel, one of the lads was reading a newspaper and happened to spot a big Dixon's advertisement for the very same camera – at a *cheaper* price. So much for the fantastic deal I negotiated. Of course, the rest of the lads thought it was hilarious, but Billy was adamant that he was more than happy with the price he paid.

Trevor Brooking, on the other hand, is exactly as people would imagine him to be from his personality on the pitch – a great ambassador for the game. He's the same now as he was when playing: totally down to earth. Anybody meeting him would not be disappointed; they'd get the Trevor Brooking they thought they knew. He is the perfect gentleman and you can't fail to be impressed by him. I'm sure he'd have had offers to move on when we were in the Second Division but West Ham obviously made him the right offer to stay and I'm glad he did. I'm sure he felt a loyalty to the club and wouldn't have been looking to move on anyway. His kids were at school and he wouldn't have wanted to uproot them.

I had the pleasure of getting to know the Brooking family and I got the impression that Hilkka, his Finnish wife, very much wore the trousers at home. I used to have her on the phone a lot, asking for pictures for Trevor to sign. 'And can you come round and do some photos of the kids?' Their house in Shenfield certainly displayed her influence because it had a very nice Scandinavian décor.

When it came to Trevor's retirement as a player, at the end of the 1983/84 season, Hilkka rang me to say that she had arranged for a video recording to be made of his final game at West Ham. He had a surprise coming when he woke up on Saturday morning, she laughed, because he was going to have a film crew in the bedroom. She asked me to help document events as well because she wanted to capture everything from the day. Typically, West Ham spoilt the script by losing 1-0 at home to Everton, who leapfrogged us in the table and pushed us down to ninth, one place behind Tottenham. But Trevor was still given an emotional send-off, carried shoulder-high on a lap of honour around the pitch. The fact is they just don't make players like him any more. For me, Trevor was one of the last really genuine blokes in the game and it's no surprise to see him reach such a prominent position in the FA as its director of football development. He always has that little laugh in his voice. And for some reason he calls me Stefan. 'All right, Stefan, ha ha!' He still does it to this day.

One of my closest friendships, however, was with Paul Brush, who remained at West Ham for another five years after suffering the bitter disappointment of being left out of the 1980 FA Cup final team and then having to play second fiddle to Frank Lampard and Steve Walford for the left-back position. He had played in the previous six FA Cup ties but John Lyall decided to go with Lampard's experience against Arsenal and I can still remember the day when I saw Brushy leaving the training ground after being told he wasn't in the team. Paul is a very genuine, mild-mannered, sensitive guy and he was in tears. In fact, he couldn't even speak to me. 'I don't want to talk,' he said.

I also got to know his wife Marilyn quite well and I took their wedding photographs when they got married at Barking Abbey. You know me – weddings, Bar Mitzvahs, cup finals... Marilyn was a barmaid and Paul had got chatting to her by chance one day. I was so delighted for the pair when Marilyn fell pregnant with their first child, Peter. But we were all devastated when, during the course of her pregnancy, it was discovered that she had leukaemia. It was terrible.

Marilyn gave birth to Peter in the early part of 1985 and

then, six months later, I received a phone call from a news-paper asking if I had any photographs of Paul and his wife available. 'Why's that?' I asked. 'So you haven't heard?' they replied. And then they told me that Marilyn had died. Apparently she'd suffered a heart attack. I was speechless. Paul soon made contact and I just didn't know what to say. He told me that the press were hounding him and that he didn't want to speak publicly at that point in time. He asked if I could help in any way, so I spoke to Trevor Smith at the *Recorder* and he said he'd try to circumnavigate things and stop the press from getting directly to Paul. It was big news, but we did our best to fend off people by telling them to talk to us if they needed any information.

I saw Paul a few times and I think he handled the situation well, but it was obviously a very sad time. He told well-wishers that they should send in cuddly toys rather than flowers, so Paul ended up with a house absolutely full of them. I remem-ber taking a picture of Paul with his son, the pair of them surrounded by cuddly toys. Alvin Martin had access to a van, so he got Ray Stewart to help him collect up the toys and take them round to the local hospitals so that lots of children could enjoy the benefit.

John Lyall did everything he could to offer his support at that difficult time and helped Paul secure a loan move to Crystal Palace, which soon became permanent; the regular first-team football did him the power of good. Ironically, Paul later married the nurse who had been looking after Marilyn and I ended up taking those wedding photographs as well. He's now in another long-term relationship with a lady called Chrissie and has continued to keep in touch, inviting me round to dinner and that kind of thing. I remember speaking to Paul in 2001 when he was offered the manager's job at Leyton Orient, where he had been coaching for seven years. He was concerned that he'd end up out of work if things didn't go well. I told him he had no choice but to accept the position – and he duly followed in the footsteps of former Hammers Pat Holland and Tommy Taylor. But sure enough, he was axed two years later. So that's what you get for listening to me!

The early 1980s were a great time for me because I was now travelling everywhere with the team, occasionally lending a helping hand with the baggage on trips, forming good relationships with the players. The club had also established itself back in the First Division with three successive top-half finishes.

Even though I don't often get too emotionally involved during games, there are, of course, exceptions – such as the 4-0 win at Tottenham shortly after we got promoted, when David Cross scored all four goals. You can't help but enjoy stuffing the old enemy! And nobody could forget the 10-0 thrashing of Bury in the League Cup in 1983, when Tony Cottee scored four times. It's a standing joke that only West Ham could put ten goals past a side and promptly sign one of their centre-backs! Of course, Paul Hilton suffered a bit of stick from the lads when he arrived, but he took it well and was a decent guy. As a photographer, the pressure was really on that night against Bury, as I knew the *Recorder* would inevitably want to publish a shot of every goal – which thankfully I managed to get. As a nice gesture we got the photographic page framed and presented to the club, because games like that don't come along too often!

By this time I was becoming familiar with being recognised by fans – both West Ham and the opposition. At the 1980 FA Cup final there was a big flag saying 'Get Your Camera

Off Our Banner' and I like to think that was addressed at me, although I'm not sure it was. But some of the fans were chanting my name and I had a friend who worked behind the scenes at the BBC who was with the producer when they picked up on this singing. The producer said, 'Who's this Stevie Bacon guy they're singing about? And my mate said, 'I know him; he's the photographer who covers West Ham.' The producer joked, 'I've got enough trouble with cameramen, I don't want to know about photographers!'

The West Ham fans recognised me as a familiar face with a distinctive frame and were very friendly, but I used to get a lot of stick from opposing supporters – not least because of my size. It was at either Anfield or Old Trafford when I was changing ends at half-time and the home fans started chanting, 'You fat bastard! You fat bastard!' I stopped in my tracks, looked over my shoulder and gestured, 'Who, me?' And they all started cheering and clapping, so that defused the situation.

Another time, at Everton, I was lying down on a plastic groundsheet while taking some abuse from some horrible little scallywags. Somebody must have taken pity on me because at half-time I received the friendly warning, 'Here, mister, you're on fire.' I looked down and there was a load of smoke coming up from between my legs where they had been flicking lighted cigarette butts at me. The plastic groundsheet had caught alight. Who says football photography doesn't have its dangers?

While we're on the subject of being set alight, I remember the time when we were on the team bus and somebody decided to set fire to young winger Bobby Barnes. His hair was really curly and all gelled up, a real Michael Jackson sort of thing, and somebody said, 'I wonder if that will ignite?' The next thing we knew his hair was smouldering. Thankfully somebody patted the flames out. I can't say I would have predicted the great things that Bobby has since achieved, following his appointment as assistant chief executive of the Professional Footballers' Association, but he was always quite articulate and well spoken.

Tony Gale likes to tell a funny story about an away game during which Bobby was getting a lot of racial stick from Newcastle fans. At half-time the boys rallied round in the dressing room and told him that the abuse he'd been getting was disgraceful. 'Just to prove we're right behind you,' said one of the players, 'you can lead us out for the second half.' They put Bobby at the front of the line-up and, as he ran out onto the pitch, the rest of the players stayed in the tunnel, leaving him out there on his own! So much for being able to rely on your mates!

Bobby scored a vital late winner against Norwich City towards the end of the 1984/85 campaign, which ultimately made all the difference to West Ham as we stayed up by just two points, while the opposition was relegated. But it's fair to suggest that expectations weren't high as the following season got underway, especially since John Lyall had lost Paul Allen to Tottenham and attempted to bolster his side with two new players from such British footballing giants as St Mirren and Oldham Athletic. Those two players, of course, were Frank McAvennie and Mark Ward – and what a difference they would make. The Hammers went on to challenge for the First Division title until the final weekend of the season, when they were finally forced to settle for a third-place finish – their best ever. As a team, they will forever be remembered as the 'Boys of '86'.

McAvennie scored twenty-six goals in forty-two league

games and twenty-eight across all competitions in his first season at Upton Park – and he developed a reputation for scoring just as frequently off the pitch. He started banging in the goals for West Ham from the outset but a broadcasting dispute meant that his face was initially kept off the television and so he remained an unknown quantity for several months. Indeed, one TV news show dragged Frank up to the centre of London to see if people could identify him and nobody had a clue. 'Is he an actor?' 'Is he a pop star?' His face quickly became familiar in celebrity haunts, however, as Frank famously liked a night out on the town. He was linked with several Page Three girls – funny how it's never their faces that I can remember – and he eventually shacked up with Jenny Blythe in Romford. In fact, he had a house in the same street as Paul Brush. Whenever you went anywhere with Frank, the girls would always be flocking around him. Even now it's the same!

We once had an evening game at Upton Park and Frank's Scottish pal Charlie Nicholas, who was with Arsenal at the time and also had a bit of a playboy image, came to watch. I was leaving the ground when Frank called me over in the car park and asked where I was off to. I told him I was going home and he said, 'You don't fancy taking me and Charlie up west, do you?' I could just imagine what John Lyall would have said if he'd found out I was taking his players into town during the week, so I gave that one a swerve.

Yet Frank was a good guy and I got on well with him. Some might think of him as a loveable rogue after some of the scrapes he's got himself into over the years, but he's got a heart of gold. He had a sponsorship deal with Puma, so he was always giving me trainers and stuff. People ask me about him having late nights when we were away but in fact it was

ABOVE I had to beg Bonzo to let me take a photo of this injury after the game – he just wanted to get home, as usual.

LEFT A rare shot of West Ham winning silverware as Billy Bonds lifts the Division Two trophy in 1981.

I got the shot! Trevor Brooking heads the winner against Arsenal in the 1980 FA Cup final at Wembley.

Tony Cottee scores against Tottenham Hotspur in his debut on New Year's Day 1983.

David Cross celebrates after scoring four goals against Spurs at White Hart Lane in 1981.

The eerie scene as West Ham play Castilla in the European Cup Winners' Cup behind closed doors at Upton Park in 1980.

Trevor Brooking is escorted off the Upton Park pitch after his final match against Everton in 1984.

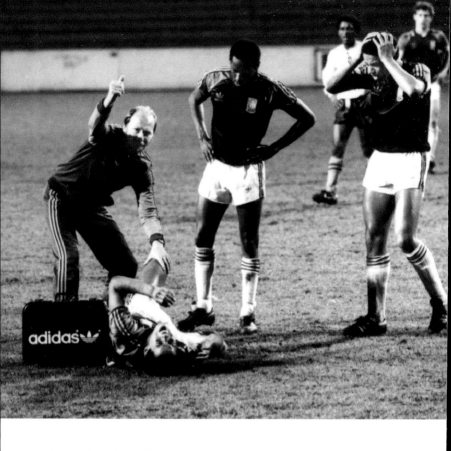

ABOVE The picture that still haunts me: Chris Ampofo reacts to seeing brother Gerhardt's horrific leg injury in a youth match at Upton Park.

LEFT David Cross somehow ended up with this impressive hammer during the parade to celebrate winning the FA Cup. East Ham Town Hall, 1980.

John Lyall is restrained by David Cross as he remonstrates with referee Clive Thomas at the end of the 1981 League Cup final, insisting that West Ham had been 'cheated'.

'I'm dreaming of a Frank Lampard...' Frank Lampard's diving header in the FA Cup semi-final replay at Elland Road in 1980.

Manager John Lyall chats with opposite number Bob Paisley as the teams take to the Wembley pitch for the 1981 League Cup final.

A nice offbeat shot of Paul Allen outside a London hotel the morning after the FA Cup win over Arsenal, as we waited to board the coach for the parade through Newham.

LEFT Ray Stewart scored a vital penalty in the FA Cup quarter-final against Aston Villa, and he was only too pleased to pose for a post-match photo on the mud bath of a pitch.

MIDDLE The Hammers have just secured their place in the 1980 FA Cup final by beating Everton at Elland Road – and Ray Stewart and dad Archie get together for a post-match celebration.

RIGHT When Paul Brush's wife Marilyn died in 1985 he requested that cuddly toys, not flowers, should be sent by well-wishers ... and the amazing response can be seen in this picture of Paul with son Peter.

Happy days... The players take a lap of honour at Wembley after the FA Cup final win over Arsenal in 1980.

Say cheese! It's August 1980 and this is the first team photo I took as official club photographer ... and with the FA Cup proudly on display too.

A very early shot of yours truly – note the chubby face, hairstyle, moustache, LED digital watch and Nikon F camera!

Paul Brush and I were ever-presents for the Hammers in the 1978/79 season, so the *Recorder* thought it would be nice to publish a photo of us in the paper.

usually Parkesy and Alan Devonshire who were reluctant to go to bed. Dev would always say it was too early to sleep, so we'd end up chatting in the bar and, even though the players wouldn't be drinking, Phil liked to puff away on a cigar.

McAvennie soon formed a fantastic striking partnership with Tony Cottee, who scored twenty-six goals himself that season. Not that TC needs telling that little fact, because he's a bit of a statistics freak. I always felt under pressure to get photographs of Tony's goals because he was famous for keeping scrapbooks of his playing career. I often went round his house to do feature-style pictures for the club programme and things like that. All his family were big West Ham fans.

Of course, TC scored on his debut, against Tottenham in 1983, which thankfully I captured on film. Somebody was doing a limited-edition type of thing using that shot a few years back and Tony gave me a signed copy. He's a good lad. I always thought of him as being like Pop Robson, one of those players who just seemed to be in the right place at the right time – a real goal-poacher. Robson scored more than a hundred goals for the Hammers during his two spells at the club and I loved him, but he had a funny habit of joining Sunderland just before we were about to win the FA Cup – as he did in 1974 and 1979.

People talk about Cottee and McAvennie being contrasting characters off the pitch, which was certainly true, but they were great friends. Indeed, they still are. And as players they just complemented each other perfectly. Helping to supply the ammunition for them that season was Mark Ward, the other new recruit. Wardy was full of life and a typical Scouser – 'Calm down! Calm down!' As has been well publicised, Mark served four years behind bars after being convicted of a cocaine-related crime in 2005 and it's fair to say he fell in with the wrong crowd. But he's a good lad really and I know he's very appreciative of what his teammates from the mid-1980s have done for him since his release from prison, in terms of raising money and trying to help him get back on his feet. I got on well with Mark during his days at West Ham and must confess to always fancying his missus at the time, who was a nice little blonde with big boobs. The couple aren't together any more, so I'm allowed to say that now ... aren't I?

Anybody looking at our results at the beginning of the 1985/86 season will see that we lost the league title when we won just one of our first seven games. You can't help but think we might have won the championship if we'd had a better start. But the main thing I remember from that period was the superb team spirit. It's incredible to think that West Ham went on from that poor start to win twelve out of fourteen league games between September and December, including nine in succession. That's just not what West Ham do.

The place was buzzing and a lot of the players still talk about the stunning 4-0 win at Chelsea, who were also in the title race, on Easter Saturday as being one of the greatest results. What a day that was! Alan Devonshire scored the opening goal and it was brilliant to see the midfielder back in league action that season after he had torn three knee ligaments in an FA Cup tie against Wigan two years earlier.

I remember taking a picture of Dev lying on the ground in agony that day and also photographing him when he returned to training a year later. I took a shot of him running straight at me and his damaged right leg was so wasted away that the difference between the two was huge. I wondered how he was ever going to return to action, but he made it and played a key role in the championship-chasing season, although it was natural for people to doubt if he could ever be the same player again.

I had a good relationship with Dev and knew his family, although I didn't see them much because they lived in Southall. He liked his betting, which didn't always work out in his favour, but the fans loved him and Tony Gale still describes him as the best player he ever appeared with. How he won only eight England caps is beyond me given his natural talent for running with the ball and beating players. And to think John Lyall paid just £5,000 to sign him in the mid-1970s.

It would have been a fitting reward for his talents if Dev had won a league title winner's medal but, being a West Ham fan, I'm not sure if I ever really thought it was likely to happen. Even the players were reluctant to openly talk about the championship for fear of jeopardising our chances. And aside from the team's slow start, the other factor that didn't do us any favours was that we lost a lot of games to the weather – in one two-month period in early 1986 we played only once in the league – so we ended up having to play catch-up towards the end of the season. Indeed, we were forced to play four games in a single week and I was thinking of doubling my usual rates. But while I like to pretend that we might just have done it had it been a level playing field, the fact is that we won six successive games during that congested climax to the campaign, so the results could not have been any better.

That closing run included an astonishing 8-1 home win against Newcastle during which Alvin Martin beat three different goalkeepers to score a unique hat-trick. Yes, the famous pub quiz question. Alvin and I have a long history because I used to cover the kids' games at Upton Park on

Monday nights and his dad Albert would come down from Bootle by train for the 7 p.m. kick-off. In Albert's own words, he'd 'tell Alvin what he'd done wrong' before jumping on the train back north for the maintenance nightshift at the National Girobank. So I got to know his family a little and have a shot of Alvin as a teenager with his rejection slip from Everton. Still, their loss was undoubtedly West Ham's gain.

Alvin is a very honest and genuine person, not to mention a great player, and he gave great service to the Hammers over a twenty-year period. He formed a brilliant centre-back partnership with Tony Gale during the 1985/86 season, inherited the captaincy from Billy Bonds and, like Devonshire, fully deserved a championship medal.

Like many other players before him, Alvin asked me to take his wedding photographs when he married his fiancée Maggie at Langtons registry office in Hornchurch. The place had some nice grounds and a lot of the West Ham players got married there. Another player from the mid-1980s who did just that was Neil Orr – or Eddie Shoestring, as we used to call him, because of his resemblance to actor Trevor Eve, with the moustache and everything. In fact, we later dubbed him Eddie Hamstring because of all the injuries he seemed to suffer. It was suggested that Neil become a physiotherapist when he stopped playing and the joke was that he wouldn't need any training because of the amount of time he'd already spent in the treatment room.

When I photographed his wedding at Langtons, there was Neil and his missus Julie, and the witnesses were Ray Stewart and a girlfriend of Julie's from Scotland. So there were only four people present and Neil told me to take as many pictures as I could. I said I could do his missus on her own, I could do the pair of them together, I could do the pair of them with Ray, then I could do the pair of them with Ray and the girl, and then I could take Ray out and do the pair of them with the girl. After that I was struggling!

Neil's name often gets overlooked when fans think about the 'Boys of '86', but he made more than forty appearances for West Ham that season as they tried to secure the league championship for the very first time in the club's history. But it wasn't to be, with the Hammers suffering heartbreak in the penultimate game at West Bromwich Albion, despite getting the win they needed. As I was shooting the game I was aware of the rumours circulating that Liverpool had dropped points at Chelsea to leave the title race wide open. But when the players got back into the dressing room they discovered that in fact Liverpool had won through a goal by player-manager Kenny Dalglish. It goes without saying that everyone was pretty down on the coach journey home as the players tried to come to terms with the fact that their title dreams were over.

I know John Lyall tried to lift spirits by getting the players to focus on what they had achieved rather than missed out on, but it was still a tremendous disappointment. And that's because everybody knew they would probably never get as good a chance again – at least not with West Ham. It was little wonder that they lost at Everton in their final game two days later, conceding second place in the table and finishing four points behind champions Liverpool.

One week later, West Ham played Tottenham in a benefit game for Gerhardt Ampofo, the young player whose career was ruined by a sickening injury. People often ask me what is the most memorable picture I've taken and suggest Trevor Brooking's goal in the 1980 FA Cup final, but the one I'll never forget was when Ampofo suffered his leg injury in a South

East Counties League game at Upton Park. That photograph still haunts me after all these years – Gerhardt is on the floor and Dave Gladstone, our assistant physio, is calling for help while Chris Ampofo has got his head in his hands in horror. He could see exactly how bad his younger brother's injury was. It was awful.

I was sitting in the dug-out with my brother Martin, who I'd invited to the game, when the incident happened and I can't truthfully remember what the challenge was like. But I can still recall the screams as Gerhardt lay on the ground with his shattered leg. The bone was sticking out and I felt sick to the stomach. When the St John Ambulance staff appeared on the scene they just looked away; they couldn't deal with it. In the end John Lyall and youth-team kit manager Stan Burke carried the player off on a stretcher. They took the kid down the tunnel and the game restarted, but we could still hear him screaming in agony. The paramedics eventually arrived, gave Gerhardt some pain relief and drove him off to hospital. It was a horrendous injury and, although Gerhardt tried to come back from it, he never really made it.

With the team having finished third, you would think the logical aim would have been to try and push on, but that wasn't really the West Ham way if the past was anything to go by. It had been an unfortunate trait of the club that they never really bought from a position of strength. We didn't make the most of the fact that we had three members of England's World Cup-winning team in 1966 and Harry Redknapp's joke that West Ham's bottom-half finishes at that time suggested how bad the rest of the side was when he was playing says it all. We won the FA Cup in 1975 but failed to build on it and were relegated three years later. And it was the same story in the late 1980s, when the

Hammers paid the ultimate price for failing to sufficiently add to the squad when good players would have been keen on joining.

I don't know if it was a board decision, but the attitude seemed to be that we'd done quite well as we were, so why fork out a lot of money? I'd have thought that John Lyall might have had a bit more clout. We also didn't help ourselves by selling Paul Goddard to Newcastle a few months into the 1986/87 season. It was an injury to Sarge that had allowed Frank McAvennie to show what he could do up front the previous season, but once he was fit again he barely had a look-in. It was typical of John to put Goddard's interests first and allow him to find first-team football elsewhere, but it left us very light in attack – especially when McAvennie's form deteriorated to the point where he had scored just twice in his final twenty-six league matches that season. It was a dramatic decline and I can't help but think that Frank's lifestyle was beginning to catch up with him. Once again, it was no surprise that John chose not to stand in his player's way when the chance arose for McAvennie to join his boyhood idols Celtic the following season.

The big-money signing we did make during the season after our third-place finish was Stewart Robson, who cost £700,000 from Arsenal in January 1987. I've got to be honest and admit that Stewart Robson is not one of my favourite people. I listen to him acting as a pundit on the radio nowadays and still can't take to him. He's very articulate and I'm sure he's very bright, but he seemed to me to have a superior attitude when he was at West Ham, maybe because he'd come from Arsenal and perhaps thought he was better than everybody else. I'm also told that he tried to stir things up in the dressing room. For example, he started trying to turn the lads against Trevor Smith, of all people. I don't know if Trevor had written something in the *Recorder* to upset him, but Robson was telling people not to talk to him or trust him. Of course, news of this quickly got back to Trevor because he had lots of friends at West Ham and Robson's ploy didn't work anyway, because all the lads knew Trevor and weren't going to allow a newcomer to poison things. To be honest, I don't really remember Robson getting close to any particular group in the dressing room. He seemed a bit of a loner. The fans must have liked him, however, because they voted the former England under-21 midfielder as their Hammer of the Year in 1987/88. But you have to remember that star performers were rather thin on the ground that year and the team finished sixteenth in the table – one place lower than the previous season.

The rot continued to set in and, to make matters worse, we sold Tony Cottee to Everton for £2.2 million in the summer of 1988, replacing him with David Kelly. When we signed Kelly from Walsall for £600,000, there were supposedly loads of clubs in hot pursuit, including Tottenham and Bayern Munich, and I initially thought we'd never get him. But we did, and when I saw him play, I really wished another club had pipped us to the post. I'll always remember his first game for us – a 4-0 defeat at Southampton. He was totally anonymous and one of the headlines was 'Has Anybody Here Seen Kelly?' – the name of an old British music hall song.

As a person, Kelly was really chirpy and cheerful. He was from the West Midlands and I jokingly used to call him a 'Brummie bastard', although I can't remember what he used to call me – something about Cockneys I would imagine. He was a friendly character, but a big disappointment as a player and the fans slaughtered him, of course. Goalkeeper

Allen McKnight was the other player who attracted a lot of criticism during the relegation season of 1988/89. I get on very well with Allen now when he comes back to West Ham to do hospitality work, but at the time I didn't seem to like him very much. Nor did the fans, who nicknamed him 'McKnightmare' for some of his poor performances.

Both players got major stick and, even though the rest of the team backed them as much as they could, they also liked to make a joke of things, which was inevitable with people like Tony Gale around. It was difficult for the rest of us because it felt uncomfortable being in the presence of Kelly and McKnight when the fans were having a dig at them. Obviously neither player was cutting it, but you've got to be seen to stick together and back each other up, even if deep down you're thinking that your teammate's recent performances have been rubbish.

The real problem was that we'd been letting quality stars go and replacing them with substandard players. And that ultimately proved to be John Lyall's downfall as West Ham plummeted to relegation. We did bring Frank McAvennie back from Celtic in March for £1.25 million, but it made no difference and it all came to a horrible head with a 5-1 defeat at Liverpool on the final day of the season, when only an unlikely win would have saved us.

I think it was Alvin Martin who asked John if the boys could have an evening out in Liverpool whatever the outcome of the game and he agreed, so we remained up there for the night. We stayed in a hotel in Kirkby that seemed more like a prison compound when they closed the big iron gates behind us. I remember Alvin saying that if you went to a party up there and you picked up a girl from Kirkby, then she was going home on her own because it wasn't the sort of area you'd want to venture back to. It was a bit dodgy. One of our youth-team players was up there with some mates and came to see us at the hotel. When he said he'd parked outside he was told to bring his car into the hotel grounds because it wasn't safe to leave it on the streets.

Needless to say, everybody was feeling very down that evening. The team had won five of their previous six games and that late spurt had given us a bit of false hope, as is always the way with West Ham. That just seemed to add insult to injury really. The lads had gone into town, so there weren't many of us at the hotel and I ended up sitting down with John Lyall and Mick McGiven. We had some sandwiches for dinner and it felt like the Last Supper – although not much of one.

Having said that, nobody stopped to think that this might have been John's last game. Despite the fact that the club had just been relegated, as far as we were concerned, getting rid of John wasn't on the agenda because it wasn't the West Ham way. When we got the call at the *Recorder* a couple of weeks later we just couldn't believe it. I remember Trevor Smith looking stunned as he put the phone down. 'They've sacked him!' he said. It seems laughable now, but Trevor then said, 'Right, I'll phone the chairman!' And he rang Len Cearns, who apparently told him, 'We haven't sacked John, we just haven't renewed his contract.' And Trevor retorted, 'Forgive me, Mr Len, but you've sacked him.' Yet the chairman was adamant that John had not been sacked; they just hadn't renewed his deal – a very technical difference, I would say.

I simply hadn't seen it coming and my reaction was one of shock and disbelief. I thought it was the wrong decision to allow John to leave the club after thirty-four years' service as a player, office boy, coach and manager. If the board didn't want him to manage the team any more, they should have offered him an upstairs role. Whether John would have accepted another position I don't know, but they should certainly have tried to keep him at the club. He simply *was* West Ham. He wasn't just the first-team manager; he ran the club from top to bottom.

Of course, that's not to suggest that John never made mistakes. Some of his later buys let him down and maybe he was too loyal to players at times. I also think he changed after Queens Park Rangers tried to secure his services in the summer of 1984. QPR had just finished fifth and requested permission to speak to John when they were looking for a successor to Terry Venables, who had subsequently taken charge of Barcelona. Len Cearns duly allowed John to speak to Rangers chairman John Gregory and, from what John told me in later years, he offered him the world compared to his existing salary at Upton Park.

It seems clear to me that there was a total misunderstanding between John and West Ham in this instance, because allowing him to speak to QPR left John with the impression that the Hammers were willing to let him go. In fact, I think the only reason that Len Cearns gave him permission to talk to Rangers was that he didn't think John really wanted to leave. When Len realised it was a genuine possibility, he started demanding compensation and John soon backed off because he felt uncomfortable being at the centre of an ugly tug-of-war. John had only a year remaining on his contract and couldn't understand why he'd been allowed to talk to Rangers if West Ham had no intention of releasing him. It was a complete failure in communication.

I don't think John was ever the same from that time onwards. It seemed that John's attitude and commitment to the club changed from that point. Until that time, John would always come back to the ground in the afternoon to do bits and pieces, but he stopped doing so and the evenings of discussion in his office after home games began to tail off. He got a bit disillusioned, in my opinion. John signed a new five-year contract with West Ham but my impression was that the QPR episode damaged his relationship with the club and things were never quite the same again after that.

I wanted to speak to John when I heard the news about his departure but it was very difficult. Trevor Smith spoke to John's wife, Yvonne, but she said, 'No, he's not speaking to anybody.' I didn't see John again after his departure until he returned to West Ham as manager of Ipswich Town in September 1990. It was no surprise that he guided Ipswich to promotion the following season (1991/92) as champions, but after leaving the club in the mid-1990s he became very reclusive and cut himself off from the game.

John had lived with his family at a house in Stanford Rivers, near Abridge in Essex, which he had renovated during the late 1980s. I visited the place on several occasions to take the 'before', 'during' and 'after' pictures and it looked amazing once it was finished. But after joining Ipswich he moved out to Tattingstone in Suffolk and I know he was very happy there. His new place was a magnificent farm property with huge grounds and John installed a lake where he would spend his time fishing. If he went down to the bottom of the garden, it would be another five minutes' walk back to the house. I guess he was just content to spend his time there. The players tried to get him out for various reunion dinners but it was very difficult.

They did, however, somehow manage to persuade John to attend a one-off function in Docklands to commemorate the

FA Cup-winning teams of 1975 and 1980. I wasn't working on that occasion, but one of West Ham's hospitality clients was desperate to have his picture taken with both John and the trophy, so I asked John if he'd mind and he was happy to agree. He was as nice as pie to everyone who met him that day and I even took the liberty of asking if I could have a picture taken with him myself. A few days later I was asked if I could get the client's print signed by John, but I didn't fancy my chances – I didn't even know when I was going to see him again.

Not long afterwards, Ian Jackson, the groundsman at the West Ham training complex in Chadwell Heath, sadly died and I saw John at the funeral. I admitted that it wasn't really the time or place, but asked John if he could sign the two prints I had with me and so we went back to his car after the service. He wrote 'thanks for all the good times' on mine and it wasn't too long after that when John died himself. So the last time I saw him was at somebody else's funeral.

Then, on the morning of 19 April 2006, I took a phone call from Ray Stewart. It must have been about eight o'clock and his first words were 'John's dead'. 'What?' I asked, in complete shock. He'd heard the news from a friend of the family and kept repeating, 'It's no' been released yet, it's no' been released yet.' He was obviously very upset and said, 'I can't talk now.' Within half an hour it was all over the radio bulletins that John had died at the age of sixty-six. He'd had a heart attack the previous night. I thought it was unbelievable. After seeing John for the final time, I'd later spoken to him when he rang to ask for somebody's telephone number. He asked me what it was like over at West Ham at that time and I told him it wasn't like it used to be. 'I think you and I have seen the best of football,' he said.

The family attended a private funeral and then had a service at a church in Ipswich where Sir Trevor Brooking and Sir Alex Ferguson undertook the readings. John's wife invited me to the service and also to the wake at Ipswich Town's ground in Portman Road. I arranged to meet some people in a nearby pub and the first person I saw was Herman Lubsen, a top ear, nose and throat surgeon in Holland whose sidekick was a Dutch journalist by the name of Jan Hermen de Bruijn, another big friend of John's. Former Tottenham managers Peter Shreeves and David Pleat soon arrived for the service along with various other football people and I spent the afternoon with a lot of the West Ham boys, such as Phil Parkes, Ray Stewart, Alan Devonshire, Alvin Martin and Tony Gale. John's brother Jimmy came over to introduce himself and thanked me for some of the things I'd said about John in the paper, which I thought was very nice. But it was obviously a very emotional day for everybody who attended.

It's incredible to think that West Ham dispensed with John's services as a manager when he was only forty-nine years of age and still had so much to offer the club. To this day, I believe he should have been given more time. He'd taken the club back up to the top flight in the early 1980s following relegation and I think he'd have done so again. For West Ham to say goodbye to John in that way just felt so wrong.

It was a fantastic time to be involved with West Ham when John Lyall was in charge. People can't really imagine what it was like because it was just so different to the way things are now. You can't get near players nowadays, but in those days there was a genuine bond between everybody at the club. We

had a great bunch of lads and a lot of the spirit and friendship they developed, which lives on to this day, came from
John's leadership. John looked for a certain type of player
and person. He always tried to find good eggs – even though
Mark Ward got into trouble many years later, he's still a
good-hearted guy.

John always made players feel so welcome at the club.
And he was a father figure to them. When John lived in
Abridge (before moving to Stanford Rivers) they would have
an annual West Ham United versus Abridge cricket match
and all the lads would turn out for him. They used to have
Christmas parties for the players' children at Upton Park
and John and Yvonne would be there serving food to the kids.

John was such a nice bloke and obviously very influential
on my career, so I've got a lot to thank him for. John gave me
my favourite saying, which is, 'It's nice to be important, but
it's important to be nice.' He held everything together and it
was the end of West Ham United as we knew it when John
left the club. It was the end of an era and we knew the club
was never going to be the same again.

CHAPTER 2

'DON'T GO, I'LL ORDER SOME MORE SANDWICHES'

When I heard that Lou Macari had been named as the sixth manager in the history of West Ham United, I was filled with trepidation. And I wasn't the only one: the players resented Lou's presence from the day he arrived at Upton Park in July 1989 and never really forgave him for replacing John Lyall, a man for whom they all had so much respect. Macari had enjoyed an excellent playing career with Celtic, Manchester United and Scotland, and, as a relatively new manager, had guided Swindon Town to two promotions, which meant the modest Wiltshire club was now rubbing shoulders with the Hammers in the Second Division. But he wasn't a West Ham man, having no previous association with the club – which I think should be a prerequisite for a manager – and had built a reputation as a strict disciplinarian. So to say that people had their reservations when his appointment was confirmed is something of an understatement.

The irony is that while many players and fans might not have great memories of Lou's short spell at Upton Park, I had an absolutely brilliant time during Macari's management of West Ham and still have regrets that he left the club midway through the 1989/90 campaign. On a personal level, the two of us just clicked – if you'll excuse another photographic pun – and we shared a similar sense of humour. He also knew I was somebody he could talk to when he felt isolated. Lou had been denied the chance to recruit his own backroom team when he accepted the post. He told me it was part of the agreement with the club to keep the existing staff – coaches such as Ronnie Boyce and Mick McGiven – in place and later admitted that it was probably one of his biggest regrets because he needed support from people he knew. But we formed a good friendship and, although there were times when that put me in an awkward position with the players – some of whom absolutely hated him – I look back on those days with great fondness.

It was always going to be difficult for Lou to follow in the footsteps of John Lyall, despite the club's recent relegation, because it seemed to be a big break from tradition to bring in a complete outsider – even though many had forgotten that had also been the case when Ron Greenwood took charge in 1961. And the many sceptics who feared that the new manager wasn't fully appreciative of West Ham's stylish play were hardly reassured when Macari suggested at his very first press conference that their current approach had not got the club very far because they had just been relegated.

More than twenty years later, history would seem to repeat itself when Sam Allardyce took charge of the Hammers after they had again lost their top-flight status. Allardyce wasn't associated with attractive football, and instead insisted that the best way to entertain fans was to win games – and Macari was much the same. 'I can't get my head around the idea of not worrying if we lose as long as it's a good game,' said Lou to me at one point, 'because winning is everything.'

It's a fair point, but it hardly endeared the new manager to the players who had been schooled by John Lyall to believe that craft was just as important as graft. Another thing that quickly put the players' noses out of joint was the change that Lou made to the food at the training ground. Trevor Smith of the *Recorder* and I would still visit Chadwell Heath every Friday and it had always been a good day to eat down there because they would have fish and chips. They had a proper deep-fat fryer in the kitchens and so it was like getting your fish from the chip shop. Lovely!

However, Lou put a stop to all the old habits he considered detrimental and insisted that the players eat healthier meals. Julian Dicks, one of John Lyall's last buys before leaving the club, loved drinking cans of Coke before games while Alvin Martin liked a bar of chocolate. But strict new rules were put in place and the players were not happy. I remember one of them coming up to me one day and saying, 'All this healthy eating, but have you seen the state of Lou's car?' He had a lovely Mercedes, his club car, but it was strewn with sweet wrappers and takeaway boxes from McDonald's and Kentucky Fried Chicken. Players would say, 'He's telling us to eat healthily but look at the stuff he eats!'

He was forced to expose his own sweet tooth when we had some kind of mechanical problem on the coach once and the lads said, 'Sod this, we're starving, let's find a shop.' The boys came back with a load of stuff that Lou frowned upon them having, yet by the time we got the coach running he was so hungry himself that he was offering Julian Dicks stupid money for a fifty-pence bag of sweets. Considering his supposedly strict regime, he was one of the most unprincipled eaters himself. And we mustn't forget he still owns the Lou Macari Chip Shop in Manchester, of course!

West Ham's first game with Lou in charge was away to Stoke City. We were in the hotel the night before the game and the routine under John Lyall had always been for the players and staff to meet at about 7 p.m. and eat together. We'd generally all have the same food – steak or whatever. So everybody went down to the dining room as usual, but when Lou saw all the players there he turned to the rest of us and said, 'We don't want to eat with them, do we? We'll eat on our own a bit later.'

I was sitting around with the rest of the backroom boys, feeling rather hungry, when Ray Stewart, who had been appointed as the players' spokesman on this occasion, emerged from the dining room to ask Lou about the menu. It was quite limited in terms of what the team could have as a main meal, but there was a choice of desserts: fruit salad or ice cream. Ray had been sent out by his teammates to ask the manager if they could have fruit salad *and* ice cream. Lou thought carefully and finally agreed. But then he started rubbing his head with his hands – which is something he made a habit of – and said, 'Fucking players, you give them the top brick off the chimney and they're still not satisfied.'

About half an hour later, we went through to sit down at a big round table and the waitress asked if she could get anyone a drink. We knew that Lou didn't drink alcohol so we all made our excuses, only for Lou to suddenly pipe up and say, 'For fuck's sake, have a drink! Just because I don't drink, doesn't mean you can't. Have a bottle of wine!' And that's what we did, which helped break the ice. But that's how the meals continued under Lou – with the backroom staff eating separately from the players.

Lou was a bit of a gambler and, believe it or not, we actually stopped the team bus in the town centre the following day so that Eddie Gillam, our kit manager, could put a bet on for him. Eddie was given a big wodge of money and told to find the nearest bookmakers. The coach was blocking the high street in Stoke and, as you can imagine, all the lads were moaning and mumbling, wondering why we've made an unscheduled stop on the way to the game. It reminds me of another time, several years later, when a player asked me to put a bet on for him before an FA Cup game at Wycombe Wanderers. Players are not allowed to bet on their own games, but the theory was that nobody would know me. I walked confidently into the crowded bar area where the bookies were. 'Hello, Steve,' said the bloke behind the counter, leaving me just a little bit red-faced!

Poor old Lou must have had an inkling that little was going to go right for him at West Ham when he watched striker Frank McAvennie break a leg in that opening game. The problems seemed to pile up from day one. He'd already seen Chelsea sign stylish midfielder Alan Dickens, who I know he was very disappointed to lose, and then he had to contend with the Paul Ince debacle. Indeed, it's been almost forgotten that Ince played in the 1-1 draw at Stoke, despite having been controversially photographed in a Manchester United shirt during the summer when still a West Ham player.

I got on fine with Paul. I first took pictures of him when Goodmayes Primary School in Ilford won a Smith's Crisps competition to play at Wembley Stadium ahead of an England versus Germany schoolboys' match. He was a talented player but a handful for West Ham as a youngster. I think the police turned up at Chadwell Heath a few times to speak to John Lyall about him. I don't know how true it was, but there was a rumour about him being involved in an arson attack at a school. I don't suppose it was a huge blaze but, as they say, there's no smoke without fire. John used to have to sort things out.

A lot was blamed on Paul's home life. Incey didn't live with his parents and I think his grandparents brought him up. I remember John saying that the boy had problems at home: his parents had split up and his mum worked in Germany as an 'exotic dancer'. One day she turned up at Chadwell Heath for a meeting with John while I was down there and there's no doubt about it, she was stunning. John was a bit embarrassed, saying to me, 'If I'm not out in half an hour, come and rescue me!'

As well as run-ins with the police, Paul also resisted club authority at times and I heard that Billy Bonds once had him pinned up against a wall during an argument at the training ground. After that, Ray Stewart went up to Incey and said, 'Look, if you don't listen to people like Billy Bonds, you've got no chance in the game.' But John Lyall did everything he could to help Paul's development and the youngster always looked destined for big things after breaking into the West Ham side in the late 1980s, not least when he scored twice in a sensational 4-1 Littlewoods Cup win against Liverpool. Lyall's departure from the club upset Ince greatly, but it was still a massive shock when we suddenly saw that unbelievable picture in the *Daily Express* of the boy wearing a Manchester United shirt while still contracted to West Ham.

An old friend of mine called Lawrence Lustig, who held a staff position on the *Daily Star*, was the man who took the infamous photograph. He's not a bad lad, even if he does support Spurs. Lawrence was on the local sporting scene when I first started taking pictures and so we'd run into each other from time to time, mostly when covering the boxing at Arbour Youth where he was friendly with future WBC flyweight champion Charlie Magri. He was asked to take a picture of a young player who was on the verge of joining Manchester United but was going on holiday; the idea being that it would only be used if the move went through in Ince's absence. All this was organised between the *Daily Star* and Ince's agent without West Ham's knowledge. Lawrence then went away himself and was, he continues to tell me, as astonished as the rest of us when he discovered the photograph had appeared prematurely. The *Express* was published by the same company as the *Star* and the sister paper somehow got its hands on the picture when the story about Paul's impending move arose – even though it had yet to go through.

Of course, all hell subsequently broke loose. Everybody was shocked by the incident because posing in another club's shirt was probably the worst thing anybody could do as a player. You just don't do that sort of thing. What made it worse was that Ince's move to Old Trafford had to then be put on hold for a couple of months because of concerns about an old hernia problem, yet Paul's position at West Ham was untenable after that picture appeared. The club was eventually forced to accept a fee of £800,000 for his transfer, with another £700,000 paid in £5,000 instalments – not a very good deal when you consider that he enjoyed six successful years with Manchester United before making a £7 million move to Inter Milan and also captained England, winning fifty-three full caps. I seem to remember that Lawrence didn't come down to West Ham for quite some time after that!

So Lou Macari had several headaches to deal with in his early days at West Ham. But he was very easy-going in lots of ways and was happy for me to continue travelling with the team, especially as I was now helping kit manager Eddie

Gillam at away games. Eddie initially sold lottery tickets for the Hammers before taking a permanent position in the commercial office, where he got involved in the travel club. It was John Lyall who asked him if he'd be interested in becoming the club's new kit manager in the late 1980s and he was delighted to accept the role. I got on famously with Eddie, who's a lovely guy, and we just set ourselves up as a team.

At one point, Eddie said to Lou, 'Of course, you know that the fans chant Steve's name, don't you?' And Lou was incredulous. 'No, I'm not having that!' Eddie insisted, 'They do! They chant, "There's only one Stevie Bacon."' And Lou couldn't believe it. 'No way!' he said. 'Why would the crowd do that?' So I joked, 'Because I'm a legend at West Ham.'

Anyway, we went to Hull City for Lou's second away game and as I came out of the dressing room before kick-off the West Ham fans were being shepherded through a walkway under the stand. Suddenly they started chanting, 'One Stevie Bacon! There's only one Stevie Bacon!' This could be heard very clearly in the dressing room and Lou apparently turned to Eddie and said, 'Fucking hell! We didn't hear it, right? If he says anything, we didn't hear it.' And Eddie replied, 'Well, I did tell you.' After the game, Eddie said to me, 'We heard the crowd singing your name.' So I tackled Lou on it. 'See, we told you about the crowd chanting my name.' 'I never heard anything,' he declared. I exclaimed, 'Yes, you bloody did, you liar!' He insisted that he'd not heard a thing for ages, but in the end he had to laugh and reluctantly admit he had.

The usual routine in John Lyall's final season, when I was spending more time in the dressing room helping Eddie, was that I'd step outside when the manager wanted to speak to the players before the game. But Lou was happy for me to remain present for his team talks. Of course, the players didn't really like Lou, and it didn't seem to me as if they showed him much respect when he was talking to them. But I'm not sure he helped himself at times. One such occasion was our next away match, at Brighton. All the players were in the dressing room waiting for Lou, who, it's been suggested, was outside watching the horse racing on the telly. When he came in, he said, 'Okay, lads, get changed.' And one of the boys asked, 'Well, who's playing?' Lou replied, 'The team's as per the programme,' leaving Tony Gale to shout, 'For fuck's sake, can somebody go out and buy a programme so that we can see who's playing?' As it happens, Galey wasn't even in the side.

There continued to be a general anti-Lou feeling in the camp. The players wouldn't or couldn't adjust to the way he did things and still blamed him for the fact that John Lyall wasn't there any more, which of course wasn't his fault since he had been brought in afterwards. But the fact that the two men were like chalk and cheese in terms of their management styles didn't help. John used to be at the training ground every day, while Lou couldn't see a problem with not being around as long as his coaches were. I remember him saying to me, 'We've got coaching staff, so why have I got to be there every day?' The players would moan, 'Bloody hell, another day off for Lou.' And he couldn't understand it. It was all too much of a culture shock for the boys and they were always complaining about the manager. Players such as Tony Gale, Mark Ward and Julian Dicks absolutely *hated* Lou. Wardy and Dicksy used to try and tackle him all the time when he made the mistake of participating in five-a-side matches in training. Dicksy still talks about how he would attempt to kick lumps out of Lou.

Meanwhile, Ronnie Boyce and Mick McGiven had also

enjoyed a close relationship with John Lyall, so I'm not sure the new manager was necessarily their cup of tea either and it left Macari with few people in whom to confide. Indeed, it probably explains why he phoned *me* so much. In one sense, you could say I became Lou's 'Mr Fixit'. Indeed, he used to call me 'Inspector Gadget'. Lou's Mercedes had a state-of-the-art radio in it and one morning he was complaining about his kids changing the station settings. When I mentioned that I had the very same kind of radio, he threw me the keys to his car and asked me to sort it out for him. And that's how the nickname came about.

Lou seemed to think I knew everything about technical equipment, so I had more than one or two calls from his home when he couldn't get his video player or television to work properly. I'd have to talk him through things and, knowing what he was like, I'd usually start off by saying, 'It *is* plugged in, isn't it?' I think on one occasion the item in question actually wasn't, so at least that was a simple problem to rectify.

Giving technical assistance was one thing, but you can imagine my surprise when he sought my advice about Nottingham Forest defender Colin Foster in the early part of the season. He rang me up and said, 'I'm thinking of buying Colin Foster; what do you reckon?' All I can remember saying was, 'Do you want him?' And he replied that he did. So I asked, 'Well, what's the problem?' He told me how much Forest were demanding for the transfer fee. 'Well, if you want him,' I declared, 'that's what you're going to have to pay.' He replied, 'Okay, I'll tell the board you said it's okay.' And I exclaimed, 'You can't buy him just because I've said so!' And he repeated, 'Yeah, I'm going to tell the board that I've spoken to you and that you've said it's okay.' I like to think he was joking...

Of course, we did indeed buy Foster and I think most fans thought that, at £750,000, we paid well over the odds for him, especially as he had left Leyton Orient for a mere £50,000 just two years earlier. So you can put that one down to me, I'm afraid!

I was happy to help Lou, but once he began talking about the players already at the club I thought it was very unfair. He'd ask what certain players were like as people and I'd say, 'Lou, you can't ask me things like that.' I think he was just trying to find out what was being said about him, but I certainly didn't want to be the one to tell him – and I didn't think it was my responsibility to do so. It simply wasn't fair, because if anything got back to the team then what would they think of me? I didn't want to be known as somebody who would go behind the players' backs. I was already in an awkward position in terms of where my support lay – with the players who I counted as friends or the manager. I tried to go with the flow most of the time, but I did take some stick from the players about my friendship with Lou and more than one of them joked that I was now picking the West Ham team.

That wasn't the case, of course, but from the first away game at Stoke I did actually become part of the team – at least as far as the hotels we stayed in were concerned. Up until that point when travelling with the club, I had always paid for my own accommodation out of my travelling expenses from the *Recorder*. But when I said that I was going to settle my bill in Stoke, Lou said, 'Settle your bill?' And I said, 'Yeah, I pay for my own room.' And Lou exclaimed, 'You don't have to pay. The club will pay for you.' Consequently, they started listing me as a player; though in truth I was a bit uncomfortable with the idea, fearing it would be fraught with problems.

A short while later, we played up at Bradford and when we checked in at the hotel the girl on the reception desk insisted that the club send through a fax to confirm the identity of the so-called 'extra player' who needed a room. 'Forget it, Lou,' I said. 'It's not worth the hassle. I'll pay.' But he said, 'You're not paying.' And he then announced that I was George Parris!

The receptionist looked unsure – as would most people, given that I don't bear the strongest resemblance to the black midfielder, who missed the trip through injury – but Lou insisted that he was the West Ham manager and so she handed over the key, with the proviso that some form of confirmation must be submitted from the club before the end of our stay. We went to check out of the hotel the following day and the receptionist said, 'Mr Parris, have you sorted things out with the club yet?' I was in the middle of telling her that nothing had come through, when club director Martin Cearns suddenly appeared behind me. I had no choice but to talk to him, and when the receptionist started calling, 'Mr Parris! Mr Parris!' I quickly turned back to the desk and quietly said, 'Look, I'll just settle the bill.' That was all I needed – for the receptionist to refer to me as George Parris in front of Martin Cearns!

The other funny thing about that weekend was that Lou had driven himself and parked close to the hotel, but couldn't remember where he'd left his car the following day. So he sent out Eddie Gillam, who couldn't find the bloody thing. Lou's shoes were in the car and I remember seeing him in the hotel immaculately dressed in a black suit, black shirt and white tie – looking just like a gangster – and a pair of trainers, which somewhat spoilt the look a little.

Lou was great when it came to making sure the club looked after me. Lou had good contacts in Limerick from his days as a player with Manchester United, a team with strong Irish connections, and in November 1989 West Ham went out to Ireland for a match against a Munster Select XI in Limerick to mark the installation of the new floodlights at Priory Park. Lou asked me if I fancied joining the Hammers on the trip and when I questioned if I could afford it, he insisted I wouldn't have to pay for anything. So I told him that I would love to. He also invited Eddie Gillam and youth team kit man Stan Burke for the jolly-up.

We flew out from Luton airport and the first thing on our itinerary was a tour of the Golden Vale Dairies in Limerick, as the company was sponsoring the game. We were then invited to a function in the boardroom at the dairy and the spread was simply phenomenal. The size of the joints of beef they were carving up were absolutely ridiculous – not that I was complaining. For some reason, Republic of Ireland playmaker Liam Brady flew out separately and all the journalists and TV crews were in attendance at this bash when somebody suddenly said, 'Liam Brady's arrived!' The place emptied as everybody shot outside to speak to Liam. We then returned to the hotel and Liam being Liam – just a nice bloke – said to Eddie, Stan and me, 'Do you want to come for a walk?' So we just went for a wander and a chat, not about football but things in general. Everyone wanted to stop Liam for his autograph and it was an unbelievable experience to be with him in his own country. He was held in such high regard; to walk with him in the streets of Limerick was like being in the presence of Jesus.

I was thrilled when West Ham signed Liam Brady. He'd had a brilliant career with Arsenal and spent seven years in Italy with top clubs such as Juventus, Sampdoria and Inter Milan before being lured to Upton Park for a mere £100,000 in the early part of 1987. He was such a special player and it was a shame that West Ham were on the slide when he signed for us. I went to Chadwell Heath to photograph him once he joined the club and we had lunch together. We'd finished eating and I was getting up to clear the plates when Liam said, 'That's all right, I'll sort these.' I stood there thinking, 'This is Liam Brady, an absolute superstar, and he's clearing my dinner plate away for me!' I must admit, I was a little bit in awe of him.

The only other time I'd felt like that in somebody's presence was many years earlier, when I was doing a news job for the *East London Advertiser*. I'd been sent to cover a cheque presentation at a sleazy little bingo hall on Bow Road where Tommy Trinder was the guest of honour. In his day – from the 1930s to the 1960s (a very long day) – he was one of Britain's best-loved comedians and a huge star, with the catchphrase 'you lucky people'. He was also the chairman of Fulham Football Club from 1959 to 1976. Anyway, I said to him, 'Mr Trinder, I hope you don't mind me asking, but what the hell are you doing here?' And he replied, 'We've all got to earn a living, boy!' Then he said, 'Come on, let's go for a walk.'

I was only about twenty at the time and couldn't believe I was walking the back streets of east London with the legendary Tommy Trinder. He told me a story about how he'd had a row with one of the big theatre groups: they refused to book him for anything and his response was to buy all the advertising space in Piccadilly Circus! I can't even begin to imagine how much that must have cost him. Talking to him on that day remains one of the highlights of my photographic career – along with spending time with Liam Brady in Ireland, of course. And no, meeting Marco Boogers doesn't run them remotely close.

While in Limerick, we were also invited to the mayor's parlour – they were taking West Ham's visit very seriously out there. There was a lovely guest book, which had been signed by all the important visitors they'd had over the years, but it was clear that some of our players didn't quite appreciate the sentiment when I got my hands on the pen and discovered that the page was full of names such as Mickey Mouse and various other cartoon characters.

On the night of the game, Limerick was hit by a fog so thick you could barely see your hand in front of your face. I sat there cursing the fact that I'd travelled all that way and couldn't even take a single picture of the game. I could hear the crowd getting excited behind me and I was thinking, 'What are you cheering? You can't see a bloody thing!' I got the impression they were making noise for the sake of it – especially as West Ham won 1-0, thanks to a Stuart Slater goal. Or so I'm led to believe...

Back at the hotel, Lou decided that he would make a bit of a speech – not that the lads were paying much attention – and suddenly he announced that there was somebody to whom he'd like to make a special presentation. 'It's to someone you all know and love,' he said, '...Stevie Bacon!' And he presented me with a white Bukta West Ham shirt, which had been signed by all the players. It was a nice thought, although I still don't know why he did that – apart from me being one of the few people in our party with whom he was friendly.

We attempted to make our journey back to London the following day, but the fog had failed to lift and when we got to Limerick airport we discovered that it was closed. Nobody could believe it – apparently fog had never caused the airport to close in its entire history. It became obvious that we'd have to remain in Limerick for a further night, but the hotel at which we'd been staying no longer had rooms available so we had to rely on some friends of Lou's to find us somewhere else.

It wasn't the best hotel in the world – dinner consisted of soup and rolls – and it was opposite a nightclub called Durty Nelly's. Lou decided he didn't want to stay at this particular place with the players, so he said to me and the rest of the backroom boys, 'Come on, this hotel's not for us, let's go to Jurys Inn,' which was much nicer and more luxurious. He knew somebody had to remain with the players, so he told Rob Jenkins, our physio, to look after them. 'No way do I want anybody going over to that nightclub!' ordered Lou. But Rob wasn't having it. 'Fuck that!' he said. 'I'm not gonna be in charge of that lot. I'm locking myself in my room!'

We headed over to Jurys, where Lou promised us a nice meal and also kindly gave me his single room, saying he'd share with Mick McGiven, while Eddie Gillam could share with Stan Burke. I loved it, thinking how great it was to spend an extra night away in a top hotel, one that I'd never be able to afford myself. I went up to my room and decided a nice bath was just what I needed before dinner. I ran the water, puffed up the foamy suds and plonked myself down in the tub, when all of a sudden the phone rang next to the bath.

'Stevie? It's Lou. The fog has lifted and we've just been told we're flying out now. We've got to be downstairs in ten minutes to head back to the airport.' I put down the phone, jumped out of the bath, sending water everywhere, and hurriedly tried to dry myself and get ready. To be honest, I think they're probably still drying out the room now, thanks to the amount of water I splashed all over the place. I threw everything into my bag and rushed downstairs, thinking I was late and holding everybody up, only to dash into the foyer where there was not a soul to be seen. Before I could think about what to do next, Eddie and Stan appeared as if they were heading off for a walk. I asked why they weren't ready and they said, 'Ready for what?' I told them the fog had lifted and that we were going home, but they simply pointed towards the window. And suddenly the penny dropped.

I approached reception and said, 'Can you tell me what number room Mr Macari is staying in, please?' The girl gave me the number and so I went and knocked on the door, only for Mick to appear. 'Where is he?' I said. 'Where's Lou?' I walked into the room and there on the bed was a vibrating mound under a blanket, which I pulled off to reveal Lou laughing his head off. 'Oh, I'm sorry,' he said. 'I meant to phone you to say that we've just heard that the fog has come down again and the airport has had to close for a second time.' I just thought, 'You bastard!'

Thankfully, the rest of the evening went well and we had a lovely dinner, followed by a good night's sleep. The next morning the fog had cleared and so we went to pick up the players en route to the airport. As we pulled up outside their hotel, however, the lads piled out of the reception sporting T-shirts, bags, golf brollies and other memorabilia, all emblazoned with the name of Durty Nelly's nightclub. So much for following the manager's instructions not to venture near the place! 'Fucking hell! Fucking hell!' said Lou in customary fashion.

Lou's little committee of local friends was waiting for us at the airport and managed to get us straight through customs. I don't know who they were but let's just say they appeared to have no shortage of influence. On the flight itself, Lou came and sat next to me and asked if I'd enjoyed myself. 'It's been great,' I beamed. 'Amazing!' And he said, 'There's loads more of these, don't you worry about that. How do you fancy America?' I insisted I'd love to go to the States and he said he was sure he could arrange a game for us out there. Indeed, he emphasised the same point to Stan Burke. 'Don't you worry, boys, there will be more of these.' Of course, subsequent events would sadly mean we would not get that opportunity.

The irony was that while we had been in Ireland with Macari talking about possible future trips, a newspaper story had appeared back in England that sowed the seeds of his demise at West Ham. The story claimed that Swindon chairman Brian Hillier had profited from a £6,500 bet made against his own club when they were beaten 5-0 in an FA Cup tie at Newcastle United in January 1988, when Lou was their manager. The FA duly announced that they were launching an investigation and there was a suggestion that Lou might have had some involvement in the scandal, thereby placing a black cloud over his head that would remain for several months.

In the meantime, West Ham were trying to challenge for promotion with a squad of players that wasn't really giving the manager their full support. It's to Lou's credit that the team had got a decent start to the campaign, losing just one of their first eight Second Division outings, but things then took a downturn and 1989 ended with a run of ten league games that produced just one win as the Hammers slid down to a disappointing mid-table position.

During this period we signed Justin Fashanu, the striker who had famously flopped after a £1 million move to Brian Clough's Nottingham Forest in the early 1980s, on a month's loan from Manchester City. This was a year before he publicly admitted to being gay, but the West Ham players all seemed to know about Justin's sexuality. Personally, I thought he was a very pleasant, polite guy and he always took time to speak to me, even though he had no particular reason to do so. I thought it was terrible when we heard in March 1998 that he had committed suicide.

But you can imagine what it was like when he arrived at West Ham nearly ten years earlier, with all the lads saying things like, 'Who's going to be unlucky and have to share a room with him?' We were staying up at Blackburn and it was Colin Foster who drew the 'short straw', as he called it. Poor old Fossie, he had a very slow delivery and it just gave you the impression that he wasn't the brightest bulb in the chandelier. Tony Gale used to take the piss out of him a lot and, for a big guy, he just seemed so soft. He wasn't happy when he got paired with Justin, though, and he was complaining about having to sleep with his back to the wall and things like that. He came down from his room the next morning and claimed he hadn't got a wink of sleep because of having to keep an eye on Fashanu all night. But when we were having our pre-match meal and Justin was missing, it was Foster who went upstairs to look for him. He returned to say that Justin was sitting in the middle of the room, eating mashed potato and doing yoga. Well, it takes all sorts.

Martin 'Mad Dog' Allen was another new signing, but Lou used to moan about him quite a bit. The midfielder had allegedly fallen out with Trevor Francis, his former boss at QPR, because he wanted to be at the birth of his baby, and Lou would say things like, 'Look at the way he behaves. And this is the man who talks about family values.' I don't think they really had too much time for each other.

It was only a matter of time before the Swindon scandal reared its ugly head again – and that duly occurred during an unforgettable visit to Torquay United in January 1990. The build-up to the FA Cup third-round game against the Division

Four outfit had been overshadowed by Mick McGiven's sudden resignation, the culmination of the coach's disillusionment with life at Upton Park now that John Lyall was no longer in charge. And the mood in the camp got even worse shortly after we arrived in Devon.

We stayed at a hotel that reminded me of *Fawlty Towers* – a privately owned place very close to the rocks. They were a bit mean with the bread, if I remember correctly. Anyway, the club had arranged to use a company's social sports facilities the day before the game and the weather was pretty terrible, so I was just sitting on the team bus and chewing the fat with Ivan, the driver, while the players were having their morning training session. The radio was on and suddenly the voice said, 'And in sports news, the FA have announced that Lou Macari has been charged with unauthorised betting in relation to his time at Swindon.'

'What shall I do?' I asked Ivan. 'Do I tell Lou or what?' I was in a bit of a quandary when Alvin Martin returned to the bus early, so I told him what had just been confirmed on the radio. 'Bloody hell, that will put him in a good mood,' he said. I asked if I should mention it to the manager, but he told me it was best not to get involved.

All of a sudden, the rest of the lads started appearing over the rise and we could see Lou being pursued by a bloke with a notepad and another guy trying to keep up with them while taking pictures. 'I think that solves our problem,' I said. 'He obviously knows now!'

Lou got on the coach. 'Fucking hell! Fucking hell!' he moaned.

'You've obviously heard then?' I said.

'Fucking hell! Fucking hell!' he groaned. 'That's all I need!'

We arrived back at the hotel and it was absolutely chock-a-block with cars, press guys and a TV van with a satellite dish on its roof. 'Fucking hell! Fucking hell!' said Lou. Then he turned to me: 'You're going to have to sneak me in there.' So I went and spoke to the owner of the hotel and we managed to smuggle Lou through the kitchens and up the back stairs to his room.

The rest of us met up for lunch while Lou remained out of sight and all the lads were talking about the scandal. We'd just finished eating when a guy came in from reception and asked if 'a Mr Bacon' was present. I was wondering what it was all about, when he said, 'Mr Macari would like to see you in his room.' I went and knocked on Lou's door and heard a voice ask who it was. 'It's Steve,' I said. He let me in and all he could say was, 'Fucking hell! Fucking hell!' That's all I could get out of him. I was surprised he had any hair left with the way he was furiously rubbing the top of his forehead.

Eventually he calmed down just enough to stop swearing. 'I shouldn't be here,' he said. 'I should be at home with my wife and kids.' I just told him not to be so stupid. 'What would *that* look like?' I said. 'You've got to be here. We're playing Torquay in the FA Cup tomorrow. You've got to be here.' So then he declared, 'Look, I need someone to talk to. I know, I'll order some sandwiches, that'll keep you here.' I was trying to tell him that I'd just had my lunch, but he picked up the phone to order two plates of chicken sandwiches. I liked the way he thought he could keep me in his room by plying me with food!

Lou kept insisting that he shouldn't be there. At one point I told him I'd better be making a move, but he said, 'Don't go, I'll order some more sandwiches.' I wouldn't mind, but I really wasn't hungry. He had the biggest room in the hotel and it had a balcony overlooking the cliffs. Suddenly, he got up and walked towards it. 'What are you doing?' I asked, rather worriedly, fearing the worst. And he told me he was going to shut the full-length windows. 'Oh,' I said, 'I thought you were going to jump!' I honestly thought for a moment that he was going to do something stupid.

Suddenly there was a tap on the door and it was Ronnie Boyce, who hadn't participated in the training session because he'd been feeling a bit Uncle Dick. (There's a bit of Cockney rhyming slang for you. Uncle Dick – sick.) 'What's been going on?' asked Ronnie as he came into the room. 'I've been ill in bed all morning and I've just been hassled by some reporter asking about this betting scandal.' Ronnie had told the journalist he knew nothing about it because he'd been laid up – and that was actually a quote in the following day's newspaper: 'West Ham's assistant manager, Ronnie Boyce, said, "I don't know anything about it. I've been in bed all day."' Thankfully, Ronnie's unexpected appearance gave me the opportunity to disappear, so I pushed him into the middle of the room and said, 'See you, Lou, I'm off!' I'd been stuck in there for a good hour – along with two plates of chicken sandwiches, of course.

Downstairs, the place was crawling with press and the players had been told not to talk to them. For some reason, former cricket umpire 'Dickie' Bird was also staying in the hotel and some of the players were having a laugh by shouting 'Howzat!' every time they saw him. Oh, what humour! We'd also decided to have a few drinks that Friday evening to celebrate Ronnie's forty-seventh birthday the following day. We eventually managed to lure Lou down from his room – via the kitchens – so that he could join us for a while, but we all avoided the subject of the FA charge, of course. I mean, we could hardly say, 'So, these allegations then – are they true or what?'

And then there was the game. It really did seem as if everything was conspiring against Lou, because when we got to Plainmoor it turned out that the dressing room was in the opposite corner to the dug-out. So poor old Lou had to trek across the pitch and you can just imagine the stick he got from the fans. 'All right, Lou? Have you put a bet on?' 'Where's your money today? Is it on West Ham to lose?' 'What are the odds?' He got the same treatment leaving the pitch at half-time and again when he returned for the second half. And just to make it worse, Torquay beat us with a late goal.

After the match, Lou emerged from the ground, surrounded by press guys, and climbed onto the coach. 'You fucking could have written that script, couldn't you?' he said to me. 'Yep!' I said. 'With the way the last few days have gone, that was a dead cert.' I almost said, 'You could have bet on it,' but thankfully thought better of it.

Seven days later, we were down in the West Country again for a league game against Plymouth Argyle. Kit manager Eddie Gillam and I had just got back from taking the team's stuff down to the ground when we saw Bill Bradshaw of the *Sunday People* in the hotel reception. Bradshaw had broken the original story and was really gunning for Lou. As soon as we saw him, I thought, 'Here we go. There's gonna be trouble.'

When we got back upstairs, I told Lou that I'd just seen Bradshaw. 'Fucking hell! Fucking hell!' he said, which by now was becoming something of a well-worn catch-phrase. We had our pre-match meal upstairs and Lou was wondering what to do, but I just thought I'd get my back-side on the coach and keep out of the way. All the players were on the bus and waiting to leave for the stadium when

Lou and Martin Cearns, who was just about to succeed his father Len as the West Ham chairman, emerged from the hotel with Bill Bradshaw and a photographer right behind them. It was so funny when one of the papers the following day ran a picture caption saying, 'Lou Macari leaves the team hotel with his blond minder.' We pissed ourselves with laughter over our new chairman being described as a 'blond minder'.

Typically, Lou boarded the coach, looked at me and said, 'Where the fucking hell were you when I needed you?' As far as I was concerned it had nothing to do with me, but apparently he'd been hoping I would help negotiate his escape from the hotel. Leave it to the 'blond minder', that's what I say.

After our game against Argyle, we played three closely fought Littlewoods Cup quarter-final games against Derby County, which we somehow edged through, but by the time the semi-final first leg at Oldham Athletic came around the following month, the FA had reached their verdict over the Swindon betting scandal and Macari was slapped with a £1,000 fine for his minimal involvement – he described it as 'a single telephone call' – while his former chairman was banned from football for six months.

It was hardly the greatest preparation for the game at Oldham's ground on 14 February, which has since become indelibly etched into West Ham's history as the 'St Valentine's Day Massacre'. It also didn't help that Boundary Park had a plastic pitch at that time; we'd travelled up to the game a day earlier than usual to undertake a training session on the surface, but that made very little difference, if the final result was anything to go by. The weather was absolutely horrendous the night before the game and the wind was almost

gale-force level. I watched the team training from the stands
and at one stage I thought the roof was going to blow off. Phil
Parkes was taking goal kicks and the ball was just flying back
over his head. The weather was equally atrocious the following evening. Young lads edged their way across the terraces
with tea urns on their backs, trying to keep the crowd warm.
To be honest, it was one of those occasions when you sit on
the touchline and just wonder what the hell you're doing
there – a feeling shared, no doubt, by the poor Hammers
supporters who were getting drenched behind the goal.
We were 3-0 down before half-time and I was embarrassed
to change ends during the break because everybody in the
crowd obviously knew I was covering West Ham. Usually, it's
when I go to places like Old Trafford and Anfield and decide
it's not worth changing positions, because it's not as if I'm
going to get any pictures of us scoring goals.

The second half was just as abysmal as the first: the
Hammers conceded another three goals to lose the game
6-0 and render the second leg a pointless encounter. It was
a horrible way for veterans such as Phil Parkes and Alan
Devonshire to end their West Ham careers. The dressing
room was a sombre place after that heavy thrashing, and I
can't help but think there were probably a few players hoping
that the result might nudge Lou towards the exit door.

Those harbouring such thoughts would not have to wait
too long. Just four days after the disaster at Oldham, the
West Ham bus headed to Swindon – yes, Macari's former
club, which had been fined £7,500 by the FA and was also
being investigated for making irregular payments to players – and Lou wasn't on it. This wasn't an immediate cause
for concern since the manager would quite often make his
own way to games. But when we arrived at the Post House

Hotel for our pre-match meal and he still hadn't appeared, we began to be worried by his absence.

Nobody had heard a word from Lou and we had new goalkeeper Luděk Mikloško, who we had just signed from Czech outfit Baník Ostrava, with us that day for the very first time. Ludo couldn't speak much English and Eddie Gillam and I would subsequently spend a lot of time trying to help him learn the language. On this occasion, all the boys were going up to Ludo and saying, 'We hope you've got your money because it looks as if the manager has done a runner.' He'd say, 'Pardon?' And they'd say, 'Your money? Did you get your money?' Poor old Ludo didn't have a clue what they were talking about – and maybe that was just as well really.

We had a tense lunch and afterwards I went to sit on the coach to keep out of the way. Mobile phones were still relatively new then and Martin Cearns, who had by now effectively succeeded his father as chairman, had always pooh-poohed them because he was a bit of a fuddy-duddy at times. I thought Martin and his wife Lorna were like chalk and cheese, because she was a real laugh and would sometimes call him a boring old fart herself. But I was talking to the coach driver when Martin suddenly appeared and said, 'I'm really sorry, you probably never thought I'd ever have to ask, but could I borrow your mobile phone, please?' I knew he was trying to get in touch with Lou. I showed him how the phone worked – Inspector Gadget, you see; Lou was right after all – and then Martin disappeared off to the far end of the car park with the phone to his ear. I don't know if he spoke to Lou or not, but he came back with the phone and thanked me. 'I never thought I'd have to ask to borrow that,' he said again.

We made our way to the County Ground, but there was still no sign of Lou. Without him, we drew the game 2-2, with recent signing Jimmy Quinn scoring twice, and after the final whistle I took a shot of Ronnie Boyce, Billy Bonds and youth team boss Tony Carr, who'd shared managerial responsibilities that afternoon, walking along the touch-line. That was the last we saw of Lou ... or wasn't the last we saw of Lou because we never actually saw him, if you know what I mean. The following day it was announced that Lou had resigned as manager of West Ham, after less than eight months in charge.

Much later, I spoke to Lou and he admitted that he regret-ted his decision, but said that he'd quit because he felt the adverse publicity was affecting the club. He didn't think it was fair that West Ham was becoming embroiled in contro-versy while his dirty laundry was being washed in public. He'd declared his intention to appeal against the fine imposed against him by the FA and was worried that this would mean the matter would drag on. Even though he later expressed his belief that he should have ridden the situation out, you have to give him credit for putting the club first.

I saw Lou at Leyton Orient a few years after his depar-ture from West Ham when he was managing Stoke City. I had nothing better to do that afternoon, so I thought I'd pop along to Brisbane Road. Jesus, I must have been bored. Before the game I went and knocked on the dressing-room door and Lou's assistant, Chic Bates, appeared. 'Is the gaffer in?' I asked. 'Tell him it's Steve from West Ham.' A few moments later, Lou appeared and gave me a big hug. 'Stevie! How are you?' he exclaimed. 'Come in and meet the boys.' So I followed him into the dressing room, only for him to say, 'Lads, lads, lads, see what I mean about training? If you don't train properly, this is how you're going to end up!' I just thought, 'You bastard!'

More recently, I ran into Lou at Manchester United's stadium, where he was working as a pundit for the club's television station. I wanted him to sign some books for somebody so he came down to the reception area and we had a brief chat before he began to make his way back upstairs. 'See that lad there?' he said with a grin as he turned back towards the corporate staff. 'Eight months at West Ham I was and he fucking got me sacked!' Cheers, Lou. Thanks very much!

I have great sympathy for Lou Macari because I think anybody who followed in the footsteps of John Lyall at West Ham was going to be on a hiding to nothing. John was so highly regarded by the players that anybody succeeding him would have had a problem. Lou had his own way of doing things and the players resisted his ideas and methods – many of which, it has to be said, have served him well throughout his managerial career.

He was in a position of having to repair a squad that had been relegated and the fact that he had few close allies made life even more difficult. But in the likes of Luděk Miklošk o, Martin Allen, Ian Bishop and Trevor Morley, in particular, he did make some very good signings for the club – all on my recommendation, of course!

The Swindon betting scandal was the last thing he needed and he did what he thought was the honourable thing by stepping down, but I still think it would have been interesting to see what would have happened if he'd remained at West Ham for longer. The results weren't going well but, knowing how the club worked at that time, they would probably have stuck by him for a while. Maybe with more new players on his side he could have turned things around, but we'll never know.

From my point of view, however, we had a thoroughly enjoyable time under his leadership and I was disappointed to see him go. Indeed, I was cursing my luck when he left, not least because I had been looking forward to that trip to America.

CHAPTER 3

'WHAT'S ALL THIS BOLLOCKS ABOUT DOING PHOTOS WITH HARRY?'

I t's August 1994 and West Ham United are on a pre-season tour of Scotland for friendly games against Dunfermline and St Johnstone. We're staying at the very comfortable Stirling Highland Hotel, at the foot of Stirling Castle, with little to worry about apart from deciding which of the sixty or so different whiskies available in the bar to sample next. If anybody completes all the stamps on their loyalty card they apparently bury them for free because they will obviously be dead by then. However, one man has rather more pressing concerns on his mind at this particular time – and that's Harry Redknapp.

I'm relaxing on a sofa in one of the hotel's splendid lounges in the early evening and Harry shakes his head as he sits down opposite me. 'I really don't know what to do, Steve,' he admits. 'I'm in such a quandary. I've got such a big decision to make.' 'What's that, Harry?' I ask.

He then proceeds to tell me that some associates of his are looking to purchase AFC Bournemouth with the expectation that he return to the south-coast club he managed for a nine-year period until 1992. He also reveals that he has just participated in a meeting upstairs in the hotel and that the West Ham directors want him to resist the offer from Bournemouth and take over as manager at Upton Park instead. 'But what would people think?' he says. 'They would think I'd stabbed Billy Bonds in the back and I wouldn't want that.'

'I really don't know what to advise you,' I say, even though I'm not sure he's necessarily looking for my advice. I assume it's just a case of Harry wanting to talk, although there's a possibility that he is trying to gauge my reaction to the possibility of him replacing Billy as manager after acting as his assistant for the past two years.

But what can I say? This is very different from Lou Macari asking me what I think about him buying a certain player. I get on well with Harry but I also like Billy, and I can see that things wouldn't look right if one replaced the other without there being a mutual agreement between them. It would indeed imply that something strange had taken place. But Harry seems genuine and, up until this point in time, the two men have been the best of buddies. They spent five years together as teammates at West Ham between 1967 and 1972 – Billy asked Harry to be his best man when he got married during that period and later invited his good friend to become his assistant at Upton Park in 1992.

So I really don't know what to say to Harry, nor do I see it as my business to influence his decision in any way. I suspect he would prefer to manage West Ham ahead of Bournemouth (I mean, who wouldn't?) but, of course, there's the Bonzo factor. 'Bill's my best mate,' he says, 'and it will look as if I've shafted him.'

Harry wanders off, his mind no clearer for having sought my counsel, and my thoughts return to which whisky stamp I fancy collecting next in the hotel bar. After that little conversation, I think I need a drink.

Less than a week later, Billy Bonds has resigned as manager of West Ham and the club is holding a press conference at the Boleyn Ground to confirm the appointment of Harry Redknapp as his successor. And that's when I really get caught in the crossfire between the two men. There are lots of other photographers present and one of them says, 'Steve, you know Harry. We'd like to take some pictures of him outside, so could you have a word?'

I speak to Harry and tell him my colleagues need to take some pictures, but he says he doesn't really feel like doing anything. He is very downbeat. 'This should be the happiest day of my life,' he shrugs, 'but now Billy has gone people are going to think I've stitched him up.' He eventually agrees to be photographed in the seats of one of the stands. 'I'm not going to smile, Steve, because this is a sad day,' he insists. And he really does look as miserable as sin.

After the photo-shoot, Harry approaches me and says, 'Steve, what do you reckon if I can get Billy to come over tomorrow for you to take some pictures of the pair of us together, so that people can see that there are no hard feelings between us?' Perhaps a little naively, I say it's fine. He says it would be good if we could do that. I return to the *Recorder* offices and then go home, where I receive a phone call from Billy Bonds in the evening. 'Steve, what's all this bollocks about me doing some photos with Harry tomorrow?' he asks. I tell Billy that it wasn't my idea and that Harry had suggested it might let everybody know that everything is all right between the two of them. 'I don't like the sound of that,' he says. 'No, I'm not going to do it.'

Billy doesn't say anything negative about Harry, just that he doesn't want to get involved – 'That's if it's all right with you,' he adds. I tell him that if he doesn't want to do it then that's fine with me. It's funny, but Billy is almost apologetic as he declares his reluctance to co-operate with the idea. And hence there are no photographs of Billy and Harry embracing and smiling for the camera as one passes the baton of West Ham's management to the other.

It was only some time later, when the dust had settled, that Billy told me what actually happened when he met chairman Terry Brown and managing director Peter Storrie in that room at the Stirling Highland Hotel. Bill was asked how he would feel about the idea of moving into an upstairs role as the club's director of football, with Harry taking over as manager. When Billy made it obvious he wasn't interested in the possibility, it was suggested that he forget it had been mentioned. 'Hang on, I can't forget it now!' he told them. 'You've just told me you don't want me as manager and that you want Harry instead, but now you're telling me to just forget it. How can I do that?'

Billy clearly believed that his position at West Ham was untenable after this conversation and that resigning would be the honourable thing to do. That's the kind of guy he is. In my opinion, there's no doubt that Harry's potential move to Bournemouth put huge pressure on the West Ham board to make a decision and it provided enough leverage to swing things in his favour. Not that I can say I played much of a role in encouraging Harry to take the job. After all, I needed to get my whisky card stamped.

In all honesty, I wasn't very pleased to see Billy Bonds leave West Ham – albeit with a healthy £500,000 pay-off – and would have been more than happy to see him continue as the club's manager. I still don't think he got the credit he deserved for guiding the Hammers to two promotions during his four years in charge. But even Billy would surely admit that certain events had left him feeling a little disillusioned with the game by the start of the 1994/95 season. And it certainly seemed that Harry Redknapp had taken on the responsibility for the wheeling and dealing in the transfer market after his arrival. That was presumably a big reason why the club's hierarchy didn't want to lose him when the Bournemouth link came up. I think Billy has gone on record and said that working in the transfer market wasn't necessarily his strongest point.

Yet none of this changes the fact that Billy Bonds was the natural choice to steady the West Ham ship after Lou Macari resigned in February 1990. I was down at the training ground when Billy held his first meeting with the players and he had a big smile on his face. 'Yes! I've got the big one!' he declared while clenching his fist. Ronnie Boyce had been acting as caretaker boss for a few days. 'Lads, I just want to thank you for all your support during my reign as manager,' he joked. 'I couldn't have asked for more!'

Billy was the logical choice to assume control on a permanent basis. He'd been running the Hammers youth team since retiring as a player four years earlier at the age of forty-one. West Ham had broken from tradition by appointing a complete outsider in Lou Macari and I think the board realised that there was only one man to get the club out of the mess they now found themselves in. And the name was Bonds, Billy Bonds. So they called for Bonzo and it just seemed natural that he would get things back to the West Ham way and turn the club's fortunes around. He was the people's choice to take over and I was pleased because I got on well with Billy and knew that I'd have no problems in terms of remaining part of the back-room set-up. Billy was clearly delighted and I congratulated him. Everyone at the club was thrilled for him.

The mood at the club changed dramatically when Billy took charge. Where the players had showed a complete lack of respect for Lou, it was the total opposite with Bonzo. Who couldn't respect Billy? He was the club's record holder for number of appearances with nearly 800 games to his name and had captained the team to two FA Cup final successes and one Second Division championship. It was obvious that Billy knew the game and he certainly had no difficulty communicating with the players. He seemed very calm and collected in what he did and always took time to think before saying anything instead of having a go at players in front of everybody else. And his popularity was reflected in improved results, with the team winning ten of their final seventeen league games to finish seventh in the Division Two table and even going halfway to overturning the six-goal deficit to Oldham in the second leg of the Littlewoods Cup semi-final.

Fortunes improved even further the following season as West Ham surged to promotion on the back of an incredible run of twenty-one unbeaten league games at the start of the campaign. There's no doubt that Billy Bonds was a natural leader of men on the pitch, but if it's possible to offer any criticism of him as a manager it's perhaps that he didn't have a lot of time for players that didn't live up to his standards. If somebody didn't produce the level of commitment that Billy had done as a player, he tended to ignore them instead of wrapping an arm around their shoulder. I remember striker Jimmy Quinn, who'd been signed shortly before Lou Macari's departure, once coming up to me and saying, 'Have you got any photos of me?' I said, 'Yes, I've got lots.' And he said, 'Can you fucking pin one on Bonzo's door so that he might remember what I look like?' I think he was struggling to start games during the 1990/91 season!

So maybe Billy's man-management could have been better at times. It was especially amusing watching him try to deal with the rumours that began circulating about a particularly close friendship that had developed between Ian Bishop and Trevor Morley, two players who had arrived hand-in-hand – well, on the same day, at least – from Manchester City in a deal that saw Mark Ward return north in December 1989. All kinds of eyebrow-raising and head-scratching theories emerged after Morley suffered a knife injury to the stomach at his home in March 1991, one of which was based on the notion that he and Bish were, er, more than just good friends.

It didn't help that people like Tony Gale were mercilessly winding up Billy about the pair of them. Galey would say things like, 'Those two have come in together again. They're always together; I wonder what they've been up to.' Billy was like, 'Bloody hell. What's going on between them?' And in the end things came to a head. One day Bonds erupted, 'Bish! Morley! In my office now!' The three of them disappeared into Bill's room while the rest of the lads listened at the door. Galey loves to tell the story of hearing Bonzo confront Bishop and Morley with the question: 'Well, are you or ain't you?' That was Billy's way of broaching the subject with them. Bish apparently told Billy that he wasn't even going to dignify that question with an answer. And Bill was like, 'Well, I've got to ask you. You're always hanging around the place together and leaving at the same time.'

Billy was very orthodox and genuine. I wouldn't call him naive, but he'd just had a normal upbringing with nothing funny going on around him. Of course, the reality was that Ian and Trevor were just good mates. They had come down from Manchester together and, when two players make the move between clubs at the same time, it's inevitable that they are going to support each other as they adapt to their new environment. I knew there was nothing going on between them, especially as they were both married – and if either of them was getting up to anything then it would be with a woman rather than another man. Indeed, that was my assumption – rightly or wrongly – because I know what footballers are like. I remember one player once saying to the other boys, 'I don't know what the fuss is about. You've got your wife; then you've got your mistress. What's wrong with that?'

However, the gay rumours refused to go away and the other players wouldn't stop making jokes about the matter. Galey was terrible. If he saw Bishop and Morley within a few yards of each other, he'd say, 'Look at them, Guv, they're at it again.' Poor old Trevor scored seventy goals over six seasons for the Hammers, but it's impossible to mention his name without people asking about Ian Bishop – it still happens to this very day. I just say there's nothing in it and that it's an urban myth.

It's funny because I took a team photograph around that time when the club wanted a big poster produced and Brian Blower, our commercial manager, selected the transparency to be used. I can remember the printer asking me if I was sure about the chosen shot and when I asked why he said, 'Because two of your players in the front row have got their hands on each other's knees.' As it turned out, it was Ian Bishop and Julian Dicks having a laugh, but you can forgive me for making the wrong assumptions!

Trevor has since insisted that the stabbing was nothing but an accident, which just makes me think he really should be more careful in the kitchen. In general, I found Trevor to be quite an intelligent, deep-thinking bloke. I met his Norwegian wife, Monica, quite a few times and she struck me as a bit of a fireball. Apparently, the couple had been out on the evening in question at a bash where Ian Bishop had also been present.

I really liked Bish, who was a very friendly guy. When he comes back to Upton Park nowadays I always get a big man-hug from him. But I have to say he was a lightweight with the booze. One pint and he'd be well away – and he was stupid with it. He was a funny drunk and giggled at everything. There was one occasion when he rolled into training while we were in Scotland and I didn't know how he could even walk, let alone train. I think Billy raised an eyebrow at him that morning. And then there was the time when he turned up for training with his hands wrapped up in bandages, as if he'd been mummified! I asked him what the hell he'd done and he told me that he'd come back from the pub, gone into his garage to get something and tripped over on his way out. He'd put his hands out to catch his fall and landed in some sharp gravel. He'd had to go to hospital to get all the stones and bits of gravel plucked out and he was in a hell of a state.

Trevor Morley's tummy troubles were sufficient for him to miss nine games and he faced a race against time to be fit for the FA Cup semi-final game against Nottingham Forest in April. On Trevor's first day back in training, the management had warned the other players not to mention the stabbing incident because it was a sensitive issue. But, typically, the lads went into the kitchen and grabbed a load of knives, which they strategically placed between the ribs of a skeleton in the medical room. So that was the first thing Trevor saw as he checked in with John Green, the physiotherapist who had taken over from Rob Jenkins. Telling the players to go easy on somebody is like waving a red rag in front of a bull: you're going to get a reaction.

Trevor did manage to make it back in time for the semi-final at Villa Park, and though his fitness was still something of a concern, it was Tony Gale who was left feeling hurt after the game. Galey was controversially sent off by referee Keith Hackett for a so-called professional foul on Gary Crosby midway through the first half, with the game still goalless at that point. It seemed a ridiculous decision but the crowd kept singing 'Billy Bonds' claret and blue army' throughout the second half. Hammers fans don't chant the manager's name as a matter of formality; it has to be earned. A whole host of managers at Upton Park have never achieved it, but the likes of John Lyall and Billy Bonds certainly did. The spirit of the West Ham faithful that day at Villa Park was just something else. Their ten-man team was getting beaten 4-0, but the fans just kept on singing. And singing...

It was one of the few times I've seen Galey struggle to raise a smile. Tony had inherited the joker's role at West Ham in the mid-1980s, but he wasn't laughing on that occasion. The pictures of the dismissal just show the look of total disbelief on Galey's face and he was still fuming about it on the coach home. Under normal circumstances, 'Reggie', as he was known, is the biggest piss-taker in the world. When Matty Holmes arrived, the first thing that Galey said to him was, 'I'm fucking glad you're here, it's taken the pressure off my big ears.' Poor old Matty just didn't know what to say. I get the same treatment from him as well. We were at a 'Boys of '86' bash in London recently and he was introducing me to the crowd. 'He's played more games for West Ham than the rest of us put together...' he said. And just before he announced my name, the tune of 'Roll out the Barrel' suddenly started playing. The cheek of it!

Thankfully, the players refused to allow the disappointment of defeat against Forest to derail their promotion efforts, but it was perhaps typical that in the end we saw the Division Two trophy snatched away from us in heartbreaking fashion. It was the final day of the season and I was heading up to the directors' box after our home game against Notts County – which we had lost – to take some pictures of the crowd that had congregated on the pitch, jubilant in the belief that we were champions. By the time I got to the upper tier of the West Stand, however, news had filtered through that we'd been pipped at the post: Oldham Athletic had scored an injury-time penalty against Sheffield Wednesday to finish top. So that was one photograph that certainly didn't need taking.

Nevertheless, it was a great achievement for Billy Bonds to lift West Ham back into the top flight in his first full season as manager, although the events of the following year had most supporters wondering why we had bothered. Few who remember those days will need reminding of the infamous Bond Scheme. If ever there was an example of a football club shooting itself in the foot then this was it. The ill-conceived scheme dictated that fans had to purchase a Hammers Bond – ranging in price from £500 to £975 – before acquiring the right to buy a season ticket. Basically, West Ham wanted to redevelop the Boleyn Ground and decided that if the fans wanted to sit in a nice modern stadium then they would have to help fund it, with the cunning plan designed to raise more than £15 million.

It seemed like extortion and I told chairman Martin Cearns that I thought the scheme was ridiculous. When he asked why, I told him that my brother Martin had been a season-ticket holder for many years but simply could not afford to buy a bond. 'Well, he can't have a season ticket then,' he retorted. I repeated that this was absurd, but he just said, 'No bond, no season ticket.' I told him it was a crazy idea and that there was no way that the fans were going to wear it. And his attitude was, 'Well, they will have to.'

To me, the whole scheme represented a massive own goal, a cynical attempt to exploit the loyalty of the fans. And I was also aware of the manager's discomfort with the concept. It might have been a case of Bonds by name, but certainly not by nature. Billy didn't really want to get involved in the promotion of the scheme, but he felt obliged to a certain extent because of his position at the club. The board wanted to take advantage of his surname to publicise the bonds and I know that Billy wasn't happy about it. I had to go to Upton Park to take a picture of him and Trevor Brooking, who had also been roped in to help sell the scheme, with a model of the revamped ground. Billy reluctantly went along with the initial launch but after that he didn't really want much to do with it.

Then, of course, the fans' demonstrations started midway through the season. I took pictures of a guy marching across the Upton Park pitch with a corner flag in his hand during a game against Everton in February 1992 and Julian Dicks standing next to him, probably discussing what a load of crap it all was. Dicksy was dead against the scheme and it's my opinion that most of the players were. I also remember taking a photograph of fans invading the pitch with a huge banner saying 'Lying Thieving Cheats'. Inevitably, Martin Cearns got terrible abuse in the directors' box. There was genuine anger about what the club was trying to impose.

The protests created an unsettling atmosphere that made life extremely hard for the players. You just didn't know what was going to happen from one game to the next. From a working point of view the demonstrations didn't worry me – as I've said, I got some memorable pictures out of it – but I was quick on my feet at the end of games to make sure I didn't get caught up in anything. There's no disguising the fact that it was a very bad time for the club and the directors totally misjudged the supporters. I just thought it was so pompous to believe the fans would blindly accept the idea. But some poor souls did indeed buy a bond and that put the club in an awkward position when they eventually decided to scrap the scheme as a prerequisite for obtaining a season ticket.

Whether West Ham would have otherwise stayed up in 1992 we'll never know, but the disruption certainly can't have helped the results, which went from bad to worse in the second half of the season and left us at the foot of the table when it ended. Of course, that didn't stop the team from beating Manchester United in their penultimate home game when they were all but relegated. Ken Brown scored the winning goal to ruin the title hopes of United manager Alex Ferguson, who famously complained about West Ham's 'obscene' amount of effort. Clearly you're not meant to try *too* hard when you play Manchester United. It was somewhat typical that West Ham rose to the occasion when it was simply too late.

It was the summer of 1992 when Billy Bonds said that he was going to bring Harry Redknapp back to West Ham to be his right-hand man. I told Bill that I'd yet to meet Harry, but he assured me that he was a great bloke and that I'd get on really well with him. He said that Harry had a great sense of humour and maybe Billy thought that might help lift spirits in the camp after what had been a thoroughly depressing campaign. He also knew that Harry would busy himself with the transfer market and provide vital support as he set about trying to get the Hammers back into the top flight again. What I didn't know at the time was that Billy had sought the advice of Trevor Brooking, who apparently suggested that perhaps it wasn't the best thing to do. If that was the case, I'm surprised that Billy didn't listen to him because he was – and still is – very good friends with Trevor.

Up until that point, Ronnie Boyce had been Billy's assistant but he would now take on the role of chief scout. Boycie had been a great player. His nickname was Ticker because he was the heartbeat of the West Ham team in the 1960s. The funny thing is that he used to get a bit of stick from some people. 'You're always going on about that goal,' they would say, because he used to love talking about his wonder-strike from near the halfway line in a 5-1 win at Manchester City in March 1970. Boycie was with us when we took the kit down to Maine Road for a game in the early 1990s and he wandered out onto the pitch. 'It was just about here it was,' he proudly declared as he stood in the centre circle. Eddie Gillam and I just said, 'For crying out loud, stop banging on about that bloody goal!'

Bonzo and Boycie used to go on scouting trips together and Billy would drive in his nice BMW 7 series car. I'm a car freak and would often try and talk to Bill about the specifications of the car, but all Bill would ever say was, 'I've got no idea; all I know is that it's the best car I've ever had.' Boycie was a big smoker and there was no way Billy would let him puff away in the car. Billy used to tell me how they would pull up for a coffee somewhere and Boycie would be jumping out to light up a cigarette before the car's wheels had even stopped turning.

Harry Redknapp has since claimed that what he saw at Upton Park on his arrival in the summer of 1992 shocked him to the core – he never was one to understate things – and he quickly made his presence felt by bringing in the likes of Peter Butler, Mark Robson and Matty Holmes, who would go on to prove hugely influential in midfield as the team pursued promotion.

The team soon began to get back to its winning ways, but I think half my pictures from that season are of Julian Dicks being sent off. There was the famous one at Wolves of Dicksy trooping off after getting involved with Steve Bull and Paul Birch. Billy had been forced to sprint down the touchline to stop his left-back from getting into even bigger trouble. Dicks also saw red at Newcastle and again at Derby, where I remember the West Ham fans cheering him as he stomped off. It's always puzzled me why supporters applaud players when they've been sent off and reduced their side to ten men, but I suppose that's football fans for you. Needless to say, Billy wasn't too impressed by Julian's antics, but he certainly never bawled him out while I was in the dressing room.

Nowadays, the security guys generally march players down the tunnel once they've been sent off, but in those days it was Eddie Gillam's role. I used to joke with Eddie that he missed most of the action from the 1992/93 season because he was always escorting Dicksy back to the dressing room. Not that Julian saw much of it himself, as he was absent for thirteen games through suspension.

It goes without saying that Dicksy was a hero to the Hammers fans, who just loved the vision of the player with his socks scrunched down around his ankles and the blood vessels bulging on his neck. He always used to rip the collars of his shirts – much to Eddie's dismay – and he personified toughness and tenacity while combining class and commitment, although composure wasn't his strong point at times.

The thing with Julian is that he is a totally different character when he is on his own – he's just a pussycat. I liked him a lot. I took a picture of him at the training ground with his daughters, Katie and Jessica, and I remember thinking that they looked like a couple of little dolls. He doted on them like any sensitive, caring father. But when he was with the other players he tended to play up to them a little bit and conform to the role of the hard man. However, I always thought Julian was easy to get on with and he was very friendly to me. He'd join in with the banter and maybe take the piss now and again. If he spotted you in the gym at Chadwell Heath he'd always try to hit you with the ball. He'd be firing these rockets at you and you'd be diving out of the way to avoid being taken out.

Dicksy also used to be murder at team photo sessions. The contract would state that you had to have three footballs in the picture, so we'd set things up before the lads came out. Of course, Julian would see these balls and just fire them as far away from the benches as physically possible. It took us a couple of years to work out that it might be better if we brought out the balls *after* the players had sat down. And then you'd have to try and get a shot where Dicksy didn't have his hand on another bloke's knee.

Dicksy was mucking about on the coach one day, swinging from the luggage racks and knocking into everybody. Eddie and I used to sit with goalkeeper Luděk Mikloško and try to help him learn English by going through his dictionary. As Dicksy was messing about, Ludo flicked through the pages of his book and leant across to point out a new word he'd just learned: 'fool'.

However, there was one occasion on which Dicksy certainly met his match. He liked to soak in the bath before matches and on this particular day he was relaxing as usual when we suddenly heard a commotion. 'What the fuck!' Dicksy leapt out of the tub as if he'd just been electrocuted. 'You fucking dirty bastard!' he screamed as he shot across the dressing room while stark bollock naked. Another player – with canine tendencies, it would seem – had only just had a big shit in the water. Poor Dicksy had suddenly opened his eyes to see a big log floating past his nose.

Much as he was loved, even Julian would admit that he had his work cut out to match the level of adoration that existed for the legendary Bobby Moore, the extent of which was evident to all when the former England and West Ham captain passed away on 24 February 1993 after losing his battle against bowel cancer. The news had yet to break when I took a phone call from somebody asking if I had been to the recent England game against San Marino at Wembley and taken a picture of Bobby during his radio commentary. I asked why and I was told that he had just died. Within an hour, Bobby's death at the age of fifty-one became public knowledge and I was devastated – as, of course, were Billy Bonds, Harry Redknapp and Ronnie Boyce, his former teammates.

Boycie used to room with Mooro for West Ham's away games and always said how immaculate he was. He'd describe how Bobby would take off his watch and put it on the bedside table all neat and tidy, as impeccable as you'd expect after seeing him on the pitch. Our old physio Rob Jenkins said that Bobby had a 'presence' about him. He believed that even if you'd never heard of Bobby Moore, when he walked into the room, you'd instantly know he was somebody special. He just had that star quality.

We all knew Bobby had been ill and wasn't looking too good, but that didn't dampen the sense of shock. I'd never really had any dealings with Mooro because he'd already left West Ham by the time I started getting heavily involved with the club in the mid-1970s, but I did see him a few times when he was working as a pundit at Upton Park and he'd always say 'All right, mate' if we bumped into each other in a corridor.

After hearing the news of Bobby's death, I went straight down to the Boleyn Ground but there were only half a dozen people there and just a few things on the railings. Up at the *Recorder* the next day, sports editor Trevor Smith was very upset because he'd been great mates with Bobby. He used to meet the likes of Mooro and Ken Brown socially for a beer now and again. He suggested I get back down to Upton Park because things had apparently gone crazy overnight. And, sure enough, there were lots more people and tons of stuff on the gates. I returned to the ground several more times during the immediate period of mourning and it was extremely emotional. I'd start reading the tributes, the tears would begin to flow and it would just get to me every time. There were messages and memorabilia from people around the entire country, not just West Ham fans, and that's what confirmed how much affection there was for England's World Cup-winning captain.

On one of these visits, I took a photograph of an old boy on crutches who was crying by an old Bobby Moore shirt. The photo appeared in the paper, and some time later, a guy rang the *Recorder* offices and told me the man was his father and that he'd just died. He said that lots of West Ham fans were going to his dad's funeral and he wondered if I'd mind them using that picture. Of course, I was more than happy to oblige and so we got some posters produced for them to display on their vehicles. But that photograph was just one of many overwhelming images as the country mourned Bobby's passing.

A few days after Bobby's death, the Hammers played out a goalless draw at Sunderland, with neither team really seeming in the mood. The flag at Roker Park was at half-mast and there was an eerie atmosphere in the ground. It was our home game against Wolves, however, that provided the real opportunity for the club and the fans to pay their respects to Bobby.

West Ham were being allowed to rest the number six shirt – which was later retired for good – so I came down to the ground early to take a photograph of Eddie Gillam hanging the tops up, showing the four, five, seven sequence. Remember, this was before squad numbers came into force: the team always ran from one to eleven. Bobby's former West Ham and England teammates Geoff Hurst and Martin Peters, along with Ron Greenwood, their manager at Upton Park, had agreed to carry a huge floral number six shirt onto the pitch. I'll always remember one of the news photographers saying, 'Oi! You mate! Can you get out of the way, please?' I couldn't believe that he was shouting at Ron Greenwood and, when I told him who he was, he just said, 'Who?' It was a brief moment of light relief in an otherwise sombre day, although the team thankfully did their bit by winning 3-1 against Wolves.

I've since met Bobby's widow, Stephanie, several times through her friendship with Brian Dear – another former Hammer with whom he was close – and her work for the Bobby Moore Fund for Cancer Research, which has brought her to Upton Park on many occasions. I've also seen Tina Moore, Bobby's first wife, a few times.

I would have liked to have known Mooro and worked with

him in the way I have with many players since his time at the club. I also think it would have been nice if Bobby had been given a chance to return to West Ham in some capacity after he retired as a player, following stints with Fulham and clubs in America.

What I'm led to believe is that there were some unsavoury hangers-on in Bobby's life and he'd also been involved in some questionable business projects. Whatever the truth, I get the impression he had some baggage that discouraged both West Ham and the Football Association from embracing him. In those days, the game wasn't marketed and promoted on the same scale it is today, but it's still a big shame that West Ham couldn't have employed Bobby in an ambassadorial role because he was the club's most famous son – and always will be. But in the event they did very little. I've found West Ham have a spectacular aptitude for misjudging things: if something can be done the wrong way, you can generally rely on them to do it. When I say that, I'm thinking of the Bond Scheme, the way they neglected Bobby Moore in the 1980s and their handling of the management situation in 1994 when Billy Bonds felt compelled to resign.

The Hammers stuttered a little towards the end of the 1992/93 campaign, but they recovered to head into their final game at home to Cambridge – who needed victory to avoid relegation – knowing they would clinch promotion behind runaway leaders Newcastle as long as they matched the result of Portsmouth, who had been on a fantastic end-of-season run. West Ham achieved what they needed with a 2-0 win, thanks in part to David Speedie, who scored the opener, taking his tally to four goals in an eleven-game loan spell. The fans hated the fiery former Chelsea striker and, even though he helped us win promotion, they still hated him

Things turned a bit ugly in 1992 with pitch protests over the club's Bond Scheme.

Frank Lampard came along to support me at the launch of my pictorial book, *Hammers in Focus*, in 1998.

This elderly Hammers fan was clearly overcome with emotion looking at the tributes left at Upton Park for Bobby Moore following his death in 1993.

Frank Lampard leads training at the WACA in Perth at the beginning of our Australian adventure.

LEFT Controversial player Marco Boogers joined West Ham in 1995 – and we got him blowing bubbles at the press conference.

RIGHT Frank Carson paid a pre-match visit to one of our home games and his gags proved a little too much, so I got local PC Geoff Martin to 'feel his collar' – just for a picture, of course!

RIGHT Billy Bonds faces the press at the gates of the Chadwell Heath training ground after his appointment as manager in 1990.

LEFT From the left: John Green, yours truly, Eddie Gillam and Ges Steinbergs. The Four Amigos.

BELOW One of my all-time favourite photos: Harry Redknapp and Billy Bonds enjoy a celebratory post-match beer having just won promotion in 1993.

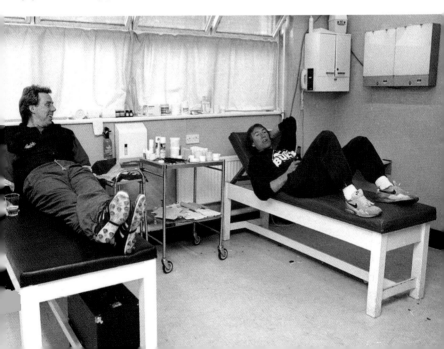

New manager Lou Macari shows his colours on the Upton Park pitch in 1989.

My all-time Hammers idol Billy Bonds welcomes another of my favourite players, Liam Brady, to West Ham in 1987.

LEFT Harry Redknapp became Hammers manager in August 1994, but he was in no mood to smile for the cameras given the circumstances surrounding his appointment.

RIGHT A very rare shot of troublesome wantaway Joey Beauchamp in West Ham kit at a pre-season friendly against Oxford City in 1994.

Pre-season in Munich in 1995 and boss Harry Redknapp (pictured here with assistant Frank Lampard) clearly doesn't like what he's seeing from the touchline.

ABOVE A fantastic souvenir from Australia – me in front of the Sydney Opera House and Sydney Harbour Bridge. Thanks to Eddie Gillam for his excellent work!

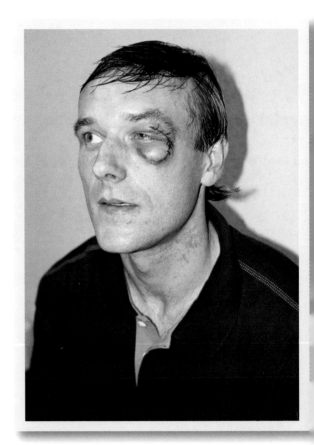

RIGHT Harry Redknapp insisted I take this photo of Luděk Mikloško's terrible eye injury, sustained at Leeds United in 1994.

I remain friends with many old players and caught up with Frank McAvennie at a 'Boys of '86' reunion dinner.

Harry Redknapp shares a joke with Coventry's Gordon Strachan and a young Frank Lampard as the latter prepares to make his Hammers debut in 1996.

The 'Boys of '86' have had several reunion dinners over the years and I found myself on the other side of the camera on this occasion.

Former manager Ron Greenwood and England teammates Geoff Hurst and Martin Peters carry a huge floral number six shirt onto the pitch at the first home match after Bobby Moore's death.

after he'd gone – which proves how much they hated him in the first place! Clive Allen scored the second goal right at the death to seal the result and moments later the crowd poured onto the pitch, forcing me to dive over the wall to escape the flood of fans. I then went up to the directors' box to take the celebratory picture we'd been denied two years earlier. It was absolutely phenomenal, with a sea of bodies washing right across the Upton Park pitch. The strange thing is that the stands still looked virtually full, so I've got no idea where all the people came from. But the club loved the picture and they placed a huge image in one of the upstairs lounges for several years.

The photograph I really treasure, however, is the one I took of Billy Bonds and Harry Redknapp after the game. I'd shot some material of the players celebrating in the dressing room, for which Billy had given me clearance. As I came out, I walked past the medical room where Harry and Bill were relaxing on the beds and chatting between themselves. I went back to get my camera, which I'd left in the dressing room with the rest of my stuff, and as I returned I could see Ken Dyer of the *Evening Standard* about to enter. 'Ken, Ken, come away,' I whispered and quickly leant around the door to fire off one shot. Of course, the flash revealed my presence, but I'd got my picture and it worked so well because it wasn't posed. It captures the two guys in a very natural way and it is still one of my very favourite pictures today. 'Come in and have a beer with us,' they said. And I did – just to be sociable, naturally.

The club had enjoyed an incredible turnaround when you consider how bad things had been just twelve months earlier and you have to give Harry Redknapp a lot of credit for that. It just seemed a really good partnership between Billy and Harry and I thought they complemented each other really well. Both men were happy with my presence in the dressing room at games and I could see that they clearly had the respect of the players. Billy would take the team talks and Harry would chip in with a few constructive comments afterwards.

We had some good times on the road under Billy and Harry because they always had plenty of tales to tell over dinner. Billy had brought John Green in as the physio, as well as Ges Steinbergs as the new club doctor, and it was a nice group of people who got on extremely well together. The relationship between Billy and Harry couldn't have been better at this time and there were plenty of laughs to be had. On one occasion, we were in a hotel for a pre-match meal and the food was brought to our table on silver trays. For some reason the serving staff wanted to lift all the chrome domes at the same time and so it was a case of 'one, two, three...' before our food was unveiled. And on Billy's plate there was just a small piece of fillet steak. Harry turned to the waiter and said, 'You can't give him a steak like that – he's an MBE!' Needless to say, the guy quickly returned with one of the biggest steaks you've ever seen.

We used to have fun on the coach journeys as well. Kevin Keen, one of our most influential players during this period, used to spend ages compiling quizzes to keep the players occupied on the team bus. For the picture round he'd go through all the Sunday magazines and cut things out. He certainly made an effort.

We had Mike Small – the 'Plaistow Pearl' I think Harry once called him – with us at that time and the striker wasn't the sharpest tool in the box. We used to have a laugh at him during the quizzes. In one of the rounds you had to pick a category and then spin for a letter – your answer would then have to begin with that letter. One question asked for a form of communication and the letter O came up. So we were all having a serious think when Mike Small suddenly said, 'Ox!' Everyone said, 'Ox? What do you mean ox? How can an ox be a form of communication?' And Small said, 'In my family's village, if you wanted to send a message, you tied it to an ox and you'd smack its arse to send it on to the next village.' I wouldn't mind, but he was born in Birmingham. Talk about playing on your roots! In the end, we had to let his answer stand.

We certainly had some characters at the club. We sold George Parris to Birmingham in early 1993, although I'd like to think he relied on more conventional forms of communication than Mike Small when he was up there. The midfielder was dubbed 'Chicken George' after the character in the *Roots* television series. He undoubtedly suffered some racist abuse during his career, but George's way of dealing with it was to treat it as banter and have a laugh about it.

Since his retirement he has confessed to a gambling addiction, but there was little evidence of that when he was at West Ham. I know he used to like a drink now and again because he'd often go to the Prince of Wales in Green Lane with Steve Potts and a few others after our trips away. George had a heart scare when he collapsed during a home game against Arsenal in 1992 and everyone was very concerned for him. I might have thought he was dying, but it still didn't stop me from taking a picture of him!

One bloke I didn't really have any time for was Mitchell Thomas. He was always dripping with gold jewellery and just had something about him that I didn't like. I suspected that he thought he was coming down a level to be with us and I used to think, 'Well, why don't you piss off back to Tottenham then?' Not my cup of tea at all.

Another character I didn't take to was Dale Gordon – or 'Disco Dale' as we used to call him. He was famous for that one step-over move, which used to encourage ironic cheers from the crowd. I always thought he was a bit flash. He used to say, 'Mortgage? What's a mortgage?' And all the lads would start to explain what it was and he'd say, 'I know what it is, it's just that I'll never need one because I've got pots of dough. If I want a place I'll just buy it.' He missed a lot of games through injury and seemed to spend a lot of time on crutches. He damaged his ankle after a buggy was over-turned on a golf course once. Of course, that got described as a 'training incident'.

Gordon does at least hold the distinction of scoring West Ham's first ever Premier League goal, in a 1-1 draw at Coventry City three games into the 1993/94 season. Clive Allen scored the next two in a 2-0 home win against Sheffield Wednesday a few days later. Clive was a really nice guy and I got on very well with him. By the time he joined us, he'd been on the books of so many London clubs – including QPR, Arsenal, Crystal Palace, Tottenham and Chelsea – that there was only one thing for it when I took his picture on arrival. 'I know it's bit corny,' I said, 'but you've played for so many capital clubs I think we should have you reading the *London A-Z*. 'Fucking hell!' he said. 'That is corny.' I asked him if he could think of anything better and, of course, he couldn't. Yet Clive didn't seem like a typical footballer and was more intelligent than most. Well, certainly brighter than Mike Small.

West Ham had picked up a few points but a 4-0 home defeat by QPR suggested we faced a long season of struggle, so the club was forced to sacrifice its best player in September 1993 in order to try and strengthen the team as a whole. That player, of course, was Julian Dicks. I have to say I was really disappointed to see him go. But everybody has to leave a club at some point. Even Bobby Moore left West Ham before his career was over and if you're getting rid of people like him then anybody can go.

But it was dramatic stuff. Harry had struck a deal for Dicks with Liverpool boss Graeme Souness that saw West Ham receive midfielder Mike Marsh and left-back David Burrows, plus a bit of extra cash to buy striker Lee Chapman from Portsmouth. I can remember the three new recruits turning up at our training ground and getting straight on the bus for a game at Blackburn Rovers the next day. I just thought, 'How the hell is this going to work?' But we won 2-0 and Chapman scored the opening goal, so we'd clearly done something right.

Returning to the coach after the game, Harry spotted Gary Firmager, the editor of the *Over Land and Sea* fanzine, and said, 'You look miserable. What's the matter? Have we fucked you up by winning and left you with nothing to complain about?' Harry was clearly upset by something that had been written and really laid into Firmager. 'You're only happy when we lose, aren't you?' he demanded. And Firmager was left stuttering, 'No, Harry. No, Harry, mate, mate, mate...' It was hilarious.

From that moment on, West Ham fans had little to moan about, as the team went on a good run, with just two defeats in eleven league games, to consolidate their position in the table. There was a period after Christmas when we seemed to draw a lot of games, but two wins over Easter – including a 4-1 victory at Tottenham – pretty much ensured we would be safe. Happy days.

However, this is West Ham and there's always one storm cloud or another lurking on the horizon. Hopes were high when the club signed Joey Beauchamp from Oxford United for a fee of £1 million in the summer of 1994, but I sensed that things weren't quite right from the moment the 23-year-old winger arrived. I went down to the Boleyn Ground to take some pictures of the player on his first day with us and could see him sitting outside in an old Ford Escort with his girlfriend. Inside the ground, I spoke to kit man Eddie and asked if Joey had been in yet, but he said he hadn't. We ended up waiting for some considerable time for him to show his face, which I thought was a bit odd.

Later, when we headed up to Scotland for our pre-season tour, right up to the moment when we boarded the plane Beauchamp was on the payphone at Heathrow to his girlfriend. Somebody said, 'Can someone go and get Joey because we need to go through now.' It was the same thing again when we landed in Scotland. He was back on the phone to his girlfriend and you could tell that something was wrong. We had a training session up there and he was standing in the middle of the field with tears in his eyes. It was so obvious that he didn't want to be with us. 'What the hell is wrong with him?' said Billy. 'I've done everything I can. I've told him he can live in Oxford if he wants to and can commute, but he's still not happy.' We tried everything with Joey, but he just didn't want to know. He was in tears all the time because he was away from his girlfriend. At one stage he appeared to be missing from the hotel and one of the players thought he might have topped himself. I don't think any of the lads could believe the way he was acting.

The team returned from Scotland and headed down to Portsmouth for another pre-season game. We were a bit late arriving at Fratton Park, so Billy and Harry told the lads to get changed quickly and get on the pitch for a warm-up. Eddie Gillam, John Green, Ges Steinbergs and I were sorting things out in the back of the dressing room when it became apparent that Joey had yet to run out and was left in the changing area with Harry and Billy. All of a sudden, we heard a door slam shut and Harry said, 'Right, you bastard!' He really tore into Beauchamp. 'You're going to lose that man his job,' he said, pointing to Billy, which some might consider ironic given the conversations that had taken place in Scotland just a few days earlier. With that, Joey burst into tears. 'Don't be such a fucking cry baby, you little shit!' said Harry. And the rest of us were hiding around the corner, saying, 'Yes! Give it to him! Give it to him!' Harry crucified him.

A couple of days later it was time for me to take the West Ham team photograph and it was so obvious that Beauchamp wasn't going to stay at the club that I mentioned his name to Billy. 'What's the scene with Joey?' I asked. 'What do you mean?' Billy countered. 'Well, do we leave him out?' And Billy said, 'We can't do that.' I told him that everybody knew Joey would soon be leaving. 'Yes,' said Billy, 'but today he's still a West Ham player so he'll have to be in the picture.' I suggested we take one shot with him and another without him, but Billy rejected the idea. 'We can't do that,' he said. 'That would look terrible. What sort of message would that send out?' So I thought, 'Okay, Billy, we'll play it your way.'

Of course, within no time at all we offloaded Beauchamp to Swindon Town, so the team photo was indeed out of date by the time it appeared. By that stage, of course, Billy had also gone, having decided he couldn't stay at West Ham after the directors had made it clear they would prefer to have Harry as their manager. I wouldn't necessarily suggest that the Beauchamp affair influenced Billy's decision, but I do think it left him feeling very disillusioned. And as I have already stated, Billy found it frustrating if players didn't live up to his standards. Joey certainly tested that frustration to the absolute limit.

Billy Bonds might have departed from West Ham in controversial circumstances, but in my view he did so with his head held high. He'd answered the club's call when they needed him in February 1990 and had led the team to two promotions. He'd endured the problems caused by the Bond Scheme and then brought Harry Redknapp back to Upton Park because he believed the club would benefit. And the fact remains that Harry and Billy did enjoy a successful management partnership for two years.

Bonds felt compelled to resign on a point of principle and nobody can criticise that. A lot of people have great sympathy for Billy after what happened at the end and you won't hear a bad word said against him. Most people I talk to are on Billy's side. He still gets the biggest cheer – apart from me, of course! – when we attend functions and people will always remember the fantastic contribution he made to West Ham as a player and boss, even if he occasionally questions if he was necessarily cut out for management.

As I write, Billy has yet to speak to Harry Redknapp following the break-up of their managerial partnership and that doesn't surprise me at all. Billy was adamant that he would never have anything to do with Harry after what happened in the summer of 1994 and I have to say I didn't doubt him. That's Bill – he doesn't change and he never will.

Of course, he still gets asked the same question by West Ham fans whenever he meets them – 'What really did happen with Harry all those years ago?' And Billy will always say, 'It's a long time ago and I don't really want to talk about it. I've got on with my life and I've certainly got better things to do than worry about him.' Now and again there might be a slight inference that he feels he was stitched up, but basically his answer is that he doesn't worry about the past and is very happy with his life. Amen, to that.

CHAPTER 4

'GET YOUR CAMERA – I'M GOING TO ROGER THE LION'

'**A**nd you, you cunt! When I tell you to do something, fucking do it!' Seconds later there was an almighty clang as a serving tray bounced off the wall, showering midfielder Don Hutchison with an assortment of sandwiches – ham, cheese and tomato, I seem to recall – as Harry Redknapp stormed out of the dressing room in a huff.

Billy Bonds had never been a ranting and raving kind of manager, whereas Harry could certainly go to town at times if things hadn't gone to his liking. On this particular occasion, in March 1995, the Hammers had drawn 1-1 at Southampton and it was Hutchison who had put us ahead with his third goal in four games, so he would appear to have been doing something right. But the former Liverpool man, known as 'Budweiser', had clearly caused Harry to lose his head in the post-match inquest – and nearly lost his own as a consequence.

My away-day routine would generally involve helping Eddie Gillam lay out the kit for the players before each game and I'd usually return to the dressing room after the final whistle because that would provide me with the easiest route back to the team bus. So we were down at The

Dell, Southampton's old ground, after this particular match and Harry was obviously not happy, because he was really bawling at the players. The dressing room was tiny and in the middle there was a medical table with a big tray of sandwiches, as well as a pot of tea.

Alvin Martin hadn't played in the game, but he was part of the travelling squad and was standing nearby while Harry was getting increasingly irate with the rest of the players. I looked at Alvin and he looked at me – and we both seemed to have the same fear that the platter of sandwiches might prove to be a bit too tempting for Harry. Indeed, Alvin discreetly started to edge the tray out of harm's way because the manager's hand kept wandering dangerously near it. However, his efforts were in vain as Harry eventually lost his rag and launched his tirade of expletives at Hutch. And with that he picked up the tray of sandwiches and hurled them at the midfielder. Food flew all over the place and poor old Hutch just sat there covered in a variety of tasty fillings as Harry stomped off to meet the press. There was a pregnant pause in the room before everyone started to laugh and joke about what had just taken place. Even Hutch managed to raise a smile.

When Harry eventually returned from the press conference, I was outside in the corridor. 'Fucking players! They don't fucking listen,' I heard him moan, then he stopped next to me and calmly said, 'Sorry about that. You didn't get any sandwiches to eat, did you?' I like the way he thought my mind would be on the food. I told him we'd scraped a few off the wall and managed to salvage them.

Most of the West Ham players had been sorry to see Billy Bonds leave in the summer of 1994 because they liked him as a manager, but it obviously helped the squad tremendously that Harry Redknapp had already been at the club for two years – it was just a case of getting on with things. Frank Lampard senior, Harry's brother-in-law, had been recruited as our assistant manager and I was delighted to see him return to the club because we'd always got on well. He used to make me laugh before games, though. Harry would say, 'Anything to add to that, Frank?' And Frank would always just say, 'Do your best, boys.' Or something along those lines. It would never be anything particularly inspiring.

It's true that Harry sometimes got really pissed off after a game and lost his temper. I wasn't a witness, but I was told about the time he allegedly booted a plastic bottle across the dressing room and caught David Unsworth with it. (That serves the Scouse left-back right for ruffling my hair every time we met!) However, most of the time Harry was a light-hearted character and there's no doubt that he is a good man-manager. He knows when to dig out a player – although Don Hutchison might view things differently – and when somebody needs to be handled in a gentle manner. Having listened to his team talks, I've always felt he knew his stuff – not that I'm any kind of expert – and was tactically aware, something he doesn't always get enough credit for. Harry was definitely a different animal to Billy after a game if things hadn't gone well, but he also had a great sense of humour and would react instinctively to situations.

There's perhaps no better example of this than when he substituted Lee Chapman during a pre-season friendly at Oxford City in 1994 and replaced the struggling striker with a member of the crowd – a bloke called Steve Davies. Poor old Chappy. He was a bit on the posh side and Tony Gale used to take the rise out of him all the time. Lee was a wine buff and Galey would always be saying, 'Where are we off to tonight, then? Some nice little wine bar for a bottle of Châteauneuf-du-Pape?' I saw Lee recently and he didn't look like the dapper character I used to know. But it reminded me of that game at Oxford when I made a few bob out of that bizarre substitution.

Chappy had been getting a bit of stick from the Hammers fans in the crowd when, all of a sudden, there was some movement on the touchline and a fan who had been talking to Harry from the terraces climbed over the wall and started putting on some kit. Apparently he'd been abusing Chapman roundly, yelling, 'Get him off, Harry; I could play better than him.' Harry duly responded, 'All right, you can have a go then.' Harry turned to Eddie Gillam and told him to get some kit ready. 'You can't let him play,' said Eddie. 'What about the insurance? What if he breaks his leg?' And Harry simply said, 'Never mind about that; just get him ready.'

So Chappy trudged off and this guy came on. I didn't have a clue what was happening but I thought I'd better take some pictures of him nonetheless. He wasn't too bad, actually. I thought no more of it really until the following day when I got a call from the picture editor of *The Sun* – a friend of mine called John Edwards – asking if I'd been working at the game. He said they were taking the guy down to the West Ham training ground to get some pictures of him with Lee Chapman and I thought, 'Well, the best of luck with that.' As it turned out, the real joke was that Chappy was oblivious to the fact that the fan had been shouting abuse at him, so he happily posed for pictures. He only realised what had really happened when the newspapers crucified him the next day. But they used my photographs from the game and I made about £500 out of that – a nice little earner at the time.

I can't imagine any manager other than Harry pull-ing such a stunt – and it was the same when we played St

Patrick's Athletic in a pre-season friendly several years later. The Dublin outfit was being run by Patrick Dolan, whose twin brother Eamonn rose through the ranks at West Ham. I photographed the pair of them as boys when they played against each other at Chadwell Heath and at that time they were like two peas in a pod. However, when I met Pat again in Dublin he was even bigger than me! He made a joke about his size and said that I might not have too much trouble distinguishing the two of them now.

On this occasion, another punter jumped out of the crowd to enter the field of play – but he wasn't wearing a West Ham shirt. In fact, he wasn't wearing anything at all. He was in the naughty, naked nude and was streaking across the pitch, waving his privates in the direction of the bench, when Harry picked up a Lucozade bottle and gave chase, trying to squirt the guy from behind. Or rather *at* his behind. It was hilarious, but that's the thing with Harry. He could be in a serious situation, looking to win a match (albeit a friendly), but then switch off and do something comical like that. Personally, I think that's a good trait to have.

Aside from Harry, if anyone liked a joke – or taking their clothes off, for that matter – it was John Moncur. The tenacious midfielder joined West Ham on the same day as Joey Beauchamp – and made us laugh for very different reasons. We went to play TSV 1860 Munich in 1995 to mark the thirtieth anniversary of West Ham's European Cup Winners' Cup final victory over the Germans and the players were warming up before the game when Moncur came over to me on the touchline with a mischievous look in his eye. 'Get your camera,' he said. 'I'm going to roger the lion!' There were lots of important dignitaries taking their seats for the big occasion and Munich's mascot was a big stuffed lion. It was a beautiful thing and obviously worth quite a bit of money. I tried to tell Moncs that he wouldn't do any such thing, but that was like a red rag to a bull. He jumped on the lion and started rolling around on the floor with it, much to the horror of the mayor of Munich and the other disapproving officials.

I took a picture during the game of Harry pulling an extremely miserable face – quite possibly because hapless Dutch striker Marco Boogers was missing open goals for fun on his debut – with Frank looking on. It's not one of Harry's favourite shots but it sums up how he felt about the 4-3 defeat – and probably Moncur's antics as well. Thankfully, Moncs managed to keep his kit on while engaging in sordid activities with the lion, but I did hear a story about him wandering naked around the hotel in Munich with a lighted cigarette positioned in a very usual place. I refuse to believe it's true, but it would not have been out of character. Somebody was also guilty of throwing a plant pot – quite an impressive centrepiece from the foyer of the hotel – into the swimming pool. I've got no idea who was responsible, but it was definitely one of our players.

Nobody will be surprised to learn that John Moncur was a great friend of Paul Gascoigne, who had something of a reputation for comical behaviour himself (if wearing plastic tits and burping into microphones makes you laugh). I'd parked up at a hotel to get on the team bus one day when I heard a voice shouting across the car park. I looked up and it was Gazza. 'Hey, photey man, you're the West Ham photey man, aren't you?' he said. So that was one of my claims to fame at that time – being recognised by England star Paul Gascoigne at the height of his popularity.

There were plenty of other opportunities for Moncur to display his propensity for taking his clothes off in public. On one occasion the decorators were in at Chadwell Heath and Moncs thought it would be funny to get stark naked and cover himself with green paint before going out to train – much to the amusement of the other players and the annoyance of the staff. On another, we were due to stay at Breadsall Priory before a game against Derby County and when we arrived there was a girl welcoming the team to the hotel. Of course, Moncur promptly dropped his strides as he was getting off the coach to give the young female a bit of a welcoming present himself. That was the time when they booked me into a room that was apparently haunted. When we checked in, no one mentioned the ghastly, ghostly rumours, but the room was a bit of a trek to reach, so Eddie said he'd swap with me. In the morning he was asked if anything strange had occurred and Eddie said, 'No, why?' He was then informed that the room was haunted. Thank heavens I didn't sleep up there!

Another funny incident involving Moncur occurred when we headed to Australia in 1995 for an end-of-season tour to mark West Ham's centenary year. We were at the Suncorp Stadium in Brisbane for our final game against the Australian under-23 side and Harry was taking the pre-match team talk. He wanted everyone who wasn't playing to make themselves scarce, but I remained in the dressing room because I was helping Eddie with the kit. Harry started talking, totally unaware that Moncur had managed to secrete himself into a small locker. God knows how he managed it but he had also succeeded in stripping off, so he was stark bollock naked in this enclosed space. Then, just as Harry was in the middle of his tactical talk, Moncur pushed open the door of the locker and burst into the middle of the room with a giant leap in the shape of a star. For once, Harry had a complete sense of humour failure and went absolutely ballistic. He chased

Moncs out of the dressing room. To say he was not amused is an understatement!

To be fair, the trip was not being taken terribly seriously. We had quite a few injuries at the time, so didn't take our best team Down Under. Julian Dicks – who had returned to the club following a difficult year with Liverpool – and Tony Cottee were both crocked, but came with us because some big names were needed to try and keep the local media happy.

When the club's summer trip to Australia had first been announced, I was absolutely desperate to be included in the party. If Lou Macari had still been in charge of West Ham it wouldn't have been a problem. But I knew that, realistically, I probably wouldn't be invited to go because there would be a lot of other people ahead of me in the pecking order. So I tried to build up my role at the club and was dropping hints all over the place. I got on quite well with Peter Storrie, West Ham's managing director – not bad for somebody who made his first connection with the club as a goalpost salesman – so I'd take the opportunity to collar him and say, 'We really need a good photographic record of this trip.' And he'd reply, 'Yeah, I can see what you're saying.' He knew what I was angling for and told me he'd speak to the rest of the board to find out what they thought.

One day Peter came up to me at a home game and said, 'By the way, as long as you're happy to supply the club with all the pictures from Australia, you're on the trip.' I was over-joyed. But we were having a bit of a rocky time with results at the time and Harry kept threatening to pull the plug on the trip. 'You can forget all about Australia because we won't be going anywhere unless you pull your fingers out!' he'd say. And I'm thinking, 'Shit! We've got the trip of a lifetime coming up and Harry's in danger of scrapping it.' John Ball, the club's stadium manager, had been told he wasn't going and was really miffed about it, so he took great delight in repeatedly telling me that the trip was off. And I, of course, fell for it every time.

Harry had experienced a difficult first season in charge of West Ham, with the team languishing at the bottom end of the Premiership table until a late flurry, in which we lost just once in the final eleven games, saw us finish fourteenth. Harry might have thought this meant his ploy had worked but, despite all his screaming and shouting, there was no way he could have called off that trip. It was ridiculous to say we weren't going to Australia when it was the club's centenary tour and we had arranged to play four games out there.

The closing week of the campaign included a 3-0 home win against Liverpool that guaranteed our top-flight safety and a final day 1-1 draw with Manchester United at Upton Park that ripped the league trophy out of Alex Ferguson's grasp and handed it over to Blackburn Rovers, for whom my old mate Tony Gale was now playing. I was delighted that Galey had won a championship medal, especially after we just missed out in 1986, but I don't remember too much about the game against United – I think my mind was on other things as we were heading to Australia the very next day.

We were all very excited about the trip, but there was a split second on the Monday when I feared I might miss the flight. While heading to Upton Park to catch the coach, I drove into the back of a car that had stopped suddenly. 'No! I haven't got time for this,' I thought. Thankfully there was little damage and the other driver was happy to forget it, so I continued on my way. Needless to say, there was a huge amount of gear to load onto the team bus at the ground because we were going to be away for three weeks.

The team bus arrived at Heathrow for our 10.40 p.m. flight with Quantas, but a few of the lads had said they would make their own way to the airport and the likes of Don Hutchison, Julian Dicks and Kenny Brown duly fell out of a stretch limousine, having obviously enjoyed a few drinks along the way. It made me wonder how many times they'd been round the M25.

We had some time to kill, so the players headed to the bar and by the time we boarded the plane it's fair to say that things were getting a bit lively. All the stewardesses were getting called 'Kylie' and everybody else was either 'Bruce' or 'Sheila'. As the flight commenced, the players were getting more and more rowdy and a few bread rolls were being slung about, so the chief cabin steward came looking for somebody with a bit of authority to take control of the situation. As he approached Eddie Gillam, Ges Steinbergs, John Green and me, we simply pointed to Frank Lampard, who was sitting in business class while the rest of us – players included – were in cattle class. Harry wasn't with us on the outbound flight because he was joining us in Australia later, so it was up to Frank to try and quieten down the players. Like a school teacher, he suggested we wouldn't be going anywhere if they didn't start behaving. 'Fucking players,' he grumbled when he came and sat next to me for a moment.

Dicksy had his leg in a cast because of a broken ankle and had ignored medical advice not to travel. Unsurprisingly, his leg started to swell up on the flight, so Ges was forced to get a knife and cut off the plaster to relieve the pain. Most of the lads were getting plastered in a different way and I just wanted to sleep, so Ges gave me a handful of strong sleeping tablets and that did the trick until we touched down the next day in Singapore, where we were staying overnight.

We were still in the airport, having found somewhere to store all the kit and everything, when Frank Lampard said he was popping outside to see where our coach was. He quickly returned looking a little on the sweaty side. 'You're not going to like it out there, it's so fucking hot it ain't true,' he said. 'I'm dripping!' We went out to get on the coach and it was as if somebody was blowing a giant hairdryer in our faces. We couldn't even breathe!

The rest of the party was going to eat at the hotel that night, but I'd set my heart on finding a place called Newton Circus, having been told by a friend that the food there was simply amazing. So I rounded up Eddie, Ges and John and we jumped in a cab, but when we arrived at this place it was more like a shanty town. It was all shacks with canvas roofs and, as the taxi drove off, the heavens opened and the most amazing thunderstorm suddenly started. It was like a monsoon! 'This doesn't look much of a place,' complained Eddie. 'But the food is absolutely brilliant,' I insisted, trying to remain positive.

We eventually located a restaurant but the only seats that appeared to be available were towards the edge of the dining area and rapidly getting wet. Nevertheless, we requested a table for four. 'No problem, no problem,' said the waiter – and with that he went over to four people eating their meals in the best part of the restaurant and threw them off their table. 'You want beer?' he asked, as we took our stolen seats. And we were quickly given a huge keg containing about four pints of Japanese lager.

The four of us ordered prawn dishes and were each served with a plate containing a single barbecued prawn. It was very nice, but that was the meal in its entirety. And I'm a growing lad! Then the waiter turned up with the bill and it was about

£50 per head – for a pint of beer and a prawn. When you consider we'd also got soaked for our efforts, it's no wonder that the rest of the lads were not particularly happy. 'Screw you and your Newton Circus, we're going back to the hotel to eat,' they declared. I must admit, I was feeling a bit peckish myself, so we ended up eating just as we would have done if we'd never gone out.

Our flight to Australia wasn't until the following evening, so we used the next day to do a bit of sightseeing and shopping. I had a fake Rolex watch that Tony Gale had once purchased on my behalf and Ges was determined to buy one as well. Eddie, Ges and I had arranged to meet Frank Lampard and his wife Pat – who is sadly no longer with us after passing away in 2008 – along with vice-chairman Martin Cearns and wife Lorna for a lunchtime drink at the famous Raffles Hotel. In the meantime, we were on the hunt for dodgy Rolexes and were just about to climb into a cab outside the hotel when another driver looked at Ges – who's not the smallest bloke in the world – and then at me and said, 'No, you boys need BIG cab.' And with that he pushed the other cabbie out of the way and pointed us towards his spacious people carrier.

He asked what we were looking for and I told him we wanted to buy a fake watch. 'You want shiny watch?' he said. 'No,' I said, 'we want *fake* watch.' He eventually got the picture and we drove off past several shopping malls before we finally ended up on the outskirts of town at a bunker-type building. It looked very dodgy and we all thought we were definitely going to get done. But we ventured into the building regardless, to find it full of designer ladies' handbags, none of which were genuine. Then a guy said, 'You want Rolex?' He opened a big drawer and there were literally hundreds of very expensive-looking watches. 'You want Cartier? You want Breitling?' It was unbelievable. Ges finally chose one he liked and seemed very pleased with his purchase.

'Now what you want?' said our driver, when we were back in his vehicle. We told him we wanted to go to Raffles but he didn't seem to be listening. 'You want women?' he asked. 'You want shiny women?' Everything had to be shiny, as far as he was concerned. 'I take you to shiny women,' he said, as we sped out of the complex. We did eventually persuade him to take us to our preferred destination – at a ridiculous cost, it should be added.

We arrived at Raffles and went into the Long Bar, which was very smart and had an air-conditioning system that was made up of struts across the ceiling with fans that looked like giant table-tennis bats. I presume it was mechanised, but I couldn't help but think it looked like something out of *It Ain't Half Hot Mum*, with somebody out the back pulling on a rope to keep it working.

We met up with Frank, Pat, Martin and Lorna and it was Singapore Slings all round, except for Eddie, who asked for a Tiger beer, which arrived in a mini yard-of-ale type of glass that we all tried to sip from without spilling any (not entirely successfully). We also tried very hard to be tidy when shelling the monkey nuts on the bar, so we were amazed when the barman, in a very smart uniform, came to replace the bowl and just brushed everything onto the floor. After that, we followed his example and just started chucking shells everywhere.

We enjoyed a few rounds of drinks and Martin Cearns made the mistake of saying he'd pay. 'I'll get these, chaps,' he smiled, although his expression quickly changed when he saw the size of the bill. He just gulped in shock. He was working for Barclays at the time and said he'd better get his card out. 'That'll do nicely!' we quipped as he showed the colour of his plastic. As we were walking out, Frank Lampard put his arms around Eddie and me and said, 'Fucking tastes a lot better when we know he's paid for it!'

Pat wanted to visit a particular temple with Frank and upon entering the building they were ordered to leave their shoes outside. When they emerged, however, somebody had clearly taken a liking to Frank's expensive shoes and they were conspicuous by their absence. They'd been nicked. Poor old Frank was forced to look around for a cheap pair of shoes and he wasn't happy.

We flew to Perth later that evening and what made me laugh when we finally arrived in Australia is that we bumped into so many Englishmen. Eddie was talking to the concierge at our first hotel and it transpired that he was from Basildon. 'Bloody hell, so am I!' said Eddie. It was the same story when we took a cab out to Fremantle, which is located at the mouth of the Swan River and is where the 1987 America's Cup was staged. It's a very picturesque port. Of course, our cab driver was from East Ham. We met a few more expats and ended up in an Irish bar where some of the guys were drinking Guinness, which I thought was preposterous when you've flown 10,000 miles. I was on the Foster's – when in Rome and all that – but I must admit we did have a cheeky McDonald's for lunch. In those first few days we were still pinching ourselves that we were in Australia.

The Hammers squad had a training session at the WACA – the Western Australian Cricket Arena – on the Thursday and were supposed to then head on to an English-style pub to meet some supporters. However, rather embarrassingly, few of the players really wanted to go. I think one or two turned up, but it was a token effort on our part.

Before dinner that evening, Frank Lampard invited a few

of us up to his room for a drink. It was a typically generous gesture by Frank – even if we did suspect that the club was paying for it! *ClubCall* reporter Khris Raistrick – or plain old Chris as he was in those days – was on the trip and not particularly liked, so Frank told us not to mention his little gathering to him. John Green told the players to programme Raistrick's phone number into their mobiles – under the name of 'Do Not Answer!' Chris was always complaining about never getting through to anybody, but I can't think why...

After dinner we were in the bar when it suddenly closed earlier than expected. There was a hotel directly opposite ours, so Ges kindly offered to nip over there to see if he could get some beers for us. We were waiting in reception when suddenly there was a big commotion and Ges came running in with a load of drinks under his arm. 'Quick! Hide these!' he said, before disappearing down the corridor only for a bunch of security guys to appear in hot pursuit. It was like something out of a comedy film. Apparently, people were not allowed to take beer off the premises from the hotel across the road. 'We're looking for a big guy,' said one of the uniformed men. 'Nobody's come this way,' we said, shaking our heads in unison. Ges finally reappeared when the coast was clear and we sat down to enjoy our extra tinnies for the night.

West Ham played their first game the following evening at the WACA, which was a huge stadium. The pitch was in front of the Lillee-Marsh Stand and I can remember asking myself, 'Lillee Marsh? Who's she?' Thankfully, the penny eventually dropped about the two Aussie cricket legends.

We wandered onto the pitch before kick-off and suddenly I could hear the fans singing my name. 'One Stevie Bacon!

There's only one Stevie Bacon!' I naturally saluted the crowd – as you do – and Tony Cottee turned round to say, 'Bloody hell, we're 10,000 miles from home and they're still chanting your name!' He claims they then started to sing 'Who ate all the pies?' but I appear to have erased that from my memory.

The game began and the Hammers twice came from behind to draw 2-2 against a Western Australia side that included winger Stan Lazaridis, who impressed enough to win a trial with West Ham and a subsequent move to Upton Park. Mark Watson, who we had recently signed from non-league outfit Sutton United, scored our second equaliser. He'd been working at a Topman clothing store and turned up for the trip with a huge, really ostentatious suitcase, which the lads inevitably gave him stick about. Mark had the biggest jolly-up of anybody on the tour and one of the lads said to him, 'I hope they've kept your job open for you, because I don't think you'll be playing for West Ham much longer.' Needless to say, the striker made just one league outing for the Hammers before being sold to Bournemouth.

We moved on to Melbourne for our second game. Whereas Perth had felt like a new city, Melbourne was far less compact and had a much older feel. I'd not won any friends over our trip to Newton Circus in Singapore, which I'd insisted we do, and I didn't manage to win over any more now we were in Australia, as I kept banging on about the fact that we could watch the FA Cup final between Manchester United and Everton even though we were on the other side of the world. Everyone else was saying, 'Well, that's the magic of television.' But I couldn't get over how good that was.

I insisted that Ges, John and Eddie watch it with me, despite the fact that the match kicked off at midnight for us. Of course, it wasn't the greatest game in the world and all the travelling and drinking had caught up with me by then, so I quickly dozed off. The lads weren't happy, so every five minutes one of them would shout, 'GOAL!' I'd wake up, only to realise they were pulling my leg. This went on throughout the match, apart from when Paul Rideout scored the winner for Everton, of course, when they decided to let me carry on snoozing.

I think most of the players had also stayed up late to watch the game, because they failed to impress in a 1-1 draw against Victoria at the Olympic Park the following afternoon (with young Danny Shipp our only scorer). From Melbourne we flew on to Sydney and I think Tony Cottee must have been out there before because he told me what side of the plane I should sit on if I wanted to see the harbour as we descended. It was an unbelievable view. Sydney Harbour Bridge and the Opera House – familiar images on television that I never thought I'd get to see in person.

We stayed in a pleasant-enough hotel in Sydney, but it was in an area called King's Cross, which is where the red-light district is located. Given the nature of the area, we'd been told to be careful and not go out on our own, but I heard that one player had been trying to secure special discount rates with the hookers, who were in plentiful supply. Our seedy location was in keeping with West Ham trying to keep the cost of the trip down as much as possible. The guy who arranged the trip for the club was known as Bongo. He had a real Black Country accent and was something of a penny-pincher. We had vouchers for meals, meaning you could have a starter and a main course, or a main course and dessert, but not all three. He was always in confrontation with the players over things. But they got their revenge on him when they procured his room number one evening and spent the rest of the night living it up at his expense by putting everything on his tab – needless to say, he wasn't best pleased when confronted with the bill.

We had more time in Sydney so we were determined to try and take in all the sights. The coach driver told us that we didn't need to go via the Sydney Harbour Bridge to get to our training sessions, but he took that route just so that we could boast that we'd been across it. Not that everybody appreciated the gesture. I think it was goalkeeper Les Sealey who said, 'When you've seen one bridge, you've seen them all.'

Eddie, John, Ges and me – the four amigos – later went to see the Opera House and we met a few of the players down there. It was good to see that at least some of them were taking in the culture. 'We're not all philistines,' insisted Martin Allen. Together we wandered around from the harbour where you catch the ferries and the Opera House was built up on a peninsula. It's quite spectacular. I don't think the Aussies were too keen on it when it was built, but they've grown to love it now.

It's fair to say we didn't see much of defender Kenny Brown on our travels in Sydney. He teamed up with a girl who worked in the condom shop in the shopping mall and we barely saw him for the five days we were there. He was a bit of a randy geezer – that's all I'll say on that one. But at least he showed his face to play in the 1-0 win against the Australian under-23 side at the Marconi Stadium, in which Malcolm McPherson scored the winner. We were forced to put out under-strength teams for these games after what had been a long, hard season and inevitably suffered a bit of criticism as a result.

There is a famous fish restaurant in Sydney called Doyles, which you can get to by ferry. Harry Redknapp, Frank

Lampard, Peter Storrie and Martin Cearns, plus their wives, all went for a meal there one evening and the rest of the backroom boys and I were a bit miffed that we hadn't been invited. I casually mentioned it to Storrie towards the end of the trip and he said, 'Oh, you could have come with us.' And I was thinking, 'You're only saying that now because we're in Brisbane!'

Some of the players returned to England after Sydney, but what made the lengthy tour more enjoyable for the rest of us was the fact that the final leg involved a game in Brisbane followed by five days' complete holiday, for which we stayed in Surfers Paradise. We flew in over the beaches of the Gold Coast to land at Coolangatta airport and you could hear the boys saying, 'This is more like it!' They had the beers out within minutes of us landing! Eddie and I were still unloading the gear off the coach outside the hotel when a load of players went running past us in their shorts towards the beach. We still had the last game to play but that set the tone for the closing stage of the tour.

We played our final game at the Suncorp Stadium and by that time we were severely depleted in numbers, so much so that Harry ended up dragging somebody off the beach to play. I know; you couldn't make it up. As it transpired, he was a former YTS player by the name of Gary Peters, who Harry knew from his days at Bournemouth. But that was so typical of Harry to give him a game – not that he was able to make much of an impression because we crashed 4-0 to the under-23 side we had beaten just three days earlier.

I seemed to spend more time taking pictures of the crowd during that match than I did the football. The players had explained that their earnings from the tour were dependent on the attendance at games – and they were convinced they were being diddled. It was quite comical really because both parties approached me separately to ask if I could supply evidence to support their case. First the players asked if I'd take some pictures of the crowd to prove how many people were there. And then Bongo asked if I could photograph the empty spaces to show there was nobody in the stadium. I don't know how the situation was resolved, but I think at one stage some of the players threatened not to play unless he coughed up the cash they wanted.

Never mind the players, though; from my point of view, our three weeks in Australia was the trip of a lifetime. It was a brilliant experience and undoubtedly one of the big highlights of my long association with West Ham United. At this point I should also mention chairman Terry Brown, who I always seemed to be sitting with on our internal flights across Australia. His wife Jean spent a lot of time knitting on the plane, and Terry's brother Ken was also on the trip.

Terry was always introducing Ken to people as if they had never met him before. 'This is my brother Ken,' he'd always say. 'So nice to see you again,' I'd reply. The rest of the back-room boys and I had a long-running quest to try and get Terry to buy us a drink in Australia. We were determined to squeeze one out of him before the trip was over. And sure enough, on the final evening in Surfers Paradise, where we had the most spectacular thunderstorm as we looked out over the sea, we were about to go in for dinner when Terry arrived in the bar with Ken.

'All right, lads?' said Terry. 'It's our last night. Would you like a drink?' And we all thought, 'Yes! We've cracked it!' 'Yes, please,' we said. 'Thank you, Terry, that's very kind of you.' 'Ken, buy the boys a drink, will you?' said Terry.

I couldn't believe it. Talk about falling at the final hurdle.

Billy Bonds had always told me that I'd get on well with Harry Redknapp and that was certainly the case. He's the best company going when you're having dinner with him and we had some entertaining nights when staying in hotels before away games. Harry and Frank Lampard would generally eat with the rest of us backroom boys, but if Martin Cearns, Terry Brown or Peter Storrie were travelling with us then the manager would feel duty bound to eat with them instead.

Harry was on another table with the chairman and a few directors one evening and it seemed obvious that he wasn't enjoying himself, because he kept making excuses and coming over to see Eddie, John, Ges and me. Harry's favourite tipple was Châteauneuf-du-Pape, which is a lovely wine but rather expensive. At one point he came over and said, 'They're driving me bloody mad over there – and to top it all, the bottle's empty and they won't order another one.' So Harry turned to me and said, 'Order a bottle for your table.' 'I can't order one!' I exclaimed, to which he replied, 'Of course you can, you're Stevie Bacon! They're not going to say anything to you.'

I duly ordered the wine and when it arrived Harry was hanging around with his empty glass, so I had to surreptitiously top it up for him. He then returned to sit with the chairman, but every now and again he'd say he needed to 'check up on the boys' and come over for a refill when his bosses weren't looking. Funnily enough, the chairman never seemed to notice how Harry would leave the table with an empty glass and return with a full one.

The two significant developments – revolutions, even – at West Ham under Harry Redknapp in the second half of the

1990s were an influx of foreign players and the rehabilitation of the club's youth scheme. Both factors contributed to the Hammers consolidating their place in the Premiership, with the team securing four top-half finishes between 1996 and 2001 – not that there weren't a few relegation scares along the way, of course. And the huge turnover of players taking place as Harry went about wheeling and dealing and shuffled his pack of cards – as has become his managerial trademark over the years – certainly made the Boleyn Ground a very interesting place. It also kept me very busy as new faces arrived on a regular basis.

The trickle of foreign players into Upton Park became something of a flood as the 1990s progressed. We'd had Belgian playmaker François Van Der Elst for a couple of seasons in the early 1980s, but after that Luděk Mikloško, signed by Lou Macari in 1990, was the first imported player to make an impression at West Ham. The fans loved the Czech goalkeeper, who dominated between the sticks for eight years – and so did I. I had a good relationship with Ludo and met his wife Ivana and son Martin on more than one occasion. He seemed very drawn and hollow-cheeked when he arrived in England – nothing like the Ludo we got to know and love. He was a bit camera-shy at first and wasn't very helpful, but he soon became more comfortable with things as he acclimatised to his new surroundings.

I'll always remember being ordered to take Ludo's picture at Leeds in December 1994. Ludo had been caught by Brian Deane – who later briefly played for the Hammers – and took a right old battering during the game. He had a nasty, circular injury around his left eye that required several stitches and Harry was absolutely raging about it. 'Get your camera and take a picture of Ludo's face!' he said when he found me after the game. Of course, the goalkeeper didn't want to be snapped, but Harry was determined to have photographic evidence. 'You let him take it, Ludo,' he insisted. 'That's disgraceful!'

Despite Ludo's success, West Ham's initial steps into the foreign transfer market were rather tentative. We had Canadian striker Alex Bunbury, who seemed to spend more time on his arse than his feet. Then there was Dutch striker Jeroen Boere, who made an instant impression by being sent off on his debut at Newcastle. He was definitely a bit of a lad and liked a drink. His best game was when he scored twice in the same 2-2 draw against Leeds during which Ludo was hurt. Years after leaving West Ham, he was forced to retire from football when he was stabbed in the eye in Japan. He died in Spain in 2007, and it was later claimed in some reports that he had committed suicide. And we mustn't forget spectacular flop Marco Boogers, another Dutch striker, who at least waited until his second game, against Manchester United, before being sent off. I took some pictures of Marco blowing bubbles when he signed for us, but amid rumours of depression he quickly Booger-ed off back to Holland and a new life in a caravan.

We had better reward with Danish defender Marc Rieper, who arrived midway through the 1994/95 campaign and enjoyed a successful few years with us. He liked a drink – having a taste for probably the best lager in the world, I would imagine – and was a very sociable guy. However, it wasn't until 1996 that the dam really burst open in terms of European imports, thanks in part to the Bosman ruling, which created more freedom of movement for players, and the greater sums of money earned by Premiership clubs as a result of Sky's generous broadcasting contract.

ABOVE Paolo Di Canio celebrates his winning goal in the FA Cup victory over Manchester United at Old Trafford in 2001.

Julian Dicks reflects in the dressing room after playing his last game at Upton Park – his testimonial match against Athletic Bilbao in 2000.

An emotional Paolo Di Canio in tears after his final home game for West Ham in 2003.

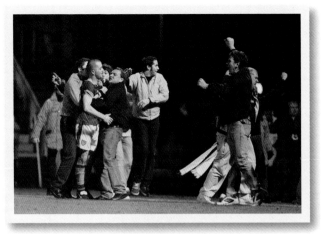

LEFT Julian Dicks is mobbed by the fans after his penalty kick gives the Hammers a 2-2 draw with Manchester United at Upton Park in 1996.

RIGHT Hammers fans get a soaking from stewards wielding fire extinguishers at Metz in the Intertoto cup in 1999.

Portuguese star Hugo Porfirio saw snow for the first time in his life when Hammers played at Wrexham in the 1997 FA Cup.

John Lyall was persuaded to attend a 1980 FA Cup final anniversary dinner in London's Docklands and is pictured here with his former players.

Joe Cole, Frank Lampard and Rio Ferdinand pictured during an England under-21 training session at London Colney.

Glenn Roeder leaves the pitch after defeat at Rotherham United in 2003 – he was sacked the following day!

Although officially on the sick list, I was invited to the promotion celebrations in 2005 and took some aerial shots from the directors' suite at the ground.

LEFT I took this picture of manager Glenn Roeder and his family to help promote his image after he took over the hot seat at Upton Park in 2001.

RIGHT Norman Wisdom poses with Bobby Moore's widow Stephanie at the unveiling of the commemorative blue plaque at Upton Park.

Actor Danny Dyer is another great Hammers fan and I had the chance to chat to him at a function in Canary Wharf.

ABOVE I met TV presenter Ben Shephard, an old friend and big Hammers fan, at a charity dinner in the city.

RIGHT Whenever Paolo Di Canio returns to Upton Park as a spectator, he always stops for a chat and gives me a big 'man hug'.

The Sun's royal photographer Arthur Edwards gave me my first break in press photography and attended my launch for *Hammers in Focus*.

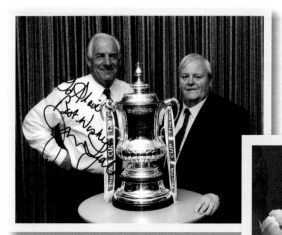

LEFT I grabbed the chance to have my photograph taken with John Lyall and the FA Cup at a reunion. John kindly signed the print for me and it's a treasured possession.

RIGHT Here it is – the Stevie Bacon Burger, available from the burger bar in Priory Road on match days, although I must admit I've never tasted one!

"WHEN WE GET INTO EUROPE STEVE, WILL YOU TAKE MY PASSPORT PHOTO...?"

Dr Martens

LEFT A cartoon of me and Ian Wright that Wrighty kindly signed and presented to me himself.

BELOW A nice happy picture on the day Ian Wright signed for West Ham. I don't think you can take a bad picture of Wrighty.

In February of that year, West Ham secured a 1-0 win at Tottenham that saw loan signing Dani score on his first full start for the club and defender Slaven Bilić make his debut. Dani was a young Portuguese striker with stunning, playboy looks – one newspaper actually ran a big picture of him with the headline 'Lock Up Your Daughters'. I was down at Chadwell Heath just after he'd signed amid all this publicity and as Dani strolled towards the showers an envious John Moncur said, 'Please don't tell me he's got a fucking huge cock as well!' But Dani was a very polite guy and after his last game – which soon became inevitable as Harry got more and more irritated by the player's partying and subsequent poor timekeeping – he gave me a hug and said it had been very nice working with me. No jokes about beauty and the beast, please.

Bilić, meanwhile, was a very bright bloke. His father was a university vice-chancellor back in Croatia and Bilić had studied law. But he was incredibly friendly too. If we were taking the kit down to an away ground he'd sometimes join us on the bus for a chat. He went back home to play for his country on one occasion and returned with a load of Croatia hats and scarves for Eddie and me. It was disappointing that he left us for Everton in the way he did the following year. It led to accusations that he was a money-grabber and damaged his image in the eyes of West Ham fans, who had previously recognised what a quality player he was.

In 1996 Harry signed Portuguese midfielder Paulo Futre. You do tend to accumulate a few bits and pieces along the way and my collection includes one of Paulo's shirts – not that I think it is worth very much. We'd all heard what a great player the former Porto, Atlético Madrid and AC Milan man was, but the Portu-geezer had a dodgy knee and was well past it by the time he came to us.

The other big-name signing in the summer of 1996 was Romanian striker Florin Răducioiu, whose international teammate Ilie Dumitrescu had arrived from Spurs earlier in the year following a protracted saga over his work permit. I thought Dumitrescu was hopeless when he finally played for us and that we shouldn't have persevered, but I can understand why Harry wanted the deal pushed through.

The two Romanian players didn't mix with the rest of the squad at all and spent most of their time together. They kept themselves to themselves and it didn't take long for Harry to become frustrated by them. We had a pre-season trip to Moretonhampstead in Devon and stayed in a lovely hotel on the edge of Dartmoor. The lads were doing something on the Sunday morning – probably a spot of light training – and Harry said he'd arranged some soup and sandwiches for when they got back. We were tucking in, when Harry entered with a look of disdain on his face. 'Fucking Eastern Europeans. Fucking Romanians! They only want the fucking lot, don't they?' he said. It transpired that Florin and Ilie weren't happy with soup and sandwiches and wanted the roast beef, Yorkshire pudding and vegetables instead, because it was a Sunday. 'What would they be eating if they were at home – cabbage soup?' said Harry. 'Now they want roast beef! Fucking Romanians...'

We played a friendly against Torquay United that turned out to be nothing of the sort and Răducioiu got smacked in the face by an elbow, which put his nose out of joint in one sense if not the other. The Torquay chairman, meanwhile, had said there would be no complimentary tickets for the game and if our players wanted extras they would have to pay for them. Their response was to tell our club secretary, Peter Barnes, that if there were no free tickets there would be no game. Needless to say, they got their tickets.

Răducioiu only started half a dozen league games for West Ham and seemed to spend more time sitting in the stands than anything. His wife was with him in the crowd on one occasion and I took a picture of Florin, but ensured that I got his missus in the shot as well – she was absolutely gorgeous! Of course, things came to a head when Răducioiu failed to turn up for our Coca-Cola Cup replay at Stockport County in December. We were waiting on the coach at the Swallow Hotel in Waltham Abbey – our usual meeting point for away games – and nobody could make contact with him. Harry was incredulous when he was told that Florin had gone shopping at Harvey Nichols instead – a legendary piece of Hammers folklore that the player has since denied. 'Fucking Harvey Nicks!' But that was Harry's answer to everything. I remember him being fed up with striker Fredi Kanouté once. 'Fucking people! Wanting to pray all day! Fucking fasting!'

That Stockport game wasn't a great day for West Ham, in all honesty. Apart from Răducioiu going AWOL, we lost 2-1 to the third-tier side after Iain Dowie – who should also have been added to the missing person's list following a terrible forty-game run without scoring – popped up with an unbelievable own goal. Iain was a very intelligent man, but there was nothing clever about that header, I can tell you. I got a great shot of him rising like a salmon to thump the ball into the back of the net. Don't ask me what I was doing at that end of the ground. Maybe I'd had a premonition.

Inevitably, Dowie was the victim of merciless stick from the fans and it even got to the stage where they were ringing West Ham and leaving hostile messages on answering machines around the club. 'What's it got to do with us?' asked somebody from the commercial office. 'It's not our fault he doesn't know which way we're kicking.' The fans never forgave him for that own goal, but my mum loved Iain and always took his side when people had a go at him. So at least there was one person sticking up for him.

If that's what British players were giving you, then perhaps it was no surprise that Harry was going foreign – even if most recruits from abroad did need a bit of time to settle in. We signed Hugo Porfírio on loan from Sporting Lisbon and were astonished to discover on the morning of an FA Cup game at Wrexham in January 1997 that he'd not seen snow before. The pitch was covered with the stuff, but the game had been given the go-ahead and we followed our usual routine of taking the kit down to the ground in the morning. 'Don't say anything negative to the players about the pitch,' said Harry. 'I don't want them to have any excuses.' When we got back, Harry asked what the surface was like. 'Bloody awful,' I said. 'Well, keep quiet about it,' he ordered. Harry then had his chat with the players in the hotel and promptly told them that the pitch was awful! It was all right for him to say it was rubbish, but not for us. As it turned out, the white stuff was the right stuff for Porfírio and he scored our equaliser in the 1-1 draw. His efforts turned out to be in vain, however, because we lost the replay.

I had a degree of sympathy for some of the foreign players – particularly youngsters such as Hugo, who I think found it difficult – because it's not easy to join in with the dressing-room banter when you don't really understand the English language or sense of humour. Eyal Berkovic certainly fell into that category. We signed the Israeli playmaker from Maccabi Haifa in the summer of 1997 following a loan spell at Southampton and he couldn't embrace the culture in the changing room at all. Eyal just wanted to come in, get changed, warm up and play. He had no time whatsoever for all the joking around and it was totally alien to him. He couldn't understand it. Once or twice he even teamed up with me in the dressing room to kick the ball about – not that he was in my league in terms of silky skills, of course – because he didn't want to get involved in what the others were doing. He was very professional in that way. Contrary to what some people might think, it was the same with Paolo Di Canio a couple of years later. The Italian might have been seen as flamboyant and charismatic, but in the dressing room he was very focused and had no time for meaningless banter.

Berkovic was a great player and a humble lad. It's a shame that fans remember his name almost as much for his famous training-ground clash with John Hartson, when he was kicked in the head, as the inventive football he played. From my point of view the pair of them enjoyed a normal relationship – I didn't detect any great friendship or animosity between them up to that point. I think the incident was just one of those things that can sometimes happen in the heat of the moment on the field.

John was a fiery Welshman and a tough character. But I thought he was a good lad – even if I did struggle to get money off him at times. He always wanted photos from me, but I could never get him to pay me for them. He'd have wads and wads of cash in his wash bag, but he'd say, 'I can't let you have any of that; I've got to get a couple of tyres for my car.' Yeah, right. Despite that, I liked him a lot and was delighted to see him make a full recovery from the cancer that seriously threatened his life in 2009.

Hartson arrived at West Ham in February 1997 in a £3.5 million move from Arsenal as the club splashed the cash in a bid to avoid relegation, the investment in Răducioiu, Dumitrescu and Futre having failed to bear fruit. Paul Kitson was also signed from Newcastle and it seemed that Harry had decided to rely on British players who could hit the ground running. The two strikers did the business on the field, but I must admit I wasn't a fan of Kitson. He'd make personal comments and snide remarks, then insist he was jesting when you knew otherwise. 'Just joking,' he'd say. I thought he was a weasel and one of the few players at West Ham I can say I really didn't take to. Just joking, of course, Paul...

One foreign player that Harry did sign the following season was striker Samassi Abou, a native of the Ivory Coast. One director said he looked as if he'd just been dragged off the beach, while Berkovic never liked changing next to him because he thought he whiffed a bit and was in need of a shower. Eyal was always complaining about him. When the fans began to chant 'Abooooou!' Samassi genuinely believed he was being booed until somebody explained things to him.

Of all the players to feature in West Ham's United Nations of the late 1990s, however, there's one man who stands head and shoulders above the rest – and that is Paolo Di Canio. I've always thought there was a fine line between genius and madness, and Paolo seemed to exist somewhere between the two. The Italian striker was an outcast at Sheffield Wednesday after pushing referee Paul Alcock to the ground during a match against Arsenal and being hit with an eleven-game ban. It was perhaps typical of Harry Redknapp's gambling nature that he would come to the player's rescue by bringing him to Upton Park. I remember when Harry told me he was trying to sign Di Canio and I asked him what he thought he was doing. 'Well, I can get him for next to nothing,' he said. 'He's a great player if you ignore what went on. You've just got to take a chance with him.' I think all managers like to think they can contain the bad boys.

But Paolo was just a law unto himself. There was never a dull moment when he was around – especially if travel was involved. On one journey up to Sunderland we'd taxied for quite some time from the Business Aviation Centre at Stansted onto the main runway before we suddenly became aware of some rumblings at the back of the plane that suggested all was not well with Di Canio. You could hear Paolo's voice, saying, 'No, no, no.' A stewardess was doing her best to placate him, but she clearly failed because the next thing we heard was, 'I will not fly today!' The stewardess rushed up the aisle to see the pilot and she must have told him there was a serious problem because the next thing we knew was that we were returning to the terminal. 'I cannot fly,' insisted Paolo. 'I don't want to die.' It's not like Di Canio to over-dramatise a situation! We eventually got him off the plane and it was Paul Aldridge, our managing director, who drew the short straw and had to drive Paolo up to the North East instead.

There was another occasion a few years later when Paolo didn't want to fly back from a game at Blackburn, so the manager at that time, Glenn Roeder, ended up having to drive him home. Stan Lazaridis was another one who got the jitters. After a few nervy moments on a windy flight up to Newcastle, he declared that he didn't want to fly back and was told he could only return by road if he scored a goal. He duly struck the winner from nearly forty yards! And it wasn't just the players who sometimes didn't have the stomach for flying. Coach Frank Burrows was gripping my seat from behind during some particularly torrid turbulence on one flight while Julian Dicks repeatedly screamed, 'We're all going to die! We're all going to die!' Frank was in a right old state. 'For fuck's sake, shut up!' he shouted as he clung on for dear life.

The incident that really made me laugh, however, was when we went to Croatia in September 1999 for a UEFA Cup first-round tie against NK Osijek. We'd switched onto a smaller plane at Zagreb for the final leg of the outbound trip and we had Croatian defender Igor Štimac with us at that point in time. Štimac was a big star in his home country and seemed to know everybody – including our pilot, who invited him to go and sit up front with him. Igor disappeared into the pilot's cabin and, of course, the rest of the players decided to tell Di Canio that his teammate was now flying the plane! Not surprisingly, this sent Di Canio into an instant panic and he jumped out of his seat and threw himself to his knees. 'No, I have babies, I have babies!' he screamed. 'We mustn't fly, I have babies!'

We settled Paolo down and he soon realised that they were pulling his leg, but it wouldn't have surprised any of us if Štimac had taken the controls of the plane given the sort of power and influence he seemed to enjoy in his home-land. He seemed to be able to make things happen with just one phone call. For example, during a spare moment, Igor asked some of the players if they wanted to shoot some guns – as you do – and several of the lads were well up for that. Štimac pulled out his mobile phone and within five minutes two huge limousines roared up to our hotel with a load of machine guns in the back. The boys went off to a clearing and started firing these guns. Štimac could get anything arranged out there.

Our hotel was riddled with shell marks and bullet holes – the scars of the Croatian War of Independence rather than wayward shooting from a bunch of West Ham players (with weapons rather than footballs). Once inside, we came across an amazing-looking black girl in the bar and it seemed obvious to us that she was a hooker. There was a rumour that Štimac had a piece of that action as well and that he gave her to Rio Ferdinand as an early birthday present. Not that you can always believe what you hear, of course!

Igor's international teammate Davor Šuker joined West Ham for a short and unsuccessful stint during the 2000/01 season and I once made the mistake of getting their names mixed up. I stupidly referred to Igor as Davor and he turned to me and said, 'Please, Steve, show me some respect.' I was full of apologies because he wasn't a man I wanted to upset. Like I said, it only takes one phone call. However, when it came to moody and temperamental characters, there was nobody to rival Paolo Di Canio. He developed a reputation for missing games that involved a lot of travel. Indeed, former Hammer Tony Gale always used to joke that we'd have to reverse the coach up north so that Di Canio wasn't aware that we were going up there.

Paolo was something of a loner at times. He was wary of food that hadn't been prepared by him or his wife, so he wouldn't eat with us at the training ground or in hotels or on the coach. I'd started to sit on the courier seat next to the driver to keep out of the way of things and, of course, Paolo decided he wanted to sit at the front of the coach. So I got turfed out and had to sit at one of the tables, which was something of a tight squeeze for me at the time, and Paolo would bring a bag of cold meats and salami and eat his own stuff up at the front. He could also be a bit paranoid about health issues. Our doctor, Ges Steinbergs, could speak Italian and Paolo was always on to him about the slightest little thing, especially if it concerned his family. 'You must come now,' he'd insist to poor Ges, who felt obliged to pander to his every whim.

Paolo was a great one for wanting photographs after

games. I'm friendly with Steve Ellis, the photographer at Sheffield Wednesday who got the shot of Di Canio pushing the referee over. We were up at Hillsborough once and I was chatting to Steve on the edge of the pitch when the players came out to warm up. Paolo went up to Steve and pointed to me. 'Fucking useless photographer,' he said. 'He never gives me any pictures.' He was joking, of course.

Paolo wasn't alone in asking for photographs – many of the players have wanted material over the years. Luděk Mikloško was one of them, but whereas many players would take material without offering anything in return, he would bring in a case of lager imported from his home country. Another appreciative player was Marc-Vivien Foé, whose transfer to West Ham along with Di Canio was paid for by the £7.5 million sale of John Hartson to Wimbledon. I produced some prints for Foé and he was so grateful that he patted his chest and said, 'I thank you from my heart. These are for my father.' It was absolutely terrible when the midfielder collapsed and died while playing for Cameroon in 2003 as a result of a heart condition.

But I always had a good relationship with Di Canio. When I asked him to sign my photographic book that was published during his time with us, he mouthed the message, 'To Steve, fucking wanker!' However, he did actually pen a very nice comment and when he comes back to Upton Park I always get a big man-hug from him. 'I will be the manager of West Ham one day,' he tells me. I'm sure a lot of the fans would love him back as the boss, but God knows what it would be like. The word chaos springs to mind.

The signings of Di Canio and Foé in the early part of 1999 helped West Ham finish fifth in the Premier League table – their second-best ever position in the top flight – to secure a place in the UEFA Intertoto Cup. I was delighted because this meant we were back in European action again and it provided the first opportunity for me to work abroad since West Ham's brief Anglo-Italian Cup adventures in 1992 (given that Australia felt more like a holiday). I'll always remember our game in Cosenza when it hammered down with rain and the Italians didn't want the match to go ahead. 'Well, we're not fucking coming back,' said manager Billy Bonds, desperate to get the meaningless competition out of the way. The whole stadium was flooded and the fire brigade had to pump water out of the stairway so that the players could gain access to the dressing room, which was below ground level – or maybe I should say sea level. Everybody thought I was mad for trying to shoot the game in atrocious conditions, but I stuck a bin-liner over my head and did my best. I got absolutely soaked.

I recall Bonzo saying he'd just tasted the best pizza he'd ever had when we were out there. 'Well, we are in Italy,' I said rather dryly. I've got to say that Billy was something of a traditionalist when it came to food. It was around the same time that he announced he was going for his very first Chinese meal. 'What's it like?' he asked. 'It's, er, like Chinese,' I replied, wondering how Billy could have reached his mid-forties without having ever nibbled noodles. He had no idea what dishes to order so we all made some suggestions and he ended up with a very big list – with a sizeable bill to match, I would imagine.

Apart from the weather, we'd had a good time in Italy and so it was great for us to return to European football seven years later. The Intertoto Cup might have forced us back into action as early as mid-July, but it did allow us to enjoy a run of games in Finland (against Jokerit in Helsinki's Olympic

Stadium), Holland (against Heerenveen) and France (at Metz) and any chance to win a trophy is not to be sniffed at – even if the prize is not much bigger than an egg cup.

We'd lost 1-0 at home to Metz in the first leg of the final so most people had written us off, but we turned on the style in the second leg to win 3-2 on aggregate thanks to goals from Trevor Sinclair, Frank Lampard and Paulo Wanchope. The game in France just happened to coincide with my birthday and the club directors presented me with a big cake, which I thought was a very nice gesture. One of my best pictures from the game was of an exuberant fan clinging on to the fencing and being hosed down with fire-extinguisher foam by one of the riot police. I loved the fact that John Ball, our stadium manager turned safety officer, told the policeman, 'Don't do that, you'll only inflame the situation.' Which wasn't the most appropriate choice of words, when you think about it.

I'm not sure whether the Intertoto Cup was too embarrassing to be seen with or just too insignificant to remember, but I recall having to ask skipper Steve Lomas at least six or seven times to pose with it during our trip to Bradford a few days later. I was in charge of the trophy and was a bit worried about losing it – not that I think it carried any great value. Nevertheless, we'd won a European trophy, and the real reward for winning the Intertoto Cup was qualification for the UEFA Cup for the first time in West Ham's history. After disposing of Osijek, we headed to Romania – yes, my favourite country – to play Steaua Bucharest. I soon had a spring in my step, however, when I discovered they were holding the *Playboy* Playmate of the Year awards for the Romanian edition of the magazine in our hotel. There were some stunning girls there. It was a media-only event, so I used my newspaper society pass to blag my way in, was able to meet the girls and obtained a goodie bag, which included a copy of the magazine. The words were difficult to understand, of course, so I just entertained myself with the pictures instead. And, as everyone knows, I've always had a great interest in photography...

On the night of the match, the police provided an escort to the Stadionul Ghencea, but as we were trying to work our way through the traffic there was one car in front of us that was reluctant to move out of the way. When we stopped at a junction the police pulled up alongside the obstructive vehicle and pointed a gun at the driver. I think it's fair to say he got the message because he posed no problems after that. The armed police also came in handy when a big gang of locals surrounded the team bus after the game to see what could be stolen, only for the guns to frighten them off. Or maybe it was the sight of Larry Hagman's ten-gallon hat. The American actor, who played oil magnate JR Ewing in *Dallas*, had been invited to the match as a special guest and then presented to the crowd. It was very strange. Next they'll be telling me that Norman Wisdom is big in Albania.

We had a message that Ilie Dumitrescu, who had only recently retired from playing at Steaua, was looking for Eddie Gillam and me after the game. However, as if I wasn't sick enough about our 2-0 defeat – thanks in part to some dodgy refereeing decisions – I suddenly started to feel really ill. We had a little chat with Ilie, but I began to feel so weak I couldn't even dismantle my equipment without some help. I was sitting next to Hammers coach Roger Cross on the flight home and he told me how awful I looked. He obviously thought it was contagious, too, because he soon made himself scarce. I honestly felt as if I was going to die, but thankfully made a rapid recovery when back on British soil. Maybe it was an allergic reaction to being in Romania!

Of course, the Intertoto Cup was not the only trophy that West Ham won in 1999; the club also triumphed in the FA Youth Cup for the third time in their history. The young Hammers thrashed Coventry 9-0 on aggregate over the two-leg final, with both Joe Cole and Michael Carrick pulling the strings in sensational style. It emphasised that West Ham's youth scheme was flourishing in the second half of the 1990s, especially with Rio Ferdinand and Frank Lampard Jr having already emerged from the ranks to establish themselves as vital first-team players with great futures ahead of them. There's no doubt that Tony Carr, the club's Academy Director, has earned and saved the club a fortune in transfer fees over the past thirty years or so. He just seems to have this knack of producing players – but don't ask me how.

As West Ham's manager, Harry Redknapp also won a lot of praise for presiding over the resurgence of the youth scheme, but I'm not sure how much credit you can necessarily give him for the players that came through at that time. I tend to think that these things go in cycles and there will be barren periods. Indeed, Matthew Rush and Danny Williamson were the only two youngsters to come through and make a significant first-team contribution during a quiet seven-year period in the late 1980s and early 1990s. In 1997 Williamson was sold to Everton for £4.5 million in a deal that included David Unsworth and the midfielder only made seventeen appearances before a long-standing foot ligament injury forced him to retire at the age of twenty-six. I think certain people at West Ham might have suspected he'd have ongoing problems, given the troubles he'd already had at Upton Park, but it was about getting a good deal for the club as well as the boy himself.

The next academy graduate to break into the first team

was Frank Lampard, who made his debut as a seventeen-year-old substitute against Coventry in January 1996. I've got a great picture of the fresh-faced youngster getting ready to come on next to Coventry's veteran midfielder Gordon Strachan, who was almost twenty-two years older than him. Harry could certainly see the funny side – he had his arms around both players and was joking with them about it.

Lampard senior was always as good as gold and that's why I got on so well with young Frank, because I knew him from a very early age and saw him growing up. I'd been taking pictures of Frank junior since he was a toddler, as his father was one of those players who would occasionally ask me round to their places to take pictures of their kids. I'd done some stuff of the two Franks having a kick-about in the back garden. Frank junior would also come to the club's Christmas parties. At one event he was chasing about with Warren – Trevor Brooking's boy – and he crashed into a table and hit his head. He was a bit of a 'buster' in those days and was always going to be a bit chunky as he was growing up. Whenever he has returned to Upton Park with Chelsea, the crowd would boo the midfielder as his name was read out but he would always turn to me and have a laugh about it.

Frank went to a private school in Brentwood and is a bright lad. Obviously he had a difficult time when he came into the West Ham first team because some of the fans believed there was a bit of favouritism towards him, with the assistant boss being his father and the manager his uncle. Nepotism? No way. I don't think Frank sought any special treatment and I certainly don't think he got it. Nobody can deny what a good player he turned out to be, having amassed ninety full England caps at the time of writing.

I think the biggest problem with Frank is that he was

critical of the Hammers after he left the club in 2001. If you do that, there are always going to be problems. He should have just gone quietly. For him to suggest that the West Ham fans were this or that was stupid, because you're never going to win that battle. And what made no sense at all was the fact that he criticised the running of the club when it was his uncle and dad that were in charge. To me, that was a crazy thing to do.

Frank's big ally as he broke into the first team was Rio Ferdinand, who made his debut against Sheffield Wednesday on the final day of the 1995/96 season. You could always see that Rio was going to be one hell of a defender. He was a good lad and I met his mum a few times. It was only going to be a matter of time before he moved on to bigger and better things, but at least we got four-and-a-half seasons out of him before he joined Leeds United for £18 million, later making a £30 million switch to Manchester United.

Rio and Frank enjoyed each other's company as teenagers and would sometimes chat up girls together. On one occasion, we were in Southampton and I had been enjoying the bar on the Friday evening when I realised I needed something from my room. As I came back down, using the back stairs, I suddenly saw Rio and Frank with two young ladies making their way up. 'You haven't seen anything,' said Frank. 'All right,' I said. And I was good to my word. After all, I didn't really feel like upsetting Frank's father or uncle.

It would be remiss of me not to mention at this point the time when a couple of young players decided to have what you could call a 'mass debate' – no, not a big discussion, but a wanking competition – at the back of the team bus. The strange thing is that they weren't making much of a secret of it and the news soon made its way through the coach. I recently told this story to my girlfriend Tash and the first thing she wanted to know was who won. And you know what? I really don't remember – or care, for that matter!

There was a buzz about Rio Ferdinand when he broke into the first team, but it was nothing compared to the sense of anticipation surrounding Joe Cole as he came through the ranks. Everybody was talking about Joe from an early age, declaring what a great player he was going to be. I've got a picture of a very young Rio presenting an even younger Joe with an award, so he was obviously showing great promise early on. I can remember Harry Redknapp saying that Joe was the best young player for his age he'd ever seen. Everyone used to watch him train because he did such amazing things. He just loved playing with the ball and would be out on the training field for ages. He had such natural ability and passion for the game, but I don't believe he's really achieved as much as he should have in his career.

Joe made his West Ham debut as a substitute in an FA Cup tie at home to Swansea in January 1999, which we drew 1-1 thanks to a late equaliser from Julian Dicks. I remember the replay well because we stayed at a dreadful hotel down on the Mumbles and I was chilling out in my room when one of the electricity sockets decided to blow up, with sparks and smoke flying out of the wall. I immediately dashed out of the room, thinking the whole place was going to go up in flames. Joe didn't play in the replay, but he trained with the rest of the lads on the beach. He had changed his footwear down there and when the session was over asked Eddie Gillam where his shoes were. 'Where did you leave them?' asked Eddie. 'On that rock over there,' said Joe. Of course, the rock was now submerged, the tide having come in somewhat. 'I think they're probably halfway out to sea by now,' said Eddie, somewhat bemused – and amused – by Joe's carelessness.

There were far more serious problems to contend with during that visit to Swansea, however – and I'm not talking about West Ham's embarrassing but entirely predictable 1-0 defeat. It was close to kick-off and I was walking along the edge of the pitch at the Vetch Field watching our stadium manager John Ball talk to his equivalent at Swansea. All of a sudden, John hit the ground. He was out cold. 'Get a doctor, get a doctor!' screamed a voice. A couple of us rushed to the West Ham dressing room and banged on the door to call for Ges Steinbergs. By the time he reached the touchline, John had stopped breathing.

Ges got down on his knees and started to give John CPR. He was pumping away and eventually brought John round, by which time the players were emerging from the tunnel for the game. John was taken to the hospital and Ges went with him, although he was back at the ground by the time the game had finished. He still had two big wet patches on his trousers from having been on his knees on the wet track.

Thankfully, Ges said he thought John would be okay. Ron Pearce, who's the current stadium manager, is John's brother-in-law and he arrived with John's missus. Everyone was praising Ges for saving John's life. The reality is that he brought him back from the brink: John had had a heart attack and had dropped stone dead. The funny thing is that Ges felt quite guilty and said, 'I think I might have bust his ribs with all that pumping.' I reassured him: 'I don't think he'll be taking you to court over that, mate. You've saved his life.'

After the FA Youth Cup final success in May 1999, Michael Carrick made his first-team debut a couple of months later.

I thought Michael was a really smashing lad. With him being a Geordie boy, people up at Newcastle would always ask about him – he was the one that got away as far as they were concerned. They could never work out how they missed him. As a youth player he'd sometimes join us on the trip up to Newcastle to get a free ride home to see his mum and dad. It was good of Harry to allow that.

Frank, Rio, Joe and Michael all went on to bigger and better things, of course, with Chelsea and Manchester United the main beneficiaries of their talents. The four players have won nearly 250 England caps between them at the time of writing. But there's another youth product of the late 1990s I've yet to mention who, in his own way, wrote a little bit of history for himself at West Ham. I am, of course, talking about Emmanuel Omoyinmi, who cost the club a place in the Worthington Cup semi-finals after coming on as a late substitute against Aston Villa in December 1999.

As has been well documented, Manny had bizarrely neglected to mention the fact that he was ineligible to appear for the Hammers in the competition, having already played in it while on loan at Gillingham. After the team were forced to play and lost a subsequent replay, it caused a huge fuss at West Ham – with the club secretary and his assistant feeling compelled to resign – and Harry Redknapp was extremely unhappy with Manny. 'Why didn't you mention it?' he kept asking him. And Manny just shrugged his shoulders.

He didn't strike me as the brightest bloke on earth. I once asked Manny how to spell his surname and he needed two attempts at it! I thought, 'If *you* don't know how to spell your name, then how the hell are *we* supposed to?' But he did have one thing going for him, I suppose. We were in the dressing room one day when he stripped off and to say he was well endowed is something of an understatement. Harry sat there, stunned, and said, 'Manny, can I borrow that for the weekend?'

One of my favourite players of that particular era has to be Ian Wright. He was such a lively character and was always laughing and joking. He was buzzing all the time. Wrighty joined us from Arsenal in the summer of 1998 and already had genuine celebrity status, long before his television career took off. He was just a mega-star. We went to Scotland for a pre-season tour and he was mobbed as we were going through Heathrow airport. Working for West Ham, you get used to seeing the reaction of the general public when they meet their heroes, but that day was something else. Ian was surrounded by a throng of people of all ages – including kids, mums and old ladies – every one of whom wanted his autograph or picture. I remember him going crazy on the touchline during one of the friendly games when he was waiting to make his debut. He was like a caged lion. I've never seen anybody so keen to get on the field – and this was a man in the twilight of his playing career.

I set up a picture of Wright posing with two smiley Hammers when he signed for us and from that moment onwards I discovered I got on well with the striker. At some stage during the season a fan sent him a caricature of the two of us. I had a camera around my neck and Ian had a bubble coming out of his mouth saying, 'If we get to Europe, will you take my passport photo?' Ian duly signed it and gave it to me, which I thought was a nice gesture.

Wrighty was such a big personality in the dressing room. I wouldn't say he got any special treatment, but Harry gave the former England star plenty of respect for what he had achieved in his career. He definitely livened up the changing room with his infectious humour and I thought that was a very good thing. This was particularly evident when Wrighty scored against Southampton at Upton Park and celebrated by re-enacting Paolo Di Canio's push on the referee, which had taken place a couple of days earlier. He got Neil Ruddock to shove him in the chest and then staggered as if he'd been shot before theatrically falling down. I thought they mimicked the original incident perfectly!

Ruddock was another controversial character and had arrived at the Boleyn Ground in the summer of 1998. The defender was similar to Wrighty in terms of having real presence – and I'm not talking about his physical size – and always being involved in whatever was going on. We were at Coventry one day and there was some argy-bargy over what music was being played on the ghetto blaster in the dressing room. There were so many players wanting so many different styles of music. Anyway, for some reason, Ruddock put on 'Take Me Home, Country Roads', the John Denver song from the early 1970s, and everybody started singing along. It was just amazing. The whole team and all the staff were singing at the top of their voices and it was really, really loud. Our door was open with the home dressing room directly opposite and I can remember Gordon Strachan – by then the Coventry manager – sticking his head out and looking quite scared. I said to the boys, 'I think we've got 'em worried!' Anybody who was there will remember that afternoon and even Harry was getting involved!

The atmosphere in the squad at that time helped bring everybody together and Wrighty and Ruddock were generally the ringleaders. We qualified for Europe at the end of the 1998/99 season and it has to be said that the two boys played their part in getting us there.

Trevor Sinclair was another lively character in the squad at that time. I seem to recall that he liked a sherbet. He gave me a bollocking once when we were on our way back from a game and the players wanted to stop at an off-licence. The boss wasn't on board to stop them but Eddie Gillam said we shouldn't really and when I muttered something in agreement Sinclair said, 'What's it got to do with you?' But I generally got on fine with him and gave him a spectacular goal-scoring photo once – in the black-and-white format he demanded.

In terms of jokers, however, goalkeeper Les Sealey was up there with the best of them. Les was the nephew of Hammers hero Alan Sealey, who scored both our goals in the 1965 European Cup Winners' Cup final win against Munich, and he used to sit with us a lot when we were away on a Friday night and have a chat.

Les would always boast about the amount of money he had. He bought houses and rented them out and we'd take the mickey out of him. I think he had properties in Luton and we often used to drop him off there after games. All the lads would joke, 'What, time to pick up all the rents then?' Now and again, if people were having a joke, Les would brag about some of things he'd done in his career – not least his appearance for Manchester United in the 1990 FA Cup final replay against Crystal Palace, which saw him collect a winner's medal. There was always banter with him. He used to bring in stuff for the lads to buy and he once said, 'These won't interest you, Steve. These are shoes. When was the last time you saw your feet?' I got my own back a couple of weeks later when he was talking about going into manage-ment with a lower league club and I said, 'You won't get a team as good as that.' We had little digs at each other, but it was all good-natured stuff.

The bizarre thing about Les is that he made his West Ham debut as a substitute striker. Julian Dicks had been sent off at Arsenal and we'd used our two outfield subs when John Moncur was forced out of action by injury. Les came on and I got a great shot of him grappling with Arsenal keeper David Seaman, which is something nobody ever thought they would see. He was always making us laugh. We were at Leicester once when Eddie opened up one of the kit bags and a mouse popped out. Les put his goalkeeping gloves on and scooped up the mouse to release him onto the Filbert Street pitch.

Les had a couple of spells at West Ham in the mid-to-late 1990s and was appointed as the club's goalkeeping coach. I used to watch him training some of the keepers and thought he was very good with them. But then one night, in August 2001, I received a phone call from my old photographer pal Lawrence Lustig, who was good friends with Les and his family. 'I've got some bad news,' he said. 'Les has died.' I must admit, his words didn't initially register properly with me. I just said, 'Les?' And he replied, 'Yeah, Les Sealey is dead.' I couldn't believe it. He'd had a heart attack at the age of forty-three.

The funeral at the City of London Cemetery and Crematorium was a very sad affair. Some of Les's old goal-keeping colleagues, including Luděk Mikloško, were the pallbearers and his coffin was interred in the catacombs. The coffin was put into the wall and we were all invited to file past. The headstone was like the plug that sealed the hole – it was very unusual. Most of the other inscriptions were very old. Both of his sons, George and Joe, were on West Ham's books as youngsters before developing their careers elsewhere.

They say you need to be slightly mad to be a goalkeeper

– and some would say Les 'The Cat' Sealey had a zany quality – but you wouldn't really put Shaka Hislop, who arrived
for the first of his two spells at West Ham in 1998, in that
category. Shaka was one of those keepers that seem like
a gentle giant. He was so laid-back it was untrue. Though
he represented Trinidad and Tobago in his international
career, having lived there as a child, he was born in Hackney
and has the most amazing accent. He was a clever bloke,
graduating in the United States with a degree in mechanical engineering and interning at NASA, but he was also a
really nice guy who could make you laugh. He went up to
John Green once and said, 'John, you're a physiotherapist.
Tell me; in your honest opinion as a medical man, do you
think I would look good in a Porsche 911?'

The last time I saw Shaka was when I bumped into him and
Craig Forrest, another former Hammers keeper, when we
played a friendly against the Major League Soccer All-Star
team in Toronto in 2008. David Beckham played against us
and that's the only thing anybody seemed interested in.

Another goalkeeper I'll never forget from Harry's days is
Neil Finn. The teenager made his one and only Hammers
appearance when he played up at Manchester City on New
Year's Day in 1996. Ludo was suspended, so Les Sealey was
expected to start in goal for the very first time, only to suffer
a calf injury the day before the game. I don't think Harry
wanted Neil to know he was actually starting the match
until the day itself because he wanted the youngster, who
had turned seventeen just three days earlier, to get a good
night's sleep. The problem was that we didn't have a jersey
for Neil, just a black shirt with a number one on the back.
Eddie had a spare number three, but couldn't find anywhere
to get it pressed onto the top. Thankfully, Ludo's wife Ivana

had travelled to the hotel on the morning of the match and offered to sew the number on for us, but with the figure one already in the middle, the final effect was very off-centre. We also needed Finn's name on the shirt, but we didn't have any letters. Conveniently, his surname was made up of characters you could make with straight lines, so John Green supplied the binding tape and Eddie and I did the rest. However, it was crudely done and as the game progressed you could see the bits of tape peeling off. Who says that West Ham do not meet the very highest standards of professionalism?

We had similar troubles when Kenny Brown was suddenly added to the Hammers squad for a game at Newcastle. Eddie had no spare shirt of any description and we were scratching our heads before somebody suggested that we go and buy one. 'The only problem,' said Eddie, 'is that we're in bloody Newcastle!' He had a point – West Ham shirts are not exactly popular items on Tyneside. Fortunately, we found a sports shop in the city centre with two mannequins displayed in the window wearing the shirts of the two sides playing that day. The shop manager wouldn't sell us the shirt but said we could have it free of charge if we arranged for the retailer's name to be broadcast over the St James' Park PA system during the game. We happily agreed and the shirt was pressed up with Brown's name and number. However, despite our assurances, we had absolutely no influence with anybody at Newcastle United and so the shop failed to get the advertising plug it was looking for.

The players almost had no kit whatsoever on another trip to Newcastle towards the end of Harry Redknapp's reign. On this occasion, Eddie and I were driving the gear up to Stansted – where we were due to meet the team – when we suffered a punctured tyre. There was no way we could jack up the loaded van with all the equipment we had in there, so we were forced to call out the AA for help. Ludo was on the phone to ask where we were and all we could say was that we were awaiting assistance on the M11. He kept ringing but in the end we just had to tell the boys to leave without us and we'd make it up there somehow.

The AA put us back on the road, but we'd missed the club's flight and the authorities at Stansted said that the only way they could get us to Newcastle was if we flew from Heathrow instead. Eddie insisted he couldn't drive to Heathrow because the return flight was to Stansted and that's where he needed the van to be. So the club arranged for us to have a people carrier, which we managed to squeeze all the gear into for the journey to Heathrow.

We struggled through the Friday evening traffic to get to Heathrow, but eventually arrived and checked all the stuff through for the flight. We had so many skips with us you'd have thought that progressive rockers Emerson, Lake & Palmer were going on tour. We had been told that a vehicle would be waiting at Newcastle airport to meet us and assumed it would be a van or a people carrier to accommodate all the kit we had. But no, a regular taxi arrived and I just looked at Eddie and said, 'Well, we're buggered!'

Eddie insisted that we could get all the gear in the car with a bit of muscle and effort, so we stuffed everything in and there was just enough room for me to squeeze in under the ceiling next to the driver. If you'd have seen all the kit on the pavement there's no way you'd have believed we could get everything into this taxi. But we somehow defied the laws of physics, with Eddie also finding a spare pocket of air to crawl into. When we arrived at the hotel, somebody came out and said, 'How the fuck did you manage to get all that in there?'

Inside, we found John Green, who had been doing some work with defender Stuart Pearce, so we joined the pair of them for a meal in the dining room. That's when I first became really impressed with Pearce, who spent a couple of seasons with us. He spoke so well about football and it was obvious to me that he'd go on to become a good club manager. As I write, he is in charge of the England under-21 side, recently had temporary control of the senior team following the resignation of Fabio Capello and managed the Great Britain side at the 2012 Olympic Games, so he hasn't done too badly, has he?

The four amigos – Eddie, John, Ges and me – had another entertaining time in the North East when the Hammers played Middlesbrough and Sunderland away within four days of each other. You might as well forget the football: we lost 4-1 against Middlesbrough midweek and then drew 0-0 on the Sunday with Sunderland in what must rank as one of the most awful games of football ever. Commentator Martin Tyler told me he'd never seen such a bad match. But we enjoyed our stay in the region between the two games.

We went to the cinema to see *Twister* and I remember Ges, who's always very generous and offering to pay for things, insisting he get us all some pick-and-mix. I didn't think it was very healthy, but looking at the pair of us it probably wasn't going to make much difference. Ges was choosing the sweets and he was eating as much as he was putting into the bag. He certainly got his money's worth because he was stealing all the chocolate brazils. He then ran off to buy some huge cups of coke but, even with all the caffeine, halfway through the film – which nobody else wanted to watch apart from me – I nodded off and started snoring. The guys weren't sure if the loud noise was the surround sound of the movie or me. Afterwards we went for a meal at an American-style diner. Ges ordered the fat-boy burger and it was absolutely huge. 'I'll finish it, don't you worry about that,' he insisted. Of course, he really struggled and the sweat was pouring off him as he refused to give in. He had just one little piece left – it was a bit like Monty Python's Mr Creosote with a wafer-thin mint. Boom!

On Saturday the boys were invited back to Middlesbrough to watch them play Coventry, but I didn't fancy it (well, can you blame me?) and decided to stay in the hotel and watch Essex play in a one-day game on the television – not that I'm much of a cricket fan. What I didn't know was that the guys would get the best seats in the house and enjoy all the hospitality that Middlesbrough FC had to offer. So the rest of them had a great nosh-up and a few drinks, watching Boro stuff four goals in against Coventry, while I was sitting in my hotel with a packet of crisps watching Essex get annihilated. It's not the first time in my life I've made the wrong call.

The undisputed highlight of Harry Redknapp's final season at West Ham was the FA Cup fourth-round victory at Manchester United in January 2001. Goalkeeper Fabien Barthez might have failed to fool Paolo Di Canio as he waved his arms around like a French traffic cop, but he certainly got the better of me because I stopped shooting in the belief that an offside flag had been waved. Then I realised Paolo had scored and I managed to get a picture of him on his knees. Like I've said before, it's sometimes better to get a picture of the celebration rather than the goal itself and that's the reason why I'll often sit in front of the West Ham fans, even if we're kicking in the opposite direction, because the players will look for their own supporters after scoring. They will also return to that end of the ground after the final whistle if they've won the game.

Eddie and I had taken the kit down to Old Trafford after breakfast and while we were there we saw Sir Alex Ferguson, who had arrived early to do an interview. Fergie noticed us in the dressing room and came in for a chat. I wasn't his biggest fan, to be honest, but I thought he was talking a lot of sense in terms of the academy system proving very expensive if it didn't produce the players the clubs wanted.

I'd already suffered my first illness through diabetes – more of which later – and had been asked by my hospital if I could get anything special for them to auction. 'In for a penny, in for a pound,' I thought. So I said to Sir Alex, 'I hope you don't mind me asking, but I've been pretty ill lately and I was trying to get something for the hospital. Is there any chance of getting a David Beckham shirt?' He sighed, 'It's always David Beckham, isn't it?' 'Before you say anything,' I quickly interjected, 'Whipps Cross Hospital was in the area where David was brought up, so I'm sure he'd have been in and out of the place in his younger days.' Suitably persuaded, Fergie asked the Manchester United kit man, Albert, to sort out a shirt, saying, 'It's Beckham, of course!' Albert told me he'd send one through to Eddie and when it subsequently arrived the great thing was that it was a match-worn shirt – which are always the ones to have – signed by Beckham on the back.

A few days later, a package arrived for me at West Ham and I opened it to discover a replica shirt signed by the entire Manchester United team, along with a certificate of authenticity. I thought that was very nice, as it could only have come from Sir Alex. I decided I'd keep the Beckham shirt and let the hospital have the one signed by the whole team. Then, about a week later, a third package arrived and this time it contained a Manchester United football that had been signed by the full squad, again with a certificate of authenticity. At the time, West Ham were doing some work with the Richard House Hospice in Canning Town so I gave them the ball to auction off and raise funds. As for my signed Beckham shirt, about a year ago someone was desperate for one and I managed to sell it for about £500! But don't tell anybody!

Clearly, Sir Alex had asked people at his club to sort a few things out for me and I thought a lot more of him after that. In 2006, he came down to Suffolk to speak at John Lyall's funeral and he later visited Upton Park for a fundraising gala night in memory of both John and Ron Greenwood. Alex was the guest of honour and, even though Manchester United were playing in Europe that week, he chartered a plane to attend the function. He spoke really well of West Ham and mentioned how we had spoilt two title campaigns for him; everyone at the club was really impressed. It was only after John's death that I began to appreciate what good friends they had actually been.

There used to be a guy called Jim who worked on the door at Upton Park in the old days and his wife Betty worked in the tea room. Jim died and Fergie must have got to hear about it, because the next time I saw Betty she said she had something to show me. She produced a letter that Fergie had sent her, saying that he was sorry to hear the news about her husband, with whom he always used to have a word when he was at West Ham. A lot of football fans tend to have a certain perception of Fergie – that he's very single-minded and that his focus is purely on Manchester United – but I think it's wonderful that he thinks of things like that. And there we are, knocking his team out of the FA Cup.

Little did we realise that Harry Redknapp would only have

another three months at Upton Park before being dispensed with by chairman Terence Brown. Terry wasn't happy about the way that funds had been spent following the £18 million sale of Rio Ferdinand to Leeds midway through a season in which the Hammers would eventually finish in fifteenth place. There was an element of shock, but I guess I shouldn't have been too surprised, given that Tony Gale had always told me that Brown would deal with Redknapp when the time was right. Galey used to talk to the chairman, who'd say, 'I've got Harry exactly where I want him.'

Personally, I was disappointed to see Harry go because I got on very well with him and thought he did a very good job at West Ham. People questioned why he bought certain players, but nobody could deny that we had a very success-ful period under his management. We finished fifth in the Premier League table, enjoyed several other top-half plac-ings and played in Europe. The football was entertaining and the club made some good profits on players in the transfer market – John Hartson, Slaven Bilić and Eyal Berkovic are just three examples.

I know Harry doesn't like to be described as a wheeler-dealer, but he's a very good one, which is probably why I've mentioned it on three occasions in this book. He's also very good at man-management. He keeps a reasonably happy ship, the training ground usually buzzes when he's about and he knows his stuff. Some people might think it was fitting the way things ended up for Harry at Upton Park given the controversial way in which he succeeded Billy Bonds in 1994. But I'd have been more than happy for him to continue at West Ham and would gladly have had him back at any time over the past ten years or so. I'm sure he'd have been inter-ested. After all, what else has he done?

CHAPTER 5

'WOULD YOU LIKE A BISCUIT?'

'Would you like a biscuit?' Glenn Roeder was playing the perfect host, pouring the tea and facing
me with the impossible dilemma of choosing
between bourbons and chocolate Hobnobs. West Ham had
appointed their new manager – the surprise successor to
Harry Redknapp – and the directors had decided that he
might benefit from some publicity. Hence I found myself
despatched to Herongate in Essex to visit the Roeder house-
hold and produce some promotional images.

There had been quite a bit of speculation as to who might
become West Ham's ninth manager following Harry's
departure, with Alan Curbishley, Steve McClaren and Alex
McLeish all apparently spurning the opportunity before
it was eventually announced that Roeder had accepted the
post on a permanent basis. The overwhelming feeling was
that Glenn, who had been on the club's coaching staff for two
years, had won the job by default – and the fact that as caretaker he had overseen a dismal 2-1 defeat at Middlesbrough
on the final day of the 2000/01 season hardly helped his case.
Indeed, he said it all by comparing himself to Foinavon, the
horse which won the 1967 Grand National as a 100-1 outsider
after the rest of the competition fell by the wayside.

Quite why nobody else seemed to want the West Ham job is something of a mystery. It's easy to talk with the benefit of hindsight, but it was obvious to most people at the time that Roeder was in for a difficult ride, not least because Harry Redknapp was a tough act to follow. The fact that he was part of the club's backroom team meant that I felt comfortable from a personal point of view, in that he was unlikely to have a problem with my presence on the team bus and in the dressing room. But the board's decision naturally dismayed supporters, who needed some convincing that Roeder was the right man for such a prestigious job. His limited credentials, achieving little as boss of Gillingham and Watford at lower levels, suggested he wasn't really up to it.

West Ham produced a publication called *Upton Park News*, which was sent out to club members, bondholders (yes, several hundred did exist) and season-ticket holders. And it was for this club paper that managing director Paul Aldridge had asked me to take some pictures of the new manager at his home. The way I read the situation was that the club's hierarchy believed Glenn lacked profile and popularity, so this was an opportunity to humanise him a little – if that's not an unkind phrase.

Glenn's wife Faith answered the door when I arrived and told me that the children were getting changed upstairs. Glenn had just come in from West Ham and Faith asked him to make the tea – and open the biscuit barrel – while she got herself ready for the photographs. It was at this point that Glenn said he knew I'd been taking pictures for a long time because he could remember me from his playing days at Orient in the 1970s. He was very pleasant, but I could tell that he was a little bit uncomfortable with the idea of being in the limelight. However, we produced a nice set of photographs, with Faith, daughter Holly and sons William and Joe pictured with Glenn in their lounge and in the garden. The idea was to show what a nice family man he was – as if that would make him a better manager. I had also been asked to take some pictures of Glenn collecting his club car in Hainault – again to try and make people think more of him.

From the team's perspective, it certainly helped that Glenn was already working at West Ham and, to be fair, the players – particularly the younger ones – always said what a good coach he was. But, in my opinion, he didn't instil great confidence in the dressing room and I think it's fair to say that some of the players were underwhelmed by his promotion to manager. I don't want to be critical of Glenn, but I don't think he had the personality, stature or respect to make a big impact with the top players. His biggest problem was trying to get his point of view across with authority.

He also looked very ill at ease with the media after games and always appeared to have a tell-tale bead of sweat on his upper lip. The press had loved Harry Redknapp because he was relaxed in their company and wasn't afraid to say what he thought. But Glenn was a different sort of character and didn't really give the media anything to work with. He was a decent man but he lacked charisma. You'd be in the hotel having a meal with him on a Friday night and there'd be no great banter. He had a sort of dry humour, but it certainly wasn't anywhere near the level of Harry.

With Frank Lampard being sold to Chelsea, Roeder was generously given £15 million to spend on new players and he signed goalkeeper David James and defender Tomáš Řepka, as well as bringing back midfielder Don Hutchison, who had been sold to Sheffield United in 1996. James was an intelligent bloke, very eloquent, and he integrated well with all the staff, which goalkeepers tend to do for some reason. We'd have chats in the hotel and that sort of thing. He was a very good artist and would always be sketching portraits of players. Řepka, meanwhile, just looked like a nutter. He had mad eyes. He was quite a decent guy to chat with, but he frightened the life out of people.

West Ham struggled at the start of Roeder's reign, winning just one of their first eight games and getting hammered 5-0 at Everton and 7-1 at Blackburn Rovers in successive outings. So you have to give Glenn credit for showing resolve in the face of initial adversity and eventually steering the team to a highly creditable seventh-place finish. It was a strong achievement in his first year. Having said that, I still thought it was crazy for West Ham to then hand him a much-improved three-year contract. Personally, if I'd have been running the club, I'd have said, 'You've done well, Glenn, but let's have a look at how things go next season.' I'd have given him another one-year deal and watched how he followed things up. What was the club afraid of, that somebody was going to come in and poach him? I hardly think so. But that's the strange thing about football – clubs just seem to want to throw money at people.

The club's board might have been impressed, but the jury was still very much out on Glenn as far as the supporters were concerned. They certainly hadn't been very impressed when the manager refused to bring long-serving defender Steve Potts onto the field as a late substitute in the 2-1 home win against Bolton in the final game of the 2001/02 season. Potts was set to leave West Ham after 399 league appearances for the club over a seventeen-year period and the fans were desperate for the popular veteran to be given the chance to reach a landmark 400 and bid an emotional farewell. Yet, incredibly, Roeder brought on John Moncur and Richard Garcia as substitutes right at the death. To this day I still cannot understand why Potts was left on the bench. I can only assume that Glenn didn't want to be seen to be pandering to the crowd – the fans were chanting Steve's name and Glenn was stubbornly thinking, 'No, I'm the manager and I make the decisions.'

I felt very disappointed for Steve because he was a good lad and I liked him very much. I've been at functions when people have asked him how he felt about being denied his 400th league appearance for West Ham and Steve is philosophical about it, but I'm sure he was gutted. Knowing Steve as I do, I think he diplomatically says the right thing and doesn't want to be seen to be holding any grudges. However, I don't think some of the other players were too impressed by Roeder's actions; he might have been comfortable on the training field, but his man-management skills left something to be desired. And, of course, the thorn in his side was always going to be Paolo Di Canio.

Di Canio was his own man and if it was going to end up being a battle of wills, you knew who was going to come out on top. It wasn't that Paolo was disruptive in the dressing room, but it was obvious – to me, at least – that he had no respect for Glenn. Things came to a head between them towards the end of the 2002/03 season as the Hammers struggled to avoid relegation. Di Canio made no secret of his displeasure when he was substituted in a 2-1 win at West Bromwich Albion in February and you could sense that their relationship was becoming untenable. The result was that the volatile Italian was frozen out of the side for a period when West Ham needed to try and win every point that was available to them. It's all right trying to show you're the boss but sometimes the team has to come first. As far as I'm concerned, you don't drop your best player when you're in the position that we were in. Some people think that Glenn was always striving to prove that he was up to the job and able to assert his authority, but if that's the case it meant that some of his decisions weren't necessarily in the club's best interests (refusing to step down being one example).

Glenn did well in his first season, but he seemed to struggle as soon as significant problems arose. We had some injuries in attack and Glenn's solution was to move defender Ian Pearce up front. All that did was open things up at the back. He didn't have the necessary experience to deal with certain issues and as things became more challenging he got found out. We failed to win a single home league game until the end of January during his second campaign and he should have been sacked long before then. It was obvious we needed to change things but the club had just given him a new contract and you have to assume that they allowed him to remain in place because of the cost of paying him off – a rather false economy, I would have thought.

It was towards the end of that fateful season that I was squeezed off the team bus for a short period of time. I was preparing to leave for an away game on Friday when I received a phone call from Glenn. I immediately wondered why he was ringing me. 'I wanted to tell you myself,' he said. 'I'm really sorry, but we just don't have room for you on the coach today.' He added that he thought it right that he should tell me himself instead of relying on kit manager Eddie Gillam to give me the news. I said that was fair enough and thanked him. I secured a ride to the game with the club secretary but I began to suspect that this might indicate how things would be from now on. I was welcome to join up with the squad at their hotel, but it looked as if my days were numbered in terms of travelling with the players to games.

Just a few weeks later, Glenn suffered his terrible collapse as a result of a brain tumour. We'd just beaten Middlesbrough 1-0 at home, keeping alive our slender hopes of Premier League survival, and I was taking the usual man-of-the-match kind of pictures that were required after the game. Suddenly I started to hear rumours that Glenn had fallen ill and had been taken to hospital. I believe Ken Dyer, the *Evening Standard* journalist, was sitting with the manager in his office when he collapsed and fortunately Ges, our doctor, was able to come to his aid. It was only later that evening that we learned more about what had actually happened. When health is the issue it puts football into perspective and it goes without saying that everybody at the club was very concerned about Glenn's welfare and anxious for him to make a full recovery.

In the meantime, West Ham had just three games to try and avoid relegation and there was only one thing the club could do – ask Trevor Brooking to fill in as caretaker boss. Brooking had returned to the club as a director in 2001 and he was the ideal candidate to try and rescue our situation. Trevor had no problem with me travelling with the squad for our game at Manchester City, but it was a different story when the time came for his team talk. Like John Lyall, Trevor was 'old school' in his approach and believed that the dressing room was the inner sanctum, so team talks had to be held in private. He therefore asked me to step outside for a few minutes while he addressed the squad, which I fully respected.

It was obvious that Trevor commanded instant respect from the players and I wasn't surprised that he came so close to keeping us up, managing to scrape seven points from the final three games. We won 1-0 at City before Di Canio – handed a recall by Brooking – struck the winner at home to Chelsea to at least give us some hope going into the final day's game at Birmingham. Di Canio scored again in the 2-2 draw at St Andrew's, but the result was to prove irrelevant. Bolton's home victory against Middlesbrough sent West Ham down with a tally of forty-two points – the highest for any club relegated from the Premier League.

To this day, people still question how we managed to get relegated with that number of points and such a talented set of players. With the likes of Paolo Di Canio, Frédéric Kanouté, David James, Joe Cole, Michael Carrick, Trevor Sinclair, Jermain Defoe, Glen Johnson and Steve Lomas in the squad, it wasn't just the best West Ham team to ever get relegated but one of the very best in the history of English football to suffer such a fate. It was typical of West Ham's luck that forty-two points proved to not be enough, but relegation should never have been allowed to happen. The situation should have been dealt with long before it became a lost cause.

The mood on the coach as we returned from Birmingham was downbeat, to say the least. But as I looked at Jermain Defoe, I would never have imagined that he was hatching a plan to submit a transfer request the very next morning. It didn't surprise me that the young striker, who was our top scorer with eleven goals that season, wanted to jump ship. But what did shock me was the speed of his actions and I thought the timing was in very poor taste.

The irony was that Defoe demanded a transfer while our

caretaker boss was Trevor Brooking, a man who remained with West Ham throughout his lengthy playing career despite the club being relegated and spending three seasons in the Second Division. To me, his was a clear example of how loyalty had disappeared from the game, something the advent of agents has had much to do with since they make a lot of money from moving players around. Attitudes have certainly changed. I can remember Ray Stewart saying, 'Why would I want to have an agent and pay him 20 per cent of what I earn?' Mind you, he is Scottish.

Defoe's written request was duly filed in the rubbish bin where it belonged and the striker was forced to remain with West Ham until midway through the following season. That surprised some people – you normally don't see a team's best players for dust once they have been relegated. The manager is also generally expected to depart – involuntarily, of course – but West Ham were in a difficult position because they knew they would attract huge criticism if they dispensed with Glenn Roeder's services while he was recuperating from brain surgery. So for that reason he was allowed to return to work for pre-season training after making a good recovery from his operation.

Personally, I still think it would have been better for everybody had Glenn left West Ham before the new season began – something should have been negotiated so that it appeared to be a mutual arrangement. I heard that the club discreetly spoke to him about the possibility of standing down but he wasn't prepared to entertain the idea. Once again, Glenn's main agenda was to try and prove he was up to the job, but we all suspected he would be released as soon as results started to go wrong. And that didn't take very long.

We were just four games into the new season when the

team suffered an embarrassing 1-0 defeat at unfashionable Rotherham – a game that will always be remembered more for the great myth it inspired than because it was Roeder's last in charge. It was common knowledge that Rotherham had tiny dressing rooms and Glenn naturally asked Eddie Gillam to let him know if all our gear could be easily accommodated when checking things out on the morning of the game. Eddie and I arrived at Millmoor and, sure enough, the dressing room was like a telephone box. There was absolutely no way that we could have squeezed all our skips, players and staff in there. So we got back to the hotel and Eddie told Glenn that things were a bit tight. Consequently, Glenn sensibly decided that the lads would get changed into their tracksuits to avoid us having to take all our gear with us.

There had been no indication of any hostility from the Rotherham staff; on the contrary, they were very friendly and had been quite apologetic about the state of the place. They had even joked about it, saying, 'I bet you're not used to this kind of thing.' But when we returned to the ground we were shocked to come up against a wall of resentment, with people accusing the players of being a bunch of big-time Charlies who didn't think the Rotherham facilities were good enough for them. The attitude was 'Who the hell do they think they are, thinking they're too good for us?' Eddie and I just couldn't believe how much the atmosphere had changed in a couple of hours. Their fans were having a go at us and their backroom boys were sneering at us.

It has since became a distorted piece of West Ham folklore that the players took one look at the dressing room, turned up their noses in disgust and ordered the team bus to make a U-turn back to the hotel. Even now, people have completely the wrong idea about what really happened that day. It does irritate me, but I would be lying if said that I lose any sleep over it! I can only assume that Rotherham's manager, Ronnie Moore, manipulated and publicised the story to motivate his team. Of course, it worked a treat because Rotherham won the game.

I've got to be honest and admit that I didn't foresee what was going to take place the following morning. I went to see my sister, who was having a Sunday barbecue in honour of my birthday, and we had the television on when it was announced that Glenn Roeder had been sacked as manager of West Ham. Even allowing for the result the previous day, I was a little surprised that Glenn had been fired quite so quickly after being allowed to start the season with us.

I have nothing personal against Glenn and I think he's a nice guy. You will hear plenty of people say that. But I have always believed he should never have been given the West Ham manager's job and that he was biting off more than he could chew. I thought that then; I still think that now. It was the wrong decision to appoint him – and West Ham certainly paid the price.

CHAPTER 6

'WHEN YOU'RE THE KING, YOU CAN DO ANYTHING'

I don't like Alan Pardew. There, I've said it. In fact, I don't think I've ever known a more arrogant person in my life. We never got on from the first moment we met – and our relationship deteriorated from there. There was one occasion when I threatened to stick a fork in his hand. I was sort of joking, but there were definitely times when I felt like swinging at him. Or telling him to fork off, if you follow my drift.

Pardew took over as West Ham's tenth permanent manager in October 2003, after Trevor Brooking – who had assumed the role of caretaker boss for a second time following the eventual dismissal of Glenn Roeder in August – had sadly insisted the job was not for him. Alan had lifted Reading into what is now known as the Championship and taken them into the previous season's play-offs, so he was considered to have the divisional knowledge required to guide the Hammers back to the Premier League at the first attempt. But having played for Crystal Palace, Charlton Athletic and Barnet, the 42-year-old had no previous association with West Ham – and that's never a good thing in my book. However, that isn't the reason I've got no time for the man.

Let me tell you a story. In fact, it's called the 'King story' among those who were present and who believe it's a perfect example of Pardew's arrogance. We were staying at a hotel in the North East ahead of a game at Sunderland during Alan's first season in charge and were about to have our Friday evening meal. The players were restricted to boiled chicken or pasta, or suchlike, whereas the rest of the West Ham party had the choice of the entire menu.

I sat down with Pardew, kit manager Eddie Gillam, physiotherapist John Green and fitness coach Tony Strudwick, who now works for Manchester United and has done very well for himself. We ordered our meals and suddenly Pardew asked us all what we were having. I think Eddie said he'd gone for the chicken, while I'd chosen the steak. Pards then turned to Struds, who revealed whatever it was he'd asked for. 'That sounds good,' said Pards. 'Tell you what; if yours is better than mine when it turns up, I'm having that.' That was one of the things he'd always say: I'm having that. 'See that bloke's haircut? I'm having that.' He said it all the time. Anyway, I wasn't 'having that' at all. So I said, 'Well, you're certainly not having my dinner. You'll get a fork in the back of your hand!' Pardew sort of laughed, before turning back to Struds and saying, 'Yeah, if yours is better than mine, I'm having that.'

Our meals eventually arrived and Pards looked at Tony and said, 'Yeah, I was right, yours definitely looks much better than mine; I'm having that.' And he went to swap the plates over. 'You can't do that!' I said. 'What do you mean?' he asked. 'You can't just take somebody else's dinner,' I said in disbelief. And he replied, without any hint of a joke, 'When you're the King, you can do anything.'

Eddie, Tony, John and I just looked at each other and there was an uncomfortable silence for a moment. Struds was a nice guy but he could be a bit of a 'yes man' at times and so he just allowed Pardew to swap the plates. However, the rest of us were flabbergasted by it all and we ended up discussing what had happened in the bar. Alan kept a straight face when referring to himself as 'the King' and I just couldn't believe the arrogance of the man.

By sheer coincidence, our next away game was at Reading, Alan's former club. Eddie and I took the team's gear down to the Madejski Stadium before the game and one of the girls from the office came out and said, 'Hello, how are you getting on with Alan Pardew?' We just mumbled, 'Yes, okay, you know...' We were putting the kit out in the dressing room when a member of the Reading backroom staff popped his head in and asked, 'So, how are you boys getting on with the King?' We burst into laughter. We couldn't believe that Alan had also used that term at Reading. 'Yeah,' the guy said, 'he always used to call himself the King.' From that moment on, that's how the West Ham backroom team began to jokingly refer to Pards behind his back. 'Seen the King yet today?'

Pardew had been placed on gardening leave at Reading for several weeks while the contractual disputes of his potential move were resolved and his appointment as West Ham's manager was finally confirmed shortly before a midweek game at home to Nottingham Forest. A journalist called Ben Kosky was covering the Hammers for the *Recorder* at the time and we'd arranged for him to visit the training ground in Chadwell Heath to talk to Alan for the first time and for me to take some pictures. When Ben told Pardew he needed a short interview, Pardew snapped, 'I haven't really got time to sit and chat to you, so you'll have to follow me around the training pitch.' I was trailing around after Alan with my camera and before I'd even finished asking if he could stop for a moment, he declared, 'I haven't got time for that. You'll just have to take what you can.' When we'd finished Ben thanked Alan and said it would be nice if he could visit the training ground every week – as he had when Glenn Roeder and Trevor Brooking had been running the show. 'Pardon?' said Alan, somewhat indignantly. Ben repeated his desire to see him weekly and Pardew made it clear that he wasn't particularly welcome. '*Weekly*? Oh, I don't know about that.'

We headed back to the car and I said, 'I don't know about you, Ben, but I don't think much of him.' Ben agreed that Pards didn't exactly seem the most helpful bloke in the world. We returned to the offices of the *Recorder* and Phil Ravitz, our sports editor, joked that I didn't like Pardew because he wasn't a 'West Ham man'. I told him that Alan simply wasn't my cup of tea and that I couldn't see us getting along too well. My initial instincts, sadly, proved to be correct.

We played Forest on the Wednesday evening and my usual routine before a home game would involve taking the young mascots into the dressing room to photograph them with some of the players. The kids were getting some autographs and I was just having a quick chat with Tim De'Ath, the club chef, who'd been sorting out the energy foods for the players, when Alan Pardew suddenly appeared and said, in quite a nasty way, 'I'm not used to seeing photographers in my dressing room.' 'Oh really?' I said. 'I'm very sorry. Would you like me to leave?' Alan proceeded to spend a short time pretending to think and then answered, 'Yes, very soon I think.'

Where's a fork when you need one? He couldn't even ask me to leave the room nicely. He could have simply said, 'Steve, when you're finished, I'd appreciate it if you didn't hang around the dressing room.' But no, he had to be nasty and sarcastic about it. I subsequently heard that Pardew had said a similar thing to Ges Steinbergs, the club doctor. The manager questioned his presence and Ges made the point that he wasn't there for the fun of it but because he might be needed. It might have been that Pardew was trying to mark his territory because it was his first game in charge, but it seemed a funny way of trying to win friends and influence people. His attitude really annoyed me, to be honest. He showed no respect and that set the tone for our relationship – or lack of one.

With a flea in my ear after the Nottingham Forest experience, I took my car to Cardiff for our next game a few days later. I didn't even ask to travel with the team because I knew what the answer would be. The players were training at the university campus so I drove down to watch the session. Afterwards, Pards said he wanted to stay and watch a youth game that was taking place down there, but the bus was taking the players straight back to the hotel. Realising he'd have no way of getting back, he asked if anybody had a car with them and Eddie mentioned that I'd driven. And so Pardew asked if I could give him a lift to the hotel, which I agreed to even though it meant having to hang around and wait for him.

When Alan had seen enough of the game he came to find me and as I began to drive us back to the hotel, it felt particularly awkward having him next to me in the car. Unsurprisingly, the conversation was rather forced. I had a blue Ford Scorpio Ultima with a personalised number plate at the time and Pards said something about me not having a bad car, so we just chatted about that. I certainly didn't want to discuss football with him.

At that point, he said, 'I understand that you've always travelled with the team.' I confirmed that had been the case since John Lyall first asked me. But I emphasised that I'd always considered it a privilege rather than a right. 'Well,' he said, 'you understand that I can't possibly have you travelling with us, don't you?' I said, 'Fine, you're the manager, that's your prerogative.' He said that I was more than welcome to join them at the hotel and stay overnight, but that he couldn't have me travelling with them. He suggested that the likes of Ges Steinbergs, club secretary Peter Barnes and I travel together by car or share a minibus – and indeed, we ended up making our own arrangements for away games and meeting the players at their hotel.

In truth, the writing had been on the wall with regard to travelling with the team from the day Glenn Roeder told me they just didn't have room. It was very different now from when John Lyall first invited me to travel with the players in the late 1970s; then the backroom team had consisted of just four people – the manager, his assistant, the physio and the kit man. By the time Pardew took charge, there were almost as many ancillary staff as there were players, so the coach was usually full. If they wanted to take a couple of extra players they would have to strap them to the roof. Trevor Brooking had kindly allowed me to travel as part of the backroom team despite the restricted space, but that was never going to continue when Pards took over – full coach or not. From that point onwards I knew that my involvement with the back-room team was going to be minimal at best. And needless to say, I never asked to travel on the team coach again.

I was very disappointed, for a number of reasons. Firstly, I'd always been made to feel a part of the set-up by John Lyall, Lou Macari, Billy Bonds, Harry Redknapp and even Glenn Roeder. I was part of the West Ham squad – so much so that Harry even made sure I received a share of the play-ers' pool when we played in a five-a-side tournament at

Wembley (although I still can't work out why he didn't let me play). I'd enjoyed a privileged position that I had fully appreciated. I'd always tried to give something back by helping Eddie – very much in an unofficial capacity – and it made the job so much more than just taking photographs. It was great to be part of the entourage as we travelled around the country together and, from a purely practical point of view, it made life easier to be taken to and from each ground on match day. But now, thanks to Alan Pardew, it was all over.

Eddie Gillam was upset for me and disappointed that our partnership had been broken up – apart from games relatively nearby where we'd drive the gear ourselves. Eddie was of the view that a lot of the people on the team bus didn't necessarily need to be there. Did we really need three masseurs and half of these guys with fancy titles who didn't seem to contribute a whole lot?

Alan was very big on the psychology side of sport. I was told that he had a motivational CD that he would listen to in his car on the way into work. He was into all that sort of thing. One of the craziest things I heard was that he thought claret was a negative colour. He couldn't understand why everything was claret and blue. They're the club's colours, for goodness' sake! We found ourselves faced with a ridiculous scenario in which the manager started putting up mottos around the walls of the training ground and the stadium. There were quotes from icons such as Muhammad Ali and Martin Luther King. (That'll be the other King then, I suppose.) Some of the lads would say, 'I don't know what that fucking means. I can't even *read* it, let alone understand it.' Don Hutchison, for example, could often be heard moaning, 'What the fuck does that mean?'

Not that Hutch was necessarily the brightest bulb in the box.

Indeed, he deliberately befriended Stephen Bywater because he felt the young goalkeeper made him look intelligent by comparison. 'At last, I've found somebody more stupid than me,' he told me. He said the two of them were out shopping one day and Hutch found some shoes. 'If they're under £50, I think I'll buy them,' he said. 'Ah,' said Bywater, 'but what if they're £49.99?' And Hutch said, 'Well, I'll fucking buy them!'

So perhaps it's not too surprising that many of Pardew's messages went over a few players' heads. Having said that, one of the signs still remains in the West Ham dressing room at Upton Park, certainly until very recently: 'Winning is what we're here for,' it says. It's a shame the players haven't taken more notice of that one over the years, but sometimes their literacy isn't the best...

What really annoyed Eddie was when Pards tried to display some of the slogans in the boot room. 'That's a load of bollocks,' said Eddie. 'You're not putting them up down here. This is my area, this is my domain.' I think that took the wind out of Pardew's sails. Somebody had stood up to him and said no. John Green, the physiotherapist, also took no nonsense from Pardew and I think that's why his position became jeopardised. However, I don't think Pardew could ever have got rid of Eddie because he was such a well-liked character that there was no way he could have tried to do that without suffering a huge backlash.

Despite having to travel independently, I continued to link up with the rest of the backroom boys at the hotel on Friday evenings during the 2003/04 season, but tried to spend as little time with Pardew – sorry, I mean 'the King' – as possible. I got on very well with our new assistant boss, Peter Grant, but I think he felt obliged to spend more time with Pards than anyone else. As far as the players were concerned, I got the feeling that there were two factions in the camp. There were those such as Hayden Mullins, Nigel Reo-Coker and Marlon Harewood who had been signed by Pardew following his arrival at West Ham and were obviously behind him – at least at first. As for the players who were already at the club, my impression was that many of them didn't particularly rate the new manager.

Pardew got off to a slow start at West Ham, having to wait until his eighth game before tasting victory, but he took the team to a fourth-place finish that saw us qualify for the promotion play-offs. Brian Deane scored a last-minute equaliser in the final league game at Wigan Athletic and I just knew that we'd shot ourselves in the foot. That goal – one that we didn't even need to score – pushed Wigan out of the play-off positions and elevated Crystal Palace, who we would eventually meet in the final at the Millennium Stadium in Cardiff. Everybody sensed that Palace were going to get the better of us – and so it proved, as they won the prize of promotion thanks to Neil Shipperley's second-half strike. And they had West Ham to thank for getting them into the play-offs in the first place!

What Pardew thought he was doing when he withdrew strikers Bobby Zamora, Marlon Harewood and David Connolly as we were chasing the game in the last twenty-five minutes I don't know. But his strange strategy didn't work and the word 'king' was certainly in my mind as the final whistle blew – 'king useless!

If West Ham were feeling poorly in the early years of the new millennium, it was nothing compared to the serious health problems I found myself fighting during this period, as my ailments escalated to the point that they became potentially life-threatening. I had first become aware that something was wrong in the first few months of 2000 when I found a spot on the bottom of my right foot that would not stop bleeding. The foot was puffy and inflamed and it eventually became very painful to walk on. West Ham were playing a home game against Wimbledon – the one in which Paolo Di Canio produced the magical strike that won the BBC goal-of-the-season award – and my foot was so sore that I went to see Sean Howlett, one of the club's doctors. He pulled a bit of a face – most people do when I take off my socks – and said, 'I think you'd best come and see me in my surgery.'

As suggested, I went to his surgery in South Woodford, where he took another look at my foot and asked for a urine sample, which I thought was a bit odd. After completing the necessary tests, he said, 'As I suspected, you're diabetic.' This was complete news to me – I'd had no idea whatsoever that was the case. He told me not to worry too much about it, but he was concerned about my foot and arranged for me to see Tom McAuliffe, the surgeon who acted as a consultant for West Ham.

Tom duly informed me that I had a serious infection. Most people would have been in terrible agony, but as a result of the diabetes I was also suffering from neuropathy, which meant I'd lost some of the feeling in my foot. That had allowed the infection to get much worse and, to my horror, Tom told me, 'I've got to be honest with you, for diabetics, these sorts of things often lead to amputation.' He did some blood tests and I remember tearfully lying in my bed that night with the words 'these things often lead to amputation' ringing in my head.

My brother and I were about to take my mother out for dinner to celebrate her birthday the following day when Tom rang and said he needed to get me into hospital – immediately. He wanted me to go to a private clinic in Buckhurst Hill but I didn't think my medical insurance would cover the costs, so Tom arranged for me to go to Whipps Cross Hospital, where he did his NHS work. I was a bit worried, particularly as I'd never spent any time in hospital before, but I packed a bag and reported to the A&E department as instructed. The receptionist insisted I couldn't just walk into A&E and ask for Mr McAuliffe, but fortunately another doctor overheard the conversation and came to my aid. 'Mr Bacon?' he said. 'Please come through. I've been expecting you.'

He took me into a cubicle, told me that he'd been made aware of the problem and that he needed to perform some tests. They tried to put a cannula in my hand, which caused a bit of a problem because they couldn't find a vein. One of the doctors – a South American called Carlos, no less – eventually managed to succeed and within twenty minutes they had found me a bed and moved me up to the ward. 'I don't know who you are,' said one of the nurses, 'but you must be special because most people end up waiting for hours to get up here from A&E.' 'I'm not special,' I insisted. 'I just know people.'

I was very hot in bed that night because I had a condition known as cellulitis and there was a danger of blood poisoning. My right leg was bright red almost up to the knee. I drifted in and out of consciousness and at one point I could see four doctors discussing my situation at the end of the bed. I knew this wasn't good but took heart from the fact that at least they weren't four priests. I was put on intravenous antibiotics as they tried to reduce the infection caused by my ulcerated foot, and they also introduced me to the diabetic team, who explained that I would need to self-administer insulin on a regular basis. Had they not been able to control the infection I could have ended up losing my leg and who knows what might have happened after that. Thankfully, after several weeks in hospital, the infection did indeed clear up and I was able to return to work after a month or so.

For the next five years I adapted to my new routine of injecting myself with insulin four times a day and being very careful about what I ate, so that helped bring my weight down. When I was first diagnosed as being diabetic, I asked how long I had been suffering from the condition and was told it was difficult to say. It's possible that I might have been diabetic for ten years. In a funny kind of way, the ulcerated foot could be counted as a blessing in disguise because otherwise I'd have continued to be oblivious to my diabetes until more serious complications arose. I could have developed a heart problem or something almost as bad.

There were symptoms of diabetes that I simply didn't recognise. I'd been getting very thirsty and would drink a two-litre bottle of Coca-Cola a night – I guess that's what you might call a serious Coke habit – so was naturally peeing a lot. I suffered from tingling sensations in my thighs and also had claw toes – very similar to hammer toes, which would have been more appropriate, I think – both of which are classic signs of diabetes.

I was now required to pay visits to the chiropody department, because I wasn't allowed to cut my own toenails for fear of inflicting any dangerous cuts or abrasions. I also had to have occasional retinal screening. I'd had problems with the blood vessels at the back of my eyes, which become very brittle and can burst when you're diabetic and have too much sugar in your system. I therefore needed laser treatment to seal the vessels – not a particularly pleasant experience as you can smell the burning. And before anybody asks, no, that doesn't explain any blurred photographs I might have taken over the years.

All was well and good until another problem occurred in the early part of 2005. Once again, I took off my sock after a game and noticed a patch of blood on it. I looked at my right foot and discovered a puncture wound, so I returned to Whipps Cross Hospital where one of the chiropodists discovered a small piece of blue shale – a tiny stone – in my shoe. I could only assume I'd picked it up from walking around the perimeter of a football pitch somewhere. The chiropodist showed me the indentation in my right shoe where the stone had been rubbing at my foot until it had punctured the skin, without my knowledge because of the lack of feeling. I was given some antibiotics but by the end of the week my leg had turned crimson again and I immediately recognised what the problem was. I was sweating in bed and feeling really ill, so I quickly found myself in Whipps Cross Hospital as an emergency case again.

This was the first time I really began to fear that my life could be in danger, because a vascular surgeon was asked to carry out some tests. It didn't help when, after a few days, I overheard one of the senior nurses speaking to a colleague and saying, 'I didn't expect Mr Bacon to still be with us this morning.' I wasn't ready to be released, so what else could she have been implying? My surgeon then appeared and informed me that, in fact, things were looking 'a little better'. I asked in what respect and he said that the infection was 'no longer life-threatening'. He insisted all was now under control, but that they needed to get to the bottom of the problem.

The hospital staff did several tests and the surgeon finally came to me and said he was fairly convinced about what the problem was. He said the infection had entered the bone in my little toe and that the only real option was to amputate it. He asked me how I felt about that and, aside from suspecting that my chances of ever kicking a ball for West Ham were looking increasingly unlikely, I thought it was a bit of a silly question. Obviously I wanted to keep the toe, but if it was the only way of solving the problem it was the only way.

The surgeon explained that they couldn't simply amputate the toe; they also had to remove the metatarsal because they couldn't ensure the infection had not gone past the joint. However, because of my poor circulation, he was worried about creating a wound on my foot that was never going to heal properly. I therefore needed to have an MRI scan and an angiogram, which involved having dye injected into my system so that an X-ray would reveal how well – or poorly – the blood was circulating in my leg. I must admit that it felt as if I had wet myself as a huge needle was stuck into my groin. But thankfully I was assured that the blood flow appeared to be sufficient to allow me to have the operation.

I had no worries about being put to sleep for the surgery – I quite enjoyed it, in fact – and although my foot bled a lot afterwards and was quite messy, I wasn't too perturbed, even when the doctor suggested I should be hooked up to a VAC (Vacuum Assisted Closure) machine in order to help keep the wound clean. The hospital even gave me a portable version of the pump so that I could be released for a weekend to attend a game at Upton Park towards the end of the 2004/05 campaign.

I remained in hospital for a few more weeks, during which time I received a phone call from former West Ham boss Lou

Macari. 'Stevie? It's Lou,' said the voice, which I must admit I didn't immediately recognise. He'd heard about my illness and wanted to wish me well. 'We are in trouble if you're laid up,' he quipped, before asking how things had been going at Upton Park. Before I even got as far as mentioning Alan Pardew's surname, he said, 'What an arrogant man he is.' I could only laugh. 'That's exactly what I was going to say.' The two men had obviously crossed paths somewhere along the way and Lou had arrived at the same conclusion as I had. Not that I was very surprised. By coincidence the nurse changing my dressings while I was on the phone was a huge Manchester United fan. She was very excited that I'd been talking to Lou – who was a big star at Old Trafford in the 1970s – and promptly told half the patients in the ward (some of whom were almost as impressed as she was).

I returned home before the season was finished, but wasn't able to attend the Championship play-off final against Preston North End because of the difficulty of getting down to Cardiff in the condition I was in. And I couldn't risk anybody standing on my foot. But it was great to see the team grab the 1-0 win – courtesy of striker Bobby Zamora, who I consider to be a real West Ham man – which took them back to the Premier League. I was certainly looking forward to returning to work at the earliest opportunity the following season.

The problem while I was recuperating at home in the second half of 2005 was that, although the infection had been removed (along with my small toe, of course), the wound wasn't healing properly. I was watching games at Upton Park from the back of the dug-out – which I suppose I should thank Alan Pardew for allowing – and was itching to get back to work. Yet the wound wasn't closing up and while that remained the case there was a big concern about the risk of new infection.

Ultimately, in the late spring of 2006, the doctors discovered that there was an infection in the next toe on my right foot and they recommended removing it along with the infected metatarsal. Obviously, that was going to mean a significant part of my foot being lost, but the only other option – which they said would *definitely* cure the problem – was a below-knee amputation. Needless to say, I suggested they just took a second toe, although I remained fearful that I would suffer the same problems all over again. They were concerned about creating another wound that was never going to heal, but I insisted that I'd grown quite fond of my right leg and would much prefer to keep it if at all possible. By the way, I've got pictures of my ailing foot if anybody would like to see them...

I went through the whole series of hospital checks once again and had another angiogram. 'I don't know how it is,' said the surgeon, 'but we've found an artery supplying blood to your foot and it's not in the place that it should be.' This was good news, even if it did make me feel a bit unusual, because it convinced the doctor that there was a good chance of the foot healing if I had a second toe removed. I subsequently had the second operation and, although there was a nasty wound, it didn't bleed as much as my previous surgery and I was only confined to the hospital for another couple of weeks before being allowed home. The stitches were taken out and everything gradually healed up nicely, I'm pleased to say.

There were several people associated with West Ham who helped me greatly during my periods in hospital. Club doctor Ges Steinbergs visited me many times and was able to explain the illness to me, so that proved a great help from a psychological point of view. Tom McAuliffe, Sean Howlett and John Green also provided valuable support and reassurance. Tom was great in terms of getting me into Whipps Cross very quickly and came to see me during my first stay in hospital. The nurse later approached me and said, 'You know who that was, don't you? You must be very important.' And again I said, 'No, I just know the right people.' When Sean came to see me, the bloke in the next bed said, 'Oi! He's my GP; I can never get in to see him. Yet he's paying you a visit!' I just said, 'It's who you know!'

Meanwhile, John Green came to my rescue when I needed to wear an Aircast boot and the chiropody department at Whipps Cross didn't have one big enough for me. John mentioned that he had some at the club and I quickly asked, 'You haven't got an extra large, by any chance?' He duly came up trumps and the guy at Whipps Cross was a bit embarrassed about the fact that the NHS couldn't supply what I needed but a football club could. Once again, I just said, 'It's who you know!'

The 'Boys of '86' also did me proud. I lost a lot of pay during my periods of incapacity, so my old friends organised a fundraising bash for me at Dagenham & Redbridge Football Club. Ray Stewart came down from Scotland, while Frank McAvennie, who missed his early morning flight from Newcastle – another late night on the town, no doubt – jumped in a car and drove down to London. I thought that was a great gesture on his part. And all the usual crew were there – people such as Phil Parkes, Alan Devonshire, Alvin Martin, Tony Cottee and Tony Gale. I owe them all a great debt of gratitude for their efforts.

My toe problems meant that I was unfit for the 2006 FA Cup final between West Ham and Liverpool, which I watched from the disabled section at the Millennium Stadium. My inability to work meant I couldn't obtain a photographer's pass, so I spoke to Gina Allen, who was the club's disabled liaison officer, and she was able to help me out. I was on crutches at the time so fellow photographers Arthur Griffiths and Avril Husband drove me down to Cardiff and we made a weekend of it. We stayed in a very unusual guesthouse, an ancient building in a little village just outside the city, and Arthur covered my club duties by visiting the team hotel and taking pictures of the players in their cup final suits, as well as the game itself. At the stadium I bumped into Phil Parkes, who was doing some radio commentary, and we had a brief chat before I took my place in the disabled seats. I'd been watching games from the dug-out at Upton Park, so I was used to observing the action without looking through the eye of the camera, but it was great to be in with the fans at Cardiff and it certainly was a different experience.

Though the Hammers had enjoyed a healthy ninth-place finish in their first season back in the Premier League, Liverpool were the hot favourites and few people fancied our chances of causing an upset by winning the FA Cup for the first time since 1980. I thought back to taking that team photo with the trophy after being handed the job by John Lyall and how much I would love the chance to restage such a shoot twenty-six years later. I knew it was a bit of an unlikely fantasy, but it started to look like a distinct possibility after Jamie Carragher's own goal and Dean Ashton gave us a shock 2-0 lead. And again when Paul Konchesky put us back in front after Djibril Cissé and Steven Gerrard had replied for Liverpool.

Like everyone else, with West Ham leading 3-2 with ninety minutes on the clock, I was gutted when the fourth official indicated four minutes of stoppage time and suddenly – crash, bang, wallop – Gerrard fired home a stunning equaliser to snatch the trophy from our grasp and take the final into extra time. When the game went to penalties after no further score, I sensed that it would not be our day, and so it proved as we went down 3-1 in the shoot-out.

I'm told it was the first time the FA Cup final had produced six goals for more than half a century and it was great for West Ham to be part of what many people still say was one of the best-ever finals. But the timing of Liverpool's third goal obviously leaves a bad memory and, although we might have enjoyed some good fortune with our goals, it's hard not to feel a bit hard done by when we were so close to winning the trophy. After all, it might be a very long time before we get such a good chance again.

Teddy Sheringham scored our one successful penalty. The former England striker had joined the Hammers two years earlier at the ripe old age of thirty-eight, but I was pleased to see such a big name arrive at the club and he was to play a big part in returning us to the top flight. I took some pictures of Teddy in the boardroom after he'd put pen to paper and was quite surprised when he recognised me. 'When did you lose the 'tache, then?' he asked. I was so taken aback he had to ask me the question again. I eventually admitted it had gone when I turned fifty, so that I could try and make myself look younger. He laughed, but I was quite impressed that he remembered I used to have a moustache.

As I recovered from my second surgery, I watched the first half of the 2006/07 season from the seats in the West Ham dug-out and had a first-class view of Alan Pardew's touchline clash with Arsenal boss Arsène Wenger after Marlon Harewood had scored our late winner. There was a bit of pushing and shoving between the two managers and, given my feelings towards Pardew, it's obvious which man I would have been cheering on had things got more physical. Amusingly, a couple of photographers wanted to know if I'd got a picture of the incident, as if I'd been secretly shooting everything from where I was sitting. I must admit, Pardew did enquire about my health now and again, so I suppose that's something. But I felt a bit cut off from things and there were times when I suspected that people were afraid to stop and talk to me in case the manager saw them.

One of my great allies had gone by this stage: physiotherapist John Green. John was certainly not a 'yes man' and I know that he didn't get on with Alan Pardew. From my understanding of the situation, Pards would ask John for his medical opinion on a player and if he didn't get the answer he was looking for he'd often discount what John had said. John would insist, 'I'm the professional here and I'm telling you that he shouldn't play.' He'd be at loggerheads with the manager for much of the time. When it came down to it, John was too strong a character for Pardew and I suppose I shouldn't have been surprised by his eventual departure. Somebody at the club leaked an email to John that confirmed his days at West Ham were numbered, with Pardew saying he wanted him out come what may. I think that helped John when it came to negotiating his settlement. It seemed a strange thing to happen because John was one of the most respected and qualified physios in the game.

I will never forget the occasion on which I resumed my match-day photographic duties for West Ham – it was the day Carlos Tévez scored his first goal for the club. That memorable moment came in a dramatic 4-3 home defeat by Tottenham Hotspur on 4 March 2007 that looked to have condemned the Hammers to almost certain relegation after what had been a pretty awful season up to that point. It had also been one of West Ham's most eventful periods, with the club changing both ownership and management within a matter of weeks while trying to avoid the drop. So when I returned to work, both chairman Terence Brown and manager Alan Pardew were no longer in office – and the club's destiny seemed to lie in the hands of an Argentinian striker who had been signed the previous summer in the most mysterious of circumstances.

When Alan Pardew unveiled the capture of Tévez and his compatriot Javier Mascherano – reportedly worth at least £30 million between them – shortly after the closure of the transfer window, my initial reaction was that something couldn't be right. As these two South Americans – one of whom had been described as 'the new Maradona' and the other 'a monster of a player' by the legend himself – appeared next to Pardew holding their West Ham shirts at the Upton Park press conference, I sensed there was far more to the situation than met the eye. 'Why the hell would these two world-class players want to come to West Ham?' I wondered to Arthur Griffiths alongside me. 'This is all going to end in tears.' It seemed patently obvious that Alan Pardew didn't have a clue what was going on. I could smell a rat.

The full details of the third-party ownership of the two players that would ultimately land West Ham in hot water with the authorities would only come to light further down the line. But it didn't take long for rumours to circulate that Kia Joorabchian, whose Media Sports Investment group co-owned the Argentinians' economic rights, had used the players as a 'sweetener' to enhance his prospects of completing a possible takeover of the Hammers. As it transpired, of course, Terry Brown decided to sell the club to an Icelandic group, headed by Landsbanki chief Björgólfur Gudmundsson and fronted by Eggert Magnússon – dubbed a 'biscuit baron' for his involvement in a bread and biscuit manufacturing firm – who became West Ham's new chairman.

A lot of fans were pleased to see the back of Brown, who wasn't the most popular of chairmen, but I'd been perfectly happy with his presence because I knew that he was a West Ham man. I'd known him for more than fifteen years since he was a familiar face in the corporate lounges of the club for some time before he joined the board and succeeded Martin Cearns in 1992. I also believe he did a reasonable job when you weigh up the positives against the negatives – even if I did struggle to get a drink out of him.

West Ham was also good for Brown: he came into the club with relatively little money and departed with a fortune following the £85 million sale in November 2006. And I can't say I was unhappy to see new people take control of the Hammers. The Icelanders' arrival had to be viewed as a positive development because Eggert – or Eggy, as he quickly became known – had excellent football credentials, having been president of the Icelandic Football Association and holding a seat on UEFA's executive committee, while Gudmundsson was a billionaire who ran a successful bank. What could possibly go wrong?

I took a liking to Magnússon and thought he was a charismatic person. I also managed to meet Gudmundsson a couple of times and he would always say hello and shake hands. The new owners organised a big bash for the staff

When I had to photograph some former players for the club, I decided to gatecrash. Geoff Pike, Trevor Brooking, Phil Parkes and Paul Allen pose with me.

RIGHT Icelandic owners Eggert Magnusson and Björgólfur Gudmundsson wave to the Upton Park crowd on their first visit to the ground.

BELOW When the Queen visited Upton Park to open the new Dr Martens Stand we managed to set up a picture of her meeting young star Joe Cole.

Ex-players join the minute's applause for former manager John Lyall at the first home match after his untimely death.

A blood-soaked fan is escorted away after the crowd trouble that marred the Carling Cup tie against Millwall in August 2009.

I was pleased to see former players Alan Curbishley and Mervyn Day return as the management team in 2006.

Playing greats Paolo Di Canio and Gianfranco Zola turn out to play in Tony Carr's testimonial match at Upton Park.

ABOVE After my appearance on *Soccer AM* I had my picture taken on the famous orange sofa with presenters Helen Chamberlain and Max Rushden.

RIGHT Who's the daddy? Undoubtedly TV and movie hard-man Ray Winstone is ... but we've been friends for many years, nevertheless.

LEFT David Hasselhoff was the special guest on *Soccer AM* the day I joined Hammers fans on the show – another shot for the album.

There may be trouble ahead... New signings Carlos Tevéz and Javier Mascherano pose with manager Alan Pardew at a press conference at Upton Park.

A bare-chested Carlos Tevéz celebrates his spectacular first goal for the Hammers against Tottenham Hotspur at Upton Park in 2007.

Manager Gianfranco Zola looks like he has the weight of the world on his shoulders as things go wrong at West Ham.

ABOVE Beleaguered boss Avram Grant looked like his time was up when Hammers took on Arsenal during his one-season spell at Upton Park.

RIGHT New co-owners David Sullivan and David Gold pose for pictures after a press conference at the ground.

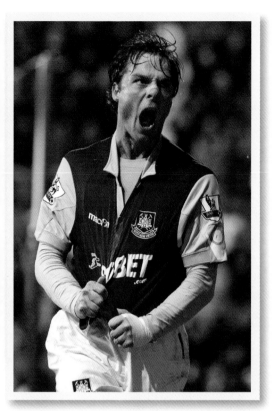

Scott Parker celebrates his goal against Wigan Athletic. He generously signed his shirt and gave it to me at the end of the game.

I travelled 3,000 miles to Toronto, Canada, to cover West Ham's match against the MLS All-Stars and young Hammer Jack Collison decides to warm up just in front of me!

RIGHT My good mate Dan Jarvis and I were at Wembley Stadium for the start of schoolboy Jonjo Heuerman's charity walk, and my old friend Sir Trevor Brooking was kind enough to pose with us in front of the Bobby Moore statue.

LEFT Although unable to cover the 2005 Championship play-off final due to ill health, I did get my hands on the winners' trophy later.

New boss Sam Allardyce shares a joke with co-chairmen David Gold (left) and David Sullivan before the pre-season friendly at Dagenham & Redbridge.

Christmas party, to which I was kindly invited, and it was a bit like meeting royalty with the way everybody was introduced. They announced 'Mr Steven Bacon' and I walked in to shake hands with Eggy and get a kiss from his wife. There was a lovely spread for everyone and, because the owners were Icelandic, it was all very fish-based, so there were lots of oysters and roll-mops, that kind of thing.

Of course, the best thing the new owners did – at least as far as I'm concerned – was getting rid of Alan Pardew as manager. Eggy had initially declared his backing for Pards, who was really struggling with the side in the early part of the 2006/07 season. The top-half finish and the run to the FA Cup final seemed a distant memory as the Hammers lost an unprecedented eight games in succession, dropping into the relegation zone, crashing out of Europe (with defeat against Palermo in the first round of the UEFA Cup) and suffering embarrassment in the Carling Cup against lowly Chesterfield. Tévez and Mascherano were struggling to start games and there was a general feeling of disharmony in the camp.

The Hammers improved a little and managed to pick up a few decent results, including that 1-0 win against Arsenal, but a 4-0 defeat at Bolton proved to be the final nail in the coffin as far as Pardew's job was concerned. Just two days later the manager was handed his P45 and I have to admit that I was delighted. John Green had always said we'd have a big party on the day Pardew left the club. I sent him a text when I heard the news and he replied with a message that said, 'Party on!'

There has been plenty of speculation about why Magnússon chose to fire Pardew as manager. I read that Eggy said he had 'reasons' that he wanted to keep to himself, but it just seemed that the more he got to know about Pards the less inclined he felt to keep him. The results at that time certainly didn't help Alan's cause and he didn't seem as popular with some of the players as he had done. I think the success of the previous two seasons – the promotion, the top-half finish and the FA Cup final – had gone to Pardew's head a little and some of the players thought he was getting a bit too flash for their liking.

I remember when the club had their victory parade to celebrate promotion in 2005 and the players appeared on the balcony of the West Stand overlooking the forecourt at Upton Park. Don Hutchison was standing behind Pardew and when the manager went out to address the crowd – as if he was the Messiah – the midfielder started shouting, 'Chocolate! Chocolate!' I asked Hutch what he'd been on about and he said that Pardew loved himself so much that 'if he was made of chocolate, he'd have eaten himself'. The team had just won promotion yet some of the players were quite literally laughing at the manager behind his back.

One thing that certainly didn't make me laugh was when Pardew produced his 'Moore than a football club' T-shirt towards the end of his first season at the club. I thought that was a disgrace. As far as I was concerned, Pardew had no right to bring Bobby Moore's name into things because he wasn't a West Ham man himself. I saw it as a cheap trick and felt sure it was going to backfire on him, which I think in the end it did really since I suspect that people recognised the cynicism of it.

People might believe I have a personal agenda against Pardew simply because he threw me off the bus and shut me out of the dressing room, but my dislike of him was more for the way he did things rather than what he did. I do give Alan credit for what he achieved at West Ham – he did enjoy a successful couple of years with the club. I'm not critical of him as a manager, more as a man. He's not the sort of guy I'd go to the pub and have a drink with – even if he was paying.

When he'd gone to Charlton Athletic, shortly after leaving West Ham, a newspaper story emerged that suggested a director at The Valley believed Alan Pardew to be one of the most arrogant men he'd ever met in his life. I scanned the headline, used Photoshop to highlight 'the most arrogant man I've ever met' and emailed it to everyone I knew, adding, 'You heard it here first!' I've since heard that he's 'gunning' for me after I was critical of him in an interview for a book about former West Ham managers. He bumped into Tim De'Ath at a game and asked if I was about. Tim was quick to say, 'No, you stopped all that, didn't you?' And Pards said, 'Well, tell him I'm gunning for him over that book.' Surely he's got more important things to worry about than what I think of him?

Given that Charlton and then Southampton both sacked him, I'd be lying if I said I wasn't surprised by how well Pardew has done as manager of Newcastle United (taking them to fifth place in the Premier League in 2012 and winning the Barclays and LMA Manager of the Year awards). Mind you, I think that goes for most people, since many thought he was extremely lucky to land that position. I also find it hard to believe that he was linked with the England job following the resignation of Fabio Capello. But at the end of the day, it's not his football credentials that concern me. I just don't like the man.

CHAPTER 7

'TWENTY-SEVEN YEARS LATER AND I'M BACK'

'Who would have thought it?' said West Ham's new manager when stepping forward to shake my hand. 'Twenty-seven years later and I'm back.' 'Yeah, I'm pleased to see you,' I said. And I sincerely meant it.

To say that the return of former midfielder Alan Curbishley as the new Hammers boss in December 2006 really made my day is something of an understatement. I'd known Alan since his playing days in the late 1970s and had always been friendly with him. I'd heard he was bringing former goalkeeper Mervyn Day back to the club with him as his assistant and thought it was fantastic that we had real West Ham people in charge of the club again after the Glenn Roeder and Alan Pardew eras. I anticipated that Curbs would always make me feel welcome at the training ground and this was confirmed when I saw him at Chadwell Heath on his first day of work and he came over to say hello.

I'd always thought it was inevitable that Alan would manage West Ham at some stage in his career, despite rejecting two opportunities to do so during his fifteen years in charge at Charlton Athletic. I think he'd felt a loyalty to Charlton in the past but having left them at the end of the previous season he was now available. Curbishley's appointment was confirmed just a couple of days after Alan Pardew's sacking and, even though he was taking control of a side that had slipped into the bottom three of the table, I was confident that Curbs would guide us to safety. He'd proved his worth as a manager at Charlton and had kept them safe in the Premier League for six seasons on relatively limited finances. West Ham was his natural home and it seemed like a perfect marriage – one that I expected to last for several years.

I was still a few months away from returning to work as a photographer, but was present in the West Ham dug-out when Alan greeted the crowd ahead of his first game – at home to Manchester United. He enjoyed the perfect start, with the Hammers securing a shock 1-0 win against Sir Alex Ferguson's team, but this may have given everybody the impression that the road to safety was going to be much less bumpy than it eventually turned out. Pardew might have gone, but many problems at the club remained, and one of them – at least as far as the fans were concerned – was Nigel Reo-Coker. The midfielder had cut a disillusioned figure during the early part of the season. West Ham had rejected interest in their skipper from bigger clubs as the summer transfer window was about to slam shut and the fans had been giving him some stick. I know that some people insist that supporters should never boo their own players, but my belief is that if people have paid their money they're entitled to voice their opinions. If players want to hear the cheers, they must accept the jeers.

Reo-Coker was presented with the perfect opportunity to win some friends when he scored the winner in the seventy-fifth minute against Manchester United, but he stupidly decided to celebrate his goal by cocking an ear towards the fans instead of sharing in their joy. It's no wonder people suggest that footballers are not the sharpest tools in the box – all he did was compound his problems. It certainly wasn't what Curbishley needed after taking over.

To be fair to Nigel, I'd always found him to be very personable and a polite, well-spoken young man. Despite being out of action, I was still spending a lot of time with kit manager Eddie Gillam in the boot room and he always enjoyed a good bit of banter with Reo-Coker. So I had no great problems with Nigel as a person. But on the field of play it was a different matter. His performances were well below par in the first few months of the 2006/07 campaign and I got the strong impression that, despite this, he felt he was too good for us. Still, he ended up playing for Bolton Wanderers and getting relegated during the 2011/12 season, so maybe he got what he deserved – with apologies to Bolton fans, of course.

Another player who gave Curbs a slight headache during his early days at the club was Anton Ferdinand. I'd known Anton since he was a little kid when he used to come over to West Ham with his brother Rio, who signed for the club before he did. I've watched him grow up and have never had a problem with him. Indeed, I had some sympathy for Anton because he was always going to get compared to his brother. I had the same thing at grammar school, where I was always being told that I wasn't as good academically as my two brothers. My oldest brother, Rod, went to university, while Martin, who I've already mentioned a couple of times, left school with several O-levels.

When you've got older siblings you're always going to be in their shadow – and that was the case with Anton, who was never going to be as good as his brother, even though Rio had told me he thought Anton might be better than him.

Whether that means Rio can't judge a player I don't know, but I wouldn't criticise Anton. He's a good defender and I certainly wouldn't complain if he found himself back at Upton Park one day. However, he let himself down when he decided to fly to the United States to celebrate his twenty-second birthday – and apparently told the club he'd visited his sick grandmother on the Isle of Wight. I thought it was a little out of character for Anton, but it seemed to suggest that there wasn't a great deal of respect for the new manager at that time. And maybe Alan didn't help himself in that respect by failing to develop closer relationships with the players, particularly in his early days at the club.

I got the impression that Curbs didn't mix particularly well with the squad. It surprised me because I'd always found him to be a good laugh and thought he was just what the club needed. Alan Pardew seemed to want to be one of the lads, but Curbs maybe went too far the other way and should have integrated with the players a bit more. There's a dining area at the training ground where the players have their meals and apparently Alan spent very little time there. He'd get his lunch and then return to his office, whereas the rest of the staff would sit with the players. He was very aloof and I could sense that there was a bit of friction.

The problems behind the scenes weren't helped by various cliques in the dressing room and, in retrospect, it's perhaps no surprise that results quickly took another downturn after that victory against Manchester United. The team embarked on a run of eleven league games without a win, which left them ten points adrift of safety with just nine fixtures remaining. Including the FA Cup game against Watford, the Hammers lost six consecutive matches – the last of which was a 4-3 home defeat by Tottenham on the day that

marked my return to West Ham as a photographer following my lengthy illness. As I've previously mentioned, it was,
of course, the match in which Carlos Tévez scored his first
goal for the club. The controversial striker had made nineteen appearances without hitting the net before firing home
a stunning free kick to give the Hammers a 2-0 lead against
Spurs. I was sitting in the photographers' pit in front of the
Dr. Martens Stand when Tévez tore off his shirt and came
leaping across the wall. I wondered where the hell he was
going, but I somehow managed to get a shot of him enjoying
his celebration with the fans.

In the end, though, West Ham lost the game 4-3 and I was
absolutely gutted. That defeat was a big kick in the nuts. Spurs
had managed to claw back two goals, bringing them level, but
victory had looked on the cards when Bobby Zamora put us
ahead by three goals to two with five minutes remaining.
Yet we still contrived to lose by conceding twice in the dying
moments in unbelievable fashion – not that we should ever
be too surprised by anything that happens at West Ham.

Defeat looked to have consigned West Ham to almost
certain relegation and just a couple of days earlier it had been
confirmed that the Premier League were charging us with
two rule breaches in relation to the signings of Tévez and his
Argentinian teammate Javier Mascherano. The latter had
recently been sold to Liverpool after being forced to play
second fiddle to Hayden Mullins and even recent signing
Nigel Quashie – prompting my suspicion that there was some
kind of financial reason as to why both Pardew and Curbishley
had been so reluctant to play the South Americans. I just
couldn't understand why both Tévez and Mascherano – two
world-class players – were not considered good enough to
start more games, especially as we were struggling.

I'd always believed their signings were too good to be true, so when it was announced that there were problems relating to their third-party ownership, I naturally responded by saying, 'Told you so!' Not that it required a genius to work out that something fishy had been going on. I didn't really understand the full complexities of the third-party ownership situation at the time, but I've since learned – along with most other observers of the case – that West Ham's big crime was to sign contracts that allowed Kia Joorabchian and MSI the right to move the players on at their discretion and to not disclose such agreements to the Premier League. It wasn't so much the third-party ownership of the players in itself, but the clauses that allowed third-party influence over their movement – and there's a crucial difference.

Towards the end of April it was announced that West Ham had been smacked with a record £5.5 million fine, which I thought was extremely harsh. But there was a huge sense of relief that the club had avoided a deduction of points, which would have condemned us to certain relegation. In truth, I think the Premier League believed we were going down anyway. We appeared to be dead and buried; nobody in their right mind really thought that we were going to stay up.

To be honest – and this might surprise a few people – I actually believe we should have had points deducted instead. My view is that financial penalties don't necessarily punish people. I think it's ridiculous when you see millionaire players being fined for their misdemeanours because it doesn't hurt them at all. What hurts them is if you stop them playing. Don't get me wrong, I was delighted we'd avoided a points-penalty, but if it had been any other club involved I'd have been adamant that they should be punished in that way. And it would be hypocritical on my part to say it should be any different just because it's West Ham – even though I'm glad it was!

The Premier League tribunal confirmed their decision and that meant we at least still had a mathematical chance of staying up. I was still finding my feet again in terms of work, so I only covered our home games in the final months of the season, plus our local trip to Arsenal. We were under the cosh for most of the game at the Emirates but somehow stole a 1-0 win thanks to a lob by Bobby Zamora on the stroke of half-time. The Gunners should have buried us, but Robert Green had a great game in goal and the result made it three wins on the spin.

Not that I suddenly believed we would stay up; like everybody else, I'd written us off. Historically, West Ham always tend to give people false hope in these situations, bringing to mind the lyrics of 'I'm Forever Blowing Bubbles': 'Just like my dreams, they fade and die...' But after defeats by Sheffield United and Chelsea, the Hammers responded with sensational wins in their final four games against Everton, Wigan, Bolton and Manchester United. Seven victories from nine outings meant we finished three places and three points above the relegation zone. It truly was the Great Escape. I wasn't able to travel to Old Trafford on the final day of the season, but I watched the game on television with friends and was absolutely delighted when we won 1-0 – although when Carlos Tévez scored that lone goal I found myself humming 'There may be trouble ahead...'

That winner took Tévez's tally to seven goals in ten games and I think we all knew that he would soon be on his way. At least I had a souvenir of his time with the Hammers since he'd signed a shirt for me down at the training ground. His English was almost non-existent, so he'd got his interpreter – a young lad who went everywhere with him – to ask me to sort out some photographs of his time at West Ham. I went through my files and produced some nice A4 prints, which I took to Chadwell Heath for him. A friend at the club had asked me to get a shirt signed by Carlos and I thought I'd take along one for myself as well when I headed down there. He loved the pictures and was more than happy to sign the shirts – and that was the last I saw of him before he joined Manchester United.

I was really keen to keep the signed Tévez shirt and refused several generous bids to sell it in the months that followed, but in the end I got offered silly money and had no choice but to let it go. I won't reveal how much I received, but let's just say I wish I'd taken along a few more shirts for Carlos to scribble his name on that day.

Inevitably, West Ham's joy at staying up was short-lived. It quickly came to light that Sheffield United, who had been relegated along with Watford and Alan Pardew's Charlton (which, needless to say, left me heartbroken), were set to challenge the decision not to take points off our tally. The threat of possible relegation still hung over us like a cloud for a few weeks and I was genuinely worried that the original verdict might be overturned. I can be the biggest pessimist going sometimes – certainly when it comes to West Ham – and generally work on the basis that if you prepare for the worst then it's a bonus if things turn out all right in the end. If not, at least you knew what was coming. Some people insisted there was nothing anybody could do to undermine our place in the Premier League, but with West Ham there's always the nagging feeling that if it *can* go wrong, it *will* go wrong.

After various appeals to different bodies, it became clear that the best Sheffield United could do was claim compensation from West Ham for their financial losses as a result of their relegation to the Championship. Their case centred on the argument that Carlos Tévez shouldn't have been allowed to play for us and that his contribution was the single most important factor in Sheffield United – who couldn't even muster a home draw against ten-man Wigan in their final game to save their skins – dropping out of the top flight.

It seems very unkind to the rest of the West Ham players to suggest our survival was solely down to Tévez. Bobby Zamora, Robert Green and Mark Noble, to name but three, all played a vital role. Former Hammer Tony Gale told me that when he gave evidence at the tribunal he had to try and convince the panel that Tévez was not the be-all and end-all in terms of how things played out. I thought it was ridiculous and I certainly don't remember Sheffield United complaining about the presence of Tévez in our side for ninety minutes when they beat West Ham 3-0 at Bramall Lane in April of that year. As a result, I was disappointed when West Ham agreed an out-of-court settlement of £20 million with Sheffield United nearly two years later, but at least we remained a Premier League club at that point. In fact, I'm surprised the Blades didn't take further legal action against us when they went down to League One in 2011 – another relegation that obviously left me devastated.

People have often asked me who I hold responsible for the whole Tévez fiasco and, much as I dislike him, I apportion no blame to Alan Pardew. He might have been the manager when the two Argentinian players were signed, but I think he was as out of touch as to what was really going on as the rest of us. So you have to look at the roles played by certain other members of the club's hierarchy – in particular, managing director Paul Aldridge and legal director Scott Duxbury.

The report published by the Premier League in the wake

of the affair was particularly critical of Aldridge, whose honesty had been called into question. I'd generally found Paul a bit of a cold fish. He had succeeded Peter Storrie as MD in 1999 and, although he was quite pleasant and would always say hello, I thought he was a bit difficult to get to know. He'd previously worked under chairman Terry Brown, who owned a holiday camp on the south coast, and some of the lads used to refer to him as 'Hi-de-Hi', after the British sitcom of the 1980s. We thought of him as being like Simon Cadell – 'Hi, I'm Paul Aldridge, the entertainments manager.'

Brown and Aldridge had left West Ham following the takeover by Björgólfur Gudmundsson, and I thought Scott Duxbury was lucky to remain at the club after his involvement in the Tévez deal. The Premier League report appeared to give him the benefit of the doubt, saying he was under pressure and had been acting under instruction, but I have to say I wasn't too keen on Duxbury.

It might seem like a silly thing on my part, but I always judge a person's character by whether they will say hello to you in any circumstance or not. A classic example of a decent guy is former Liverpool midfielder Jamie Redknapp, who I got to know through his father Harry. If Jamie is at a game, whether working as a pundit for Sky Sports or just with friends, he'll always stop and say hello, irrespective of who he might be with. Somebody like Scott Duxbury, however, will say hello to you one minute and then totally ignore you the next. If he's with other people he won't talk to you, so I wasn't that keen on him. Bearing in mind that he was a lawyer by trade and came to us from Manchester United, I'd have assumed he was shrewd enough to realise the potential problems we were going to have with the Tévez and Mascherano contracts. But maybe not...

When Eggert Magnússon stepped down from his post as chairman of West Ham in the autumn of 2007, it appeared to create a power vacuum and Duxbury seemed to be running the show. People assumed the Icelandic owners would get rid of him, but he ended up with even more power and I thought it went to his head a bit. He had the nice car and the tasty blonde on his arm. I had no real dealings with him, but I didn't like the way he used to strut around the club as if he owned it and I thought he looked like a slippery customer.

There were big changes to the backroom staff in the summer of 2007 as Alan Curbishley moved the furniture around in preparation for his first full season in charge. Several people were recruited from Alan's former club, Charlton, including a new kit manager following the retirement of Eddie Gillam. Eddie had seen a lot at West Ham since the 1980s and I knew he wasn't happy during Alan Pardew's reign. We all thought things would improve under Alan Curbishley, but I think Eddie was still rather disillusioned with the club and thought it was the right time to leave. I was naturally disappointed to see him go because he's been a great friend over the years and I miss him now that he lives in Devon.

West Ham made several big signings during that close season as owner Björgólfur Gudmundsson invested heavily to try and improve the club's fortunes. The club sold a number of players, including Nigel Reo-Coker, Marlon Harewood and Yossi Benayoun, while Carlos Tévez eventually secured his protracted move to Manchester United. We'd already signed Matthew Upson, Lucas Neill and Luís Boa Morte in January to assist the fight against relegation and big money was spent on recruiting Scott Parker, Kieron Dyer, Craig Bellamy, Julien Faubert and Freddie Ljungberg in the summer. The sales helped recoup much of the transfer expenditure, but the club's wage bill went through the roof and we seemed to be paying stupid money to players.

The club organised a big press conference to announce the £3 million signing of Ljungberg from Arsenal and as Eggert Magnússon happily posed for pictures with the Swedish midfielder, I sensed that the chairman just loved him. Indeed, it wasn't long before I got a call from Eggy's PA saying that he was very keen to see the photos from the day, so he was clearly a huge fan. Indeed, it made me wonder whose decision it was to buy the thirty-year-old in the first place. Whether my suspicions were correct or not, it was to prove a disastrous signing and the club was forced to pay him a fortune a year later to rip up his contract after he'd made just twenty-two league starts.

Thankfully, we had rather more success with the £7 million capture of Scott Parker from Newcastle United. Curbs had been at Charlton when they reluctantly sold Scotty to Chelsea three years earlier and I took a good picture of him pretending to throttle the midfielder at a press conference after questions were asked about their relationship.

The club seemed to be throwing a lot of money about at that time and this extended to various big-name ex-players being recruited as ambassadors on match days. Of course, it all caught up with Eggy in the end and he was soon on his way after his relatively small shareholding was bought out. Little did we know, however, what serious financial problems were lurking just over the horizon.

From knowing Alan Curbishley I can say that he can be quite a laugh at times, but West Ham fans tend to view him very differently because they see the football we played under his management as an extension of his character. And there's no doubt that the 2007/08 season was rather boring.

The Hammers are usually fighting against relegation or trying to win promotion, but we had a very uneventful season and my main memory of that time is that we seemed to sit in tenth place for months on end. I also have to admit that the football itself seemed pretty dull and I wasn't really enjoying it very much. The injury problems we suffered didn't help, but I just got the feeling that Curbs was playing things very safe and never really taking any chances. His management style seemed very cautious and conservative and, although such an approach worked for Charlton, it wasn't what the West Ham fans really wanted.

I find it difficult to imagine that Alan wasn't aware of the demands of the fans given his playing career at Upton Park and the fact he'd been working for fifteen years at another London club just across the Thames. He's also a very bright bloke. But he stuck with the formula that had always served him well as a manager and the result was a relatively flat season for West Ham – not that anybody would complain about a top-ten finish in the Premier League at the moment.

Though the football was dull, that season was notable for the return of Dean Ashton from injury. The striker, who became the club's record signing when making a £7.25 million move from Norwich in January 2006, had missed the previous campaign after breaking an ankle while on England duty, but he fought his way back to score eleven goals and I was pleased for him because he'd had a difficult time. I got on well with Dean. He was always very polite and would use your name in conversation. He was a nice guy and it was such a shame that we never really saw the best of him – he continued to be plagued by ankle problems and was sadly forced to announce his retirement in 2009 at the age of just twenty-six.

It just goes to show that you never know what the future holds and Alan Curbishley would certainly agree with that after resigning from his post at West Ham just a few games into the 2008/09 season. When Anton Ferdinand and George McCartney were both sold to Sunderland against his wishes – for fees that amounted to £14 million – I knew that Alan's position at Upton Park was untenable. It was patently obvious that decisions were being made behind his back and over his head, if that makes any sense. And knowing Curbs as I do, as a man of principle, I could see he would not be able to carry on under those circumstances. Therefore, I was not surprised when Alan tendered his resignation and I would never hold it against him. I have a lot of sympathy for him, in fact; you can't be the manager of a club and allow players to be sold without your permission, because it leaves you with no authority. After Ferdinand went, Curbs had insisted that nobody else would be leaving, only to see McCartney follow him up to the Stadium of Light less than a week later. I honestly don't think Alan had any choice but to quit and I think he did the honourable thing.

I also believe Alan was vindicated when he eventually won his claim for constructive dismissal and agreed a settlement of around £2.2 million with the club. His contract stated that he had control over transfers and so West Ham had clearly been in breach. Maybe some of Alan's signings didn't work out – we should have known that Kieron Dyer was an injury liability, for example – but ultimately he presided over the Great Escape, guided us to a comfortable tenth-place finish and remained true to his principles when resigning. That's not a bad record in the short time he was at West Ham and I'm sure he still feels there's unfinished work for him at the club. I know some fans have suggested he should pay the money back if he ever wants to return to the club as manager, but I think that's ridiculous. He was forced into resigning. I would welcome him back to Upton Park – and he can keep the cash.

What has surprised me is that it has taken Alan so long to return to management. There were reports of him only being prepared to take charge of a Premier League club, and such an attitude is very restrictive. I can understand his desire to manage in the top flight but, at the end of the day, if you want a job you want a job. I know he's been doing plenty of media work and maybe he's been in a position where he hasn't needed a full-time job, but at the time of writing it's been nearly four years and that's a long time out of football management. Clubs are entitled to question your hunger. I'm sure he'll return at some stage – maybe by the time you're reading this – but if he's only prepared to manage a Premier League club it could be a very long wait.

CHAPTER 8

'YOU CAME A BIT OF A CROPPER THERE, DIDN'T YOU?'

When I think of Gianfranco Zola's reign as West Ham manager, I think of trouble. Financial trouble; terrace trouble; relegation trouble. Trouble, trouble, trouble. Which is perhaps ironic given that, as a man, Zola isn't trouble in the slightest. In fact, he's one of the nicest and most easy-going people you could ever wish to meet. But he managed the Hammers at a time when things were going wrong both on the pitch and off and it was evident from Gianfranco's receding hairline (which has staged something of a surprise fightback of late) that the stresses and strains of the job were taking their toll.

I had a bit of a troubled brow myself when Zola was appointed as Alan Curbishley's successor in September 2008. I'd always admired the Italian as a player and from what I'd seen of him in television interviews it was obvious that he was a friendly guy. But I was concerned about his managerial credentials – he had previously only been an assistant to Italy's under-21 coach, Pierluigi Casiraghi, and we know from the past that great players don't necessarily make great managers. I was also a little worried about the fact that he was such a Chelsea legend because, as you might have realised by now, I do like my managers to have West Ham connections. With Zola, however, what you see is basically what you get. He's a really nice man and when he was unveiled as the club's new manager at Upton Park he was full of smiles and very friendly with everybody. He's a very likeable person.

In truth, it's a reflection of how things had changed for me at West Ham that I can't say I really got to know Gianfranco very well. I was no longer travelling with the team and staying overnight with them in hotels; my good friend Eddie Gillam had left the club so there was no real reason to visit the training ground on a weekly basis; and I simply had a lot less contact with the management. Gianfranco was perfectly pleasant when we did meet, but there was no real interaction with him. I'm told that Zola's assistant, Steve Clarke, who he lured from Chelsea, is also a very nice guy, but I don't think he ever spoke to me. In truth, I thought he seemed a little aloof and never saw him participate in any banter down at Chadwell Heath or the Boleyn Ground.

The style of football might have been a little sunnier under Zola, but there were major storm clouds hovering over Upton Park from a financial point of view. Firstly, the club's shirt sponsor, XL (no, that doesn't stand for extra large), went bust, meaning the players had to run around with an embarrassing patch on their chests, which looked simply awful. They stuck numbers on them but we still looked like a park football team. And then chairman Björgólfur Gudmundsson's Icelandic banking empire collapsed towards the end of 2008, meaning there was nobody to subsidise the losses the club was making as a result of the heavy spending that had taken place. Add in Sheffield United's £20 million compensation claim and Alan Curbishley's complaint against constructive dismissal and suddenly the club's financial state looked rather perilous. I thought to myself that such a turnaround could only happen to West Ham. No other club could be taken over by a billionaire only to see his mountain of wealth blow up in smoke. It was just typical West Ham.

Inevitably, there was a lot of concern at the club as staff in various departments worried about their jobs and there was a very real fear that we could even be forced into administration. The club eventually found itself being passed into the hands of Straumur, an Icelandic banking entity that had been one of the major creditors of Gudmundsson's holding company, who were in dire straits themselves. Needless to say, I decided it probably wasn't a good time to ask for a wage rise.

It was no surprise that West Ham considered it prudent to sell striker Craig Bellamy in January 2009 when Manchester City offered £14 million, but eyebrows were raised when the club subsequently decided to invest at least £5 million of that cash on a relatively unknown commodity by the name of Savio Nsereko. The club stressed that the nineteen-year-old Ugandan-born Germany under-20 international was one for the future, but it seemed a very strange deal given the situation we were in. Why spend what little money we had available on an unproven youngster when the team had just lost one of its best players?

The signing of Savio was overseen by Gianluca Nani, the club's technical director, who had been appointed towards the end of Alan Curbishley's reign as manager. He was supposed to have an excellent knowledge of the European transfer market, yet when he needed to buy a player following Bellamy's sale he simply went back to his old club Brescia, whose president was his father-in-law. It all looked very dubious and the signing of Savio soon turned out to be a disaster, as predicted. The youngster made just one league start and ten substitute appearances before being offloaded to Fiorentina. He's recently been playing in Bulgaria and Romania, which says it all really.

I can remember when Nani arrived at the club and we did some pictures of the Italian on the Upton Park pitch. He appeared with his surname on the back of a West Ham shirt and made some quip about not being the Nani who played for Manchester United. Oh how we roared.

My opinion is that his influence on the club was not particularly healthy. Things started going wrong from the moment he arrived and I got the impression that people were being recruited just because he knew them. We had a Greek doctor arrive in a senior position and it then came to light that he wasn't registered with the General Medical Council. That was also the beginning of the end for club doctor Ges Steinbergs, who had been an important figure at West Ham over the previous decade or so and a good friend. It seemed that Nani was making a lot of the decisions at the club – in tandem with chief executive Scott Duxbury – and that he had an influence over Zola that wasn't necessarily positive. Not that anybody was complaining after West Ham finished ninth in the Premier League in 2009 and just missed out on a European place, however. But as we saw with Glenn Roeder seven years earlier, you can't necessarily judge a manager's qualities after one decent season.

When the police come knocking at your door, it's never a nice feeling. That was the case during Gianfranco Zola's second season in charge of West Ham when the boys in blue (rather than claret and blue) paid a visit to my office in the aftermath of the explosive Carling Cup second-round game at home to local rivals Millwall in August 2009. There was a huge build-up to the game and a lot of banter on social networking websites such as Facebook and Twitter – on which I'm very active – and I feared there was going to be trouble. Indeed, it was inevitable really given the fact that the two clubs hadn't faced each other for a few years.

I usually try to get to any game about two hours before kick-off, but on this occasion I arrived at Upton Park even earlier, probably around 5 p.m. I suspected there might be problems outside the stadium and wanted to get into the ground safely. A friend of mine, who is a reporter and had turned up with his brother and prospective father-in-law, rang me to ask if I could help them get in because they hadn't been able to buy any tickets and were being held in an area by the police for safety reasons. I couldn't believe a reasonably intelligent guy thought the club would be selling tickets on the night for a game like that. There was nothing I could do for him and the three of them apparently took hours to get home because of the security around the ground.

When the game started, I positioned myself towards the Trevor Brooking Stand and did my best to focus on the football, but I do find it difficult to concentrate when we play the likes of Millwall. I'm constantly aware of what's going on in the crowd and the hostile feeling between the two sets of fans. At half-time I moved towards the other end of the pitch and after Junior Stanislas scored West Ham's late equaliser to take the game into extra time, things began to escalate. The game boiled over when the Hammers subsequently scored twice to win the tie and there were several pitch invasions, as well as problems in the north-west corner of the ground where a group of fans spilled over the wall.

I don't enjoy taking pictures of pitch invasions or crowd disturbances, but I do have an obligation in those circumstances. Firstly, the *Recorder* expects me to document events; secondly, the club needs material for identification purposes. So I just have to shoot whatever I can and hope I don't get coshed over the head, which was certainly the case for one particular supporter who was dragged the length of the touchline by police with blood streaming down his face from a head wound. Of course, I had to take some pictures of that because it was such a dramatic image – one that was fully exploited by the national media in the days that followed.

As soon as we heard that a Millwall fan had been stabbed in the streets outside the ground we knew it was inevitable that the newspapers would make the most of the story. It was portrayed as a riot inside the stadium, when the reality was that the pitch encroachments were more celebratory than anything else. There was a chap with a young child on his shoulders and girls swinging their handbags. But we all know the media don't like the truth to get in the way of a good story.

A few days after the game, West Ham told me that they needed my pictures so that they could produce some posters of those fans who had run onto the pitch. They were like 'wanted' posters, featuring little headshots of people, although the quality was never going to be very good given the distance of the shots and the fact that it was a night game. I duly supplied the images and was told that I'd probably be hearing from the police because they might want to do something similar or need evidence if they wanted to bring charges against people. I then received a phone call from an officer who told me that he wanted to use some of my material and take a statement from me.

And so I found myself being quizzed by the cops – not as a suspect, of course, but as a potential witness – and it proved a lengthy process. I had to answer a multitude of questions for well over an hour and I was told that the police needed their cases to be watertight if they went to court. I had to confirm that the images were originals, where they had been stored and whether they were on a compact flash card or an SD card. I then had to sign an affidavit confirming that the images had not been retouched in any way. It was a hell of a process and the officer explained that it needed to be that way so that – in his words – 'no smart-arse lawyer' could wriggle anybody out of it.

I'd been asked to supply photographic evidence on a few other occasions during my career. There had been a pitch invasion at a match against Birmingham in the early 1980s and I was contacted by a fan who seemed to think I could help him after he'd been arrested. We didn't shoot digitally in those days so I had to produce a print and write on the back that I certified that the image had been taken at a specific place and time and had not been retouched in any way. There was another incident when somebody approached me to establish when a picture of some crowd trouble was actually taken and, because the digital image had an imprint confirming the time and date, we were able to prove a person's innocence.

The inquest after the Millwall game was the most intense I've ever experienced and I was warned that I might even have to go to court to give evidence if necessary – not that I was ultimately required to, thankfully. As a West Ham fan, I must admit to having mixed emotions about getting involved in possible prosecutions. The joke in the *Recorder* offices was that the 'wanted' posters included my photo byline, so any hooligans would know who to come after to seek retribution. You do start to worry a bit. But at the end of the day, these people are not necessarily friends of mine and it's not my fault if they've done something wrong. The only thing that concerned me was the fact that most of the activity inside the ground was quite good-humoured. But given the history of hostility between West Ham and Millwall, it was foolish for anybody to run onto the pitch because it's obvious the authorities would come down heavily on them. Everybody knows that it's an offence to trespass on the playing surface nowadays and there's no grey area about that. It's black and white (well, the pictorial evidence is in colour) and you're caught bang to rights.

I have a lot of correspondence on Facebook and Twitter and most of my followers are West Ham fans, so I see a lot of different threads. From what I've read, several people are serving bans because of what took place that evening, although I don't know if my pictures played a part. Not that it's anything I should lose any sleep over, because there's nothing I can do about it anyway. I'm legally obliged to submit my material to the authorities if they request it. I do feel that the penalties are harsh in some cases, but there are others where people have deserved to have their collars felt. And I can fully understand why West Ham need to be seen to be pro-active in terms of identifying fans who have run onto the pitch: they have to cover their own back, otherwise the club will get punished as well. They have to keep the Football Association happy. But I hate those types of games and am relieved that they seem to be few and far between nowadays.

In my opinion, the police were asking for trouble by allowing the Queens pub in Green Street to remain open on the evening of the Millwall game. It's common sense that all pubs within walking distance of the ground should be closed several hours before we play such matches. The games against Millwall should always have early kick-off times if possible and I don't have a problem with the suggestion that away fans should be banned from both Upton Park and The Den. Innocent fans would complain about being unfairly punished, but if it was a reciprocal arrangement between the two clubs I wouldn't argue – especially if the games were aired live on television. People might say that's easy for me to say because I can still gain access to the away games as a photographer, but that doesn't mean I don't fear for my safety when we visit Millwall. It was even worse at the old Den, although thankfully we only went there on a handful of occasions.

There was one game, during John Lyall's days in the late 1970s, when we went for a pre-match meal at the hotel next to Tower Bridge. We were expecting a police escort to arrive after we'd finished eating, but the steaks had just been served when a policeman wearing riot gear came into the restaurant and said, 'Right, we're going now!' John Lyall pointed out that we hadn't eaten yet and the copper just told us that if we didn't board the team bus within two minutes we wouldn't be going to the game at all. We got onto the coach and the police vehicle that escorted us was like something we used to see on the news from Northern Ireland. The Land Rover was covered in armour plating and had blacked-out windows with grills. And off to war-torn Millwall with rumbling stomachs we headed.

At the end of the game, I wanted to use the players' tunnel to return to the coach but the security guys wouldn't allow me through. Consequently, I walked up the terracing to use an exit with the idea of walking round to where the team bus was parked. The steward pushed me out onto the street and suddenly I saw two groups of Millwall and West Ham fans glaring at each other from either side – and I was stuck in the middle. Incredibly, the West Ham fans started chanting, 'One Stevie Bacon, there's only one Stevie Bacon...' But all I could think was, 'Fuck this for a game of soldiers, I'm getting out of here!' And so I started banging on the door and demanded to be allowed back in, only for the steward to say I couldn't go back into the ground. 'You just watch me,' I said and dived past him to head back to the tunnel, where they thankfully let me through once I'd explained that it was about to kick off outside.

You've got to be careful with Millwall fans. I remember the time I went up to a game at Newcastle when hooliganism was at its worst and somebody threw a petrol-soaked scarf – described as a 'firebomb' by some people when recalling the tale – into the West Ham end. I left the game early and travelled back by train with my brother only to run into some returning Millwall fans, who were buzzing about the act of violence that had taken place at St James' Park. 'Wish we'd thought of that!' said one of them – and I got the distinct impression he wasn't joking.

West Ham's rivalry with Millwall never seems to go away, irrespective of whether we're playing them on a regular basis or not. In fact, the longer between the games, the worse the tension seems to get. It certainly doesn't help when you've got people making movies about the gang warfare between the two clubs. I am, of course, talking about *Green Street* (2005), which, apart from being a pretty rubbish film, totally blackened our name and was hardly the sort of publicity the club needed. West Ham clearly had no idea what the film was really about when they allowed the makers to shoot footage during a home game against Gillingham – and neither did I when I was asked to take some pictures of Elijah Wood. I'm still not sure why anybody thought the bloke who played Frodo Baggins in the *Lord of the Rings* trilogy would make a good football hooligan, but thankfully my involvement in the sorry episode was limited to meeting Elijah and taking a few shots of him. Unsurprisingly, certain people at West Ham were rather embarrassed when the film finally emerged and the club was subsequently forced to try and distance itself from it.

The troubles surrounding Millwall's visit to Upton Park in 2009 were still relatively fresh in the memory when the south London club returned to West Ham for a league game in February 2012. Thankfully, the match took place without major incident, but I was extremely disappointed that circumstances dictated that we were not able to hold a minute's silence for former goalkeeper and coach Ernie Gregory, who passed away at the age of ninety just two weeks beforehand. It was unfortunate that our next home game just happened to be against Millwall, whose fans were never likely to show much sympathy for a Hammers legend, and so the players simply wore black armbands in honour of his memory to avoid any embarrassments. Ernie deserved a minute's silence, he really did, but the truth is that we live in a sad world and some people simply can't be trusted.

Some fans might beg to differ, especially when West Ham were relegated from the Premier League in 2011, but I genuinely believe that the purchase of the club by David Gold and David Sullivan in January 2010 was the best thing that could have happened to us at that point in time. It was never a comfortable situation with Straumur running the club and it's no secret that we were in serious financial trouble – it was subsequently revealed that our debts had risen to £110 million.

There was a lot of correspondence on Twitter about the potential interest of Tony Fernandes, who subsequently bought QPR instead, but at the end of the day Gold and Sullivan put their money on the table and I was very pleased they did. As far as I am concerned, they rescued the club from the financial abyss and for that we should always be grateful. Gold and Sullivan might have owned Birmingham City for seventeen years, but they were true West Ham people and there was something romantic about their return to Green Street. Despite my famous pessimism, I envisaged everything coming good and, although we've had problems since their arrival, I still feel just a little safer with them at the club.

I photographed the two Davids as they surveyed their new empire at the Boleyn Ground and have since got to know Mr Gold a little bit as I see him at every home game. He's a good guy who generally comes down to say hello and always calls me by my name. I sometimes end up taking his picture with people in various parts of the ground and I must admit to having had an embarrassing experience at a recent game. I was bringing some match sponsors downstairs and one bloke kept saying how he couldn't believe that Stevie Bacon was taking his picture. 'How long have you been here?' he asked. 'You're a legend.' He was with a girl who was being presented with an award of some kind and she asked if I could take her picture with David Gold. I was about to take the shot when the bloke jumped into the frame and said, 'I can't believe Stevie Bacon is taking my picture. He's a legend, you know.' And David Gold said, 'Yeah, Stevie's been here a long time.'

I was starting to feel a bit old at this point, but what made me laugh was the fact that this guy was far more impressed by me taking his picture than he was by being photographed alongside David Gold. I reckon he had his priorities all wrong myself, but these things do happen from time to time.

There was another time when I was in a corporate lounge after a game and the sponsors were waiting for one of the players to show his face. It's not always easy persuading top stars to come up and on this occasion one of the youth team players was sent out to say hello. I can't even remember who he was, but he had a woolly hat pulled down over his face and he looked like he was about to mug someone. I took a group photo and one of the chaps turned to the commercial manager and said, 'Any chance I can have a picture with Stevie Bacon now? At least we know who he is!'

There was one game towards the end of the 2009/10 campaign, however, when I became the centre of attention for all the wrong reasons. We were having a terrible time in Gianfranco Zola's second season at the club and were suffering a run of losses that would eventually extend to six consecutive games. However, the midweek 3-1 home defeat by Wolves – in what had previously been dubbed a must-win game – on this occasion was the least of my problems.

It's standard procedure for me to go onto the pitch just before kick-off to take a picture of the two captains with the mascots. As usual, I got the shot, gave the referee the thumbs up and turned to start walking off the pitch. I was trudging off towards the sidelines when one of the mascots – and it had to be the youngest one, of course – came running off without really looking where she was going. She bumped into me from behind and clipped my standing foot to send me flying. It was definitely a red card offence. I went crashing down and landed heavily on my camera, which caused me a lot of pain, although my immediate feeling was one of embarrassment more than anything else.

Quite apart from my size and my dodgy feet, I also have bad knees, so I was struggling to get up, hoping that not too many people in the 33,988-strong crowd had seen me. But, of course, everybody had witnessed what happened and, to compound my shame, the woman who played Bubbles the Bear came over to help me up. I was feeling rather winded and sore, but managed to make my way to the photographers' dug-out, only to hear somebody in the crowd say, 'You took a bit of tumble there, didn't you?'

My mobile phone then rang and it was the mother of a friend saying that her son had just sent her a text message to tell her that he was in fits of laughter over what he'd just seen. Then I got a call from one of the match-day hostesses, whose brother was in one of the executive boxes with a load of people who were all in hysterics. Apparently they were all wetting themselves. She had wondered what was so funny and was told that Steve Bacon had been wiped out by a seven-year-old mascot and then rescued by Bubbles the Bear. I later made my way up to one of the lounges and former Hammers star Bobby Gould was the guest for the night. 'All right, mate?' he said, and it seemed for a moment as if he wasn't going to say anything about my little incident. But then he said, 'You came a bit of a cropper there, didn't you? Was it that little mascot?' To make it worse, yet more people arrived and started laughing at me as well.

I had no idea at the time but it later transpired that I had cracked a rib, which explained why I was in so much pain. My chest was black with bruising by the end of the night and I was in agony as I tried to get some sleep. I phoned

Ges Steinbergs, the club doctor, the next day and he told me that there was little I could do about it. It was simply a case of having to grin and bear it – and that's not a reference to Bubbles the bloody Bear, by the way.

The following Saturday I was at home watching television when *Soccer AM* came on and I said, only half joking, to my brother that I could be appearing on the Third Eye section. He told me not to be so stupid and that I wasn't important enough but, lo and behold, presenter Helen Chamberlain then announced that they were heading to Upton Park. 'Have a look at the photographer on the pitch getting wiped out by the two-foot mascot,' she gleefully said, before the clip was played over and over again to much laughter from the guests in the studio. I took some consolation from the fact it was a long shot of the incident and my face couldn't really be seen – until they suddenly zoomed in to show Bubbles helping me to my feet. 'And he's a big fellow, as well,' added Helen, just to set the seal on the matter. The Facebook and Twitter banter didn't stop for weeks after that. The moment has also been captured for posterity on YouTube, under 'Stevie Bacon takes a tumble', just in case anybody is interested.

Later in the year, I appeared on *Soccer AM* in person when a Facebook friend by the name of Dan Jarvis, who lives in Gravesend, told me that he was going on the show with a group of West Ham fans and that they wanted me to join them. I laughed at the idea but reluctantly agreed and got down to the club shop to buy myself a Hammers shirt. After all, if they had tops to fit heavyweight flop Benni McCarthy – who really did prove a fat lot of good for West Ham at that time – I didn't think I'd have too much of a problem finding my size. Having said that, the shorts were a bit on the tight side!

When we arrived at the Sky studios in Isleworth I told the lads that I was worried about the programme showing the clip of me being wiped out by a mascot and they admitted that they had mentioned it. 'Thanks very much,' I said, fearing the worst. We were in the restaurant before the show when a producer came up to me and said, 'Steve, I'm really sorry, but we've got "The Hoff" on the programme today, so we're not going to have time to show your clip.' He was very apologetic, but I was more than happy to hear that and told him not to worry about it.

I was starting to relax a bit when, about five minutes before transmission, another guy with headphones and a clipboard approached me and asked, 'What game was that when you fell over?' I told him they weren't showing the clip, but he just said, 'No, I know, I just wondered what game it was.' Needless to say, I spent the rest of the show sweating over the whole thing, but thankfully the presence of David Hasselhoff saved my bacon, if you know what I mean.

When the time came for our team to play the car-park game, where you try and score goals through a circular target, we proved to be totally useless – I think we got about two in total – and I was as bad as anybody. I really did feel like Benni McCarthy. But we had some pictures taken with 'The Hoff' and former Tottenham goalkeeper Erik Thorstvedt, who was also on the show, as well as Helen Chamberlain and co-presenter Max Rushden. 'We did have your clip,' smiled Helen, 'but we ran out of time.' I accepted her apologies and let out a huge sigh of relief. Despite my initial reservations, it had been a great day.

Thankfully West Ham picked up towards the end of the 2009/10 season and were able to avoid relegation, but it seemed like one of the worst secrets in football that Gianfranco Zola would soon be on his way, since there was strong speculation that the new owners wanted their own man in charge. Gianfranco retained his dignity throughout the final weeks and even pulled on his shooting boots once again to make an appearance in a testimonial game for the club's youth academy boss, Tony Carr, who was celebrating nearly thirty years of dedicated service in his role.

I've known Tony ever since he's been involved with West Ham and believe he fully merited his MBE, which he was awarded in June 2010. It's great that he has had the recognition he deserves because he's been brilliant at developing young players. We don't do a lot of things right at West Ham, but they seem to have got that side of things sorted.

In Tony's honour, West Ham played an Academy All-stars side and it was great to see Rio Ferdinand, Frank Lampard and Joe Cole show their faces on the night. Even Chelsea captain John Terry found himself pictured in a West Ham shirt, but the photographs of the night – as far as I was concerned – were always going to be those of Zola playing alongside Paolo Di Canio. The two Italians had a bit of a laugh together when they came onto the field and it was a fantastic occasion.

Later that week, the Hammers played their final game of the season – a 1-1 home draw with Manchester City – and Zola's twenty-month reign was brought to an end. Personally, I thought Gianfranco should have been given more time to prove himself. At the end of the day, he did keep West Ham up – although maybe we should thank Iain Dowie for that. The former Hammers striker guided Hull City to relegation that season with a record of one win in nine games as their 'football management consultant'. It had been a long time since that own goal at Stockport in 1996, but I think Iain might have repaid us at last given that we finished just one place above the drop zone.

Zola was an honourable man, but maybe his lack of experience told in the end. It had been a close call in terms of avoiding relegation and I can see why David Sullivan and David Gold – who had also kicked Gianluca Nani into touch – didn't want to run the risk of us going through that experience again. They believed they were doing the right thing, but it's just a shame that they got their next managerial appointment – a bloke known as 'Mr Toad' behind his back – so spectacularly wrong.

CHAPTER 9

'ME AND STEVIE GO BACK THIRTY YEARS'

Avram Grant is a miserable character. I was walking along one of the corridors of the Boleyn Ground in the early part of the 2010/11 season when the manager suddenly appeared from around the corner and started heading towards me. 'Good morning,' I said as we crossed paths, only for the Israeli to totally ignore me as he continued on his way.

Sadly, that is my abiding memory of Avram Grant, the Hammers boss who never once spoke to me in his entire period at the club. When you consider the close relationships I enjoyed with some of his predecessors – John Lyall, Lou Macari, Billy Bonds and Harry Redknapp – it was extremely disappointing. But I realised at the press conference that heralded his arrival in the summer of 2010 that we were never likely to end up as the best of mates. To mark the occasion, I took some pictures of Grant on the pitch at Upton Park and, in stark contrast to previous manager Gianfranco Zola, who had been all smiles when he met the media, the new man showed no personality whatsoever and looked very sour-faced. He never said a word to me on that first day and that set the scene for the entire season.

I know it's easy to speak with the benefit of hindsight, but I didn't think he was a good appointment at the time. Yes, he'd taken Chelsea to the Champions League final in 2008, but anybody could have achieved that with the squad he had at his disposal following the departure of José Mourinho. And I know he guided Portsmouth to the FA Cup final only a few months before joining us, but he'd also just been relegated – so I wasn't particularly happy to see him get the job at West Ham.

I never socialised with the man, so maybe I'm doing him a disservice, but I just couldn't see how a manager with his personality and character could inspire players. He seemed to have all the charisma of a toad, and that's what some people referred to him as – Mr Toad. I believe that his general demeanour had a lot to do with his downfall at Upton Park, because I can't for the life of me see how he would have been able to get the best out of our players.

We lost our first four league games under Grant's command and spent the rest of the season trying to recover from such a poor start. Indeed, we were still at the bottom of the table when Arsenal visited Upton Park in January. The popular view was that the game would be Grant's last in charge of the Hammers, irrespective of the result, with former Leicester City, Celtic and Aston Villa boss Martin O'Neill strongly linked to his position. I joined the rest of the photographers in focusing on the manager after the game – a dismal 3-0 defeat – and when he threw his scarf into the crowd it certainly seemed to be a farewell gesture. But then we heard O'Neill was unhappy that news of his potential appointment had been leaked and it appears that West Ham had mucked things up again. O'Neill withdrew his interest and Grant, purely by default, managed to remain in office.

For me, it was a monumentally bad decision not to change the manager before the end of the season. I can't believe the owners could not see what was going to happen if they didn't.

It was obvious that we would end up getting relegated if we didn't get rid of Grant. But they ended up allowing him to recruit more players – including Robbie Keane, Demba Ba and Wayne Bridge – and hoped that would make the difference instead. With a lot of managers it probably would have done, because they were good players, but this is Avram Grant we're talking about. And although we briefly climbed out of the bottom three for a fortnight in March, we slumped back to the bottom of the table and eventually found ourselves facing relegation since we only managed to collect two points from our final nine games.

The point of no return came at fellow strugglers Wigan Athletic in our penultimate match when we threw away a 2-0 lead – courtesy of two Demba Ba goals – that should have condemned our opponents to the drop and kept our survival hopes alive. Historically, 2-0 has been a dangerous scoreline for West Ham because it seems we've only got to concede one goal and then we crumble. Our worst fears came to fruition when Wigan hit back with three second-half goals to give themselves a lifeline and send us down instead.

I can't say I feel sorry for Grant over the way that David Sullivan took him into a room immediately after the final whistle and told him he was fired. I didn't like the guy so he's never going to get any sympathy from me. People might say it's not the West Ham way of doing things, but I'm not sure if there is a West Ham way of doing things any more. The game seems to have moved on. It's obvious that Sullivan couldn't wait to get rid of Grant, so why had he allowed things to get to that stage? Why not make the change when there was time for a new man to give us a chance? I can only assume that it was cheaper to sack Grant after relegation, but that seems like a false economy when you consider the many millions of pounds the club lost by dropping into the Championship. The fact is that West Ham were relegated for the second time in eight years with a squad that should easily have been good enough to stay up. As with Glenn Roeder in 2003, you have to lay the blame firmly at the manager's door and say that Grant has to be held responsible.

We all heard about Scott Parker providing a half-time team talk to inspire an unlikely comeback from three goals down at West Bromwich Albion in February and I've been told by several insiders that the manager wasn't exactly full of words in the dressing room at the best of times. And when he was he didn't necessarily get the response he was looking for. There was one occasion when Grant was telling the players that they wouldn't be going down because there were ten teams worse than West Ham. 'Yeah,' said one player, 'but we've lost to eight of them!'

That Grant faced the press after the game at Wigan and refused to admit he'd been sacked just summed things up really. He couldn't even go properly. It was a mistake to appoint him in the first place, but the club's gamble to keep him on backfired big time and they paid a heavy price.

It's unbelievable when you consider that we had four England internationals (five if you include Bridge on loan) on the team, two of whom departed in the summer of 2011. I was disappointed to see Scott Parker leave the club but it was inevitable that he would move on for the sake of his England career. Scotty is what I would describe as an old-school type of player in terms of how helpful and co-operative he is. I get a lot of people asking me to get things signed by the players and in the old days it was never a problem. It's become rather more difficult now, but I could always rely on Parker to do the honours.

Scotty once did me a huge favour when I wanted to give a good friend of mine, Dan Jarvis, a special eighteenth-birthday gift and asked Scott if I could have one of his shirts after he'd played in it. He said it would be no problem, but when I went to see him after our next game it transpired that all the team's shirts were going to be auctioned for charity because they had poppies on them to mark Armistice Day. Scott was very apologetic but insisted I could have his shirt from the next home game, which happened to be against Wigan. He actually scored in the 3-1 win and I took a nice shot of him pulling his shirt down as he ran towards the touchline in celebration. I walked down to the dressing room after the game and spoke to one of the security guys, who seemed to think that Scott had walked in bare-chested. I feared that he'd forgotten about our arrangement and thrown his shirt into the crowd, but Scott duly appeared with the prized item in his hand, having already signed the back for me. Like I say, he's Mr Reliable.

Considering Scott is such a decent guy, I was very disappointed that he got a bit of stick when it became obvious that he was going to sign for Tottenham Hotspur. Surely people should just remember the way the midfielder performed for us during his four years at the club. He was named as the Football Writers' Association Player of the Year in 2011 and won the Hammer of the Year in his final three seasons at Upton Park, so that says it all. For me, he was the spiritual captain of the side and can take no blame for the way things went in the end. I thought he was a talismanic sort of player and far more of a leader than Matthew Upson, who was not one of my favourite players if I'm honest. I thought he was very lucky to be the captain of West Ham. I didn't find him to be particularly helpful. There was one occasion when the club's press officer had arranged for me to take a picture and, when I knocked on the dressing-room door, Upson came out. He said he knew nothing about the arrangement and that he didn't have time, which I thought was a bit rude given that he was probably only listening to music. As far as I'm concerned, the club should have stripped the defender of the captaincy as soon as he refused to sign a new contract. If he wasn't committed to the club, how could he be trusted to lead with authority? He joined Stoke City after his deal expired and barely played for them, so maybe the grass isn't always greener after all.

Goalkeeper Robert Green and striker Carlton Cole were also expected to leave after the club's relegation, but thankfully they both stayed to help us back up again the following season. Green stopped talking to the media after he suffered some criticism for the embarrassing goal he conceded against the USA at the World Cup finals in 2010 and whether I've felt the effects of that I don't really know, but he's never struck me as being the most approachable of guys. The bottom line is that I work for the club and yet he hasn't always wanted to play ball. As for Carlton, I haven't had too many dealings with him but he's another gentle giant. He strikes me as one of those players who does all the hard work on the pitch but gets it wrong when he has time to think. We've had a few of those over the years.

It saddens me a little that it's no longer possible to get to know the players in the way I used to in the 1980s and 1990s. Even ignoring the fact that I no longer travel with the squad, the reality is that players just don't remain at clubs long enough nowadays to establish any real friendships with them. They're here for a couple of years and then they're off. I'm also disappointed that the fans don't get the access to players that they used to. I leave games quite some time after the final whistle and I can still see fans pushing their autograph books through the railings only for players to sometimes ignore them. That really annoys me, especially as supporters are not allowed down to the training ground any more. Kids could go into the car park to get signatures in the past, but it's like Fort Knox down there nowadays. I totally understand why security needs to be tighter than it used to be, but there seems to be a lot of secrecy about things and I'm not sure that a lot of it is particularly necessary.

I've got to admit that Sam Allardyce wasn't my first choice to become West Ham's new manager following the sacking of Avram Grant in the summer of 2011. In fact, he wasn't second on my list, either. But I had a brief chat with Sam down at the training ground after his appointment and in that one moment I'd had more contact with him than with Grant during his entire period in charge. He seemed very personable and, for that alone, he won a place in my good books, although I reserved judgement on whether he was the right man for West Ham until we could see if the team was going to win promotion or not.

Personally, I'd have liked Chris Hughton to take charge of the Hammers. Chris was a Newham boy, so I'd seen him at local level as a youngster and, after spending most of his playing career at Tottenham, he joined West Ham to help us win promotion in 1991 as a replacement for injured left-back Julian Dicks. I got on very well with him and thought he was one of the more intelligent footballers I'd come across. He'd done very well guiding Newcastle United back into the

Premier League in 2010 after their relegation and I saw no reason why he couldn't repeat the trick at Upton Park. I imagine he'd have got us playing in a style more associated with West Ham than Sam Allardyce subsequently did. But after harshly getting the sack at St James' Park, he took charge of Birmingham City and steered them to fourth position in the Championship table in 2012, before losing to Blackpool in the play-offs. Chris will always stop for a chat whenever we bump into each other and he is one of the game's good guys.

I would also have been very happy to see former boss Alan Curbishley return to Upton Park because, despite everything that had happened a few years earlier, he was a West Ham man through and through. And you certainly couldn't say that about Sam Allardyce, who had no past connection with the club and was saddled with a reputation for producing teams that played a functional rather than flamboyant style of football. His approach was the total opposite to what the Hammers were supposed to represent, but Sam made a good point when he said that the West Ham way clearly hadn't worked because we'd been relegated.

I'd be lying if I said I thought the quality of football was anything to write home about during the 2011/12 season, but I was prepared to tolerate it and accept it as a necessary sacrifice if we won promotion. I think a lot of fans shared that view. Sam's job was to get us back into the Premier League and everything else was secondary. Whether you necessarily need to play that particular way to get out of the division was a matter of debate, with the likes of Swansea City and Norwich City playing stylish football on the way to promotion the previous year, but we had to keep our fingers crossed and hope.

We were looking on course for automatic promotion for

most of the season, but a disappointing run of seven home games without a win – six of which were draws – towards the end of the campaign proved costly as Reading and Southampton snapped up the top two places. I can't help but think we under-achieved by finishing third with the squad we had, which was surely the best in the division, but it was only our home form that let us down because the team set an incredible club record for winning thirteen away league games (fourteen if you include the play-off semi-final victory at Cardiff City). That's a big break from tradition – we're supposed to be rubbish north of Watford!

Sadly, I was unable to work at the final half a dozen home games, including the play-off semi-final second leg against Cardiff (we won 5-0 on aggregate), because I was suffering problems with both of my knees. I twisted my left knee when we played at Watford very early in the season and was in agony the whole game. It was so painful that I couldn't sleep for the next few nights. The discomfort settled down for a few months before getting worse again and although I was able to fulfil my desk duties at the *Recorder,* I struggled at matches because of all the moving around required and eventually had to stop shooting the games.

I had an MRI scan and X-rays, which revealed serious wear and tear in my left knee, to the extent that there was virtually nothing left of the cartilage and bone was rubbing on bone. Now I know how Julian Dicks felt with his knee problems in the early 1990s. I was told that I needed a total knee replacement and, as if that wasn't bad enough, my surgeon advised me that because of the extra pressure I'd been putting on my better knee, the right one was also going to need doing fairly soon afterwards. I was hoping to have the first operation in the summer of 2012, but as I write it's impossible to know how soon I'll be back at Upton Park to cover games – hopefully at the start of the 2012/13 season.

My knee problems meant that, as had been the case in 2005, I was unable to attend the Championship play-off final. Since I'd been working when we lost to Crystal Palace in the 2004 final, a few of my friends were actually rather happy for me to stay away from our big Wembley date against Blackpool in the belief that my presence would not bring the best of luck! I managed to get my girlfriend Tash and her father some tickets, but settled down to watch the game on television at home. And my absence appeared to do the trick – the Hammers won 2-1 thanks to goals from Carlton Cole and Ricardo Vaz Tê. Tom Ince – son of former Hammer Paul – scored Blackpool's equaliser shortly after half-time and I wasn't feeling very confident as we rode our luck and suffered a few scares in the second period. Even after Vaz Tê struck West Ham's second goal with just a few minutes remaining, I was still reluctant to believe we'd actually won promotion until the final whistle went – and then I started to wonder who was going to threaten some kind of legal challenge, seeing as that seems to happen whenever we think we've achieved something.

I still believe we should have returned to the Premier League without having to endure the nail-biting stress of the play-offs, but plenty of people will say that winning at Wembley – and it was our first game there since 1981 – is the best way of winning promotion. At the end of the day, Sam Allardyce fulfilled his brief and took us back up on the first attempt, and we have to be grateful for that. We now need to enjoy a safe season in the Premier League; I don't think we can afford to go down again. We must stay in the top flight because that's where we belong and hopefully the club's financial burdens will be considerably eased, although you can end up spending a lot of money simply trying to compete.

Winning promotion wasn't the only battle the club was involved in at that point in time. The Hammers were also trying to secure the right to play in the Olympic Stadium from 2014. Opinion over the prospective move was divided from the very start and I was firmly in the group that wanted the club to remain at Upton Park. I'm a traditionalist and have spent most of my working life at the Boleyn Ground, so it shouldn't surprise people to learn that I like the stadium and would prefer to stay there. I know there are lots of problems in terms of redeveloping certain parts of the ground if the club wants to increase its capacity, but that would be my ideal solution rather than move away from Green Street.

Having said that, I was talking to Billy Bonds about the subject a while back and he told me he wasn't particularly against the idea of the club moving because it wasn't as if we'd be leaving the Boleyn Ground we all knew and loved. The Chicken Run has gone, the atmosphere isn't what it used to be and it's just not the same any more since it was redeveloped as an all-seater stadium in the 1990s.

He's got a point, but I remain convinced that Upton Park is our natural home. I also had massive worries about the Olympic Stadium itself: the crowd would be so far away from the pitch because of the running track and it's a huge number of seats to try and fill. I just can't see where we're going to get 60,000 fans from. If we need to reduce admission prices to attract more supporters, it defeats the purpose of moving to a bigger stadium, as far I'm concerned. I still think 40,000 would be the right capacity for West Ham and that can surely be achieved by redeveloping Upton Park.

Therefore, with all this in mind, I was disappointed when the

Olympic Park Legacy Committee provisionally awarded the new stadium to West Ham after approving their joint bid with Newham Council in February 2011. It wasn't a decision I wanted but it was one that I came to accept – unlike rival bidders Tottenham Hotspur, who did everything possible to contest the verdict. Spurs had planned to demolish the stadium rather than have it adapted for football and I could never see how that was going to be allowed to happen. The OPLC must have agreed because they voted 14-0 in favour of the West Ham/Newham bid.

Personally, I always suspected that Tottenham had ulterior motives and their challenge against the decision had more to do with trying to put pressure on various authorities to support their building of a new stadium in their own borough. And as for Leyton Orient, who also stuck their oar in and tried to block the move, I can't help but think that chairman Barry Hearn was looking for financial compensation more than anything else. I don't think he had a legitimate complaint about West Ham moving closer to Brisbane Road – we would still be in the borough of Newham and the competition for support between the two clubs already existed.

I was astonished when it was announced in October 2011 that West Ham's bid for the Olympic Stadium had collapsed because of the subsequent legal challenges and that a new procedure was being set up for interested parties to apply for purely rental use instead. Once again, West Ham confirmed their intention to bid for use of the stadium but my concerns became even greater now that the club would be leaving Upton Park for a place they wouldn't even own. You just don't know what might happen further down the line and there's also the issue of the club losing the right to earn additional revenue from the stadium because of only playing there as tenants. I believed the situation was fraught with problems.

It was announced that the identity of the leasing tenants would be announced in May 2012, but then the London Legacy Development Corporation declared that the decision was going to be delayed at least a couple of months. I can't say I was devastated, but I still think the way the whole affair has been conducted by the authorities is ridiculous. Time will tell if the final decision this year is the right one for West Ham.

I suppose it's inevitable that I am so nostalgic about the Boleyn Ground after taking photographs there for nearly forty years. The terraces used to be much closer to the pitch, so wherever I positioned myself, whether in front of the North Bank or South Bank, the crowd would be right behind me, literally breathing down my neck. You'd build up a repartee with different people who would stand in the same place at every game. In the South Bank, for example, there were a couple of old girls – and I mean old – who would always be there in their usual spot with their claret and blue scarves around their necks. They used to appear in the opening credits of *The Big Match*. They would give me a cup of tea from their flask at half-time or offer some cake. I suppose I did develop something of a cake habit.

With the crowd so close to the pitch – especially in the Lower East Stand, otherwise known as the Chicken Run – there was always an electric atmosphere for evening games at Upton Park. It's no accident that some of West Ham's most memorable results have been in midweek matches. Everyone talks about the great nights under the floodlights, but the fact is that the lights were never very good from a photographer's point of view. The floodlights were upgraded when more games started appearing on television, but they've never been brilliant. There was a massive improvement when they built the Bobby Moore Stand and the Trevor Brooking Stand, but when they added the roof extensions after the rebuilding of the West Stand, the floodlights remained in their old position. The pitch was moved but the lights were no longer level with the corner flags and so the corners do tend to be a bit dark.

My match-day routine at home games has changed a lot over the years and I'm much busier than I used to be. As I've said, I try to arrive at Upton Park about two hours before kick-off and my first job is to meet the mascots, of which there can be up to a dozen. They get changed into their West Ham kits and we do a variety of pictures, with the kids sitting in the dug-out, standing in the tunnel with the West Ham crest behind them and having a kick-about on the pitch. When the players have arrived I'm allowed to take the mascots into the dressing room for some pictures. And just before kick-off, we lead them into the centre circle and they pose for the camera with the team captains and the match officials.

It can sometimes be an overwhelming experience for young children to stand in the middle of a packed stadium with lots of players around them, so I have a word with them beforehand and tell them to just look at the camera and ignore any distractions. It's always difficult trying to get an entire group of people to look at you perfectly for a photograph and it's even harder when 30,000 spectators are watching and time is of the essence. I get a maximum of three attempts and that's it, then I have to try and get off the pitch without being taken out by one of the youngsters (thankfully the Wolves game was a one-off to date).

I also have to take pictures of various sponsors and

corporate clients during the build-up to each game. The commercial staff will bring people down to the pitch for photographs and occasionally there will be a presentation being made to somebody that needs to be captured by the camera. We generally tend to have special guests – former athlete Kriss Akabusi, for example – who will be interviewed by announcer Jeremy Nicholas and sometimes allowed to read out the team-sheet (if they can be trusted). Again, I have to get pictures of everything that's going on before the game.

I always feel happier once the pre-match obligations have been met and I can concentrate on the game itself. Photographers traditionally sit by the touchline between the goal and the corner flag to get the best vantage point. But with the advent of advertising hoardings, we've since been pushed into various different areas around the pitch. I used to work with two different cameras: one with a short lens to shoot across the goal and another with a long lens to shoot down the pitch. But most clubs only allow photographers to work from the sides now, so I favour working with one camera with a 300mm lens, which gives me a good sweep across to the nearest goal and also down the pitch. It means I can shoot both goalmouths if required, although I'm obviously tighter on the action if the play is up at my end.

We have two dug-outs in the West Stand – or the Alpari Stand, as it is now known – and they are level with the perimeter line of each eighteen-yard box. It's not a bad position but the sight lines are very low and you do tend to have a worm's-eye view. In the past, we always used to kick towards the Trevor Brooking Stand in the first half if possible, but for some reason that changed in 2011 when captain Kevin Nolan opted to play towards the Bobby Moore Stand instead. He's caught me out on a few occasions and I've either had to leg it down to the other end or work from where I am and hope for the best.

For a Premier League game at Upton Park, there are around forty photographers at work whereas in the old days there would just be five or six of us covering a match. There was a lot of camaraderie on the touchline in the 1970s; we'd all exchange tips and have a real laugh. You had the doyen of sports photography, a guy called Monte Fresco who worked for the *Daily Mirror*; then there was Peter Jay, who worked for *The Sun* and is sadly no longer with us; Lawrence Lustig started his career around the same time as me; and you'd also see Kent Gavin, another famous name in sports photography, as well as Reg Lancaster. These guys were pretty famous Fleet Street photographers but they were so helpful if you were a new boy on the touchline.

In the old days, goals were the most important thing to capture during a game, but now celebration shots tend to get used more often. I'll also look to capture key incidents, such as bookings, red cards, disputes between players and injuries. A player might limp off with the physio and be out for six months, so suddenly that picture takes on a greater significance. You have to try and cover everything. Once upon a time, I'd get through about three rolls of film of thirty-six exposures, so would have around 120 pictures, but now I shoot digitally and can bash away to my heart's content and take a couple of hundred shots if I want to. If I've got time at the break, I sometimes edit things down by deleting stuff.

After a goal has been scored, you will generally see a lot of photographers looking at the back of their cameras to see if they have got the big shot or not. You might wonder why they would bother given they can't exactly re-wind time and try again. But what happens is that a lot of photographers swap material. If you've got a bunch of guys working together in that way, it means everybody gets the shot they're looking for.

The newspapers are fully aware that it goes on but they don't usually have a problem because it guarantees that they're not going to miss out on the picture that really matters. I know the sports editor at the *Daily Mail* at one particular time told his photographer not to get involved in such arrangements, but he soon changed his mind after a couple of months when he realised he wasn't getting the shots he wanted. You can't always get every picture and sometimes you've got the shot, sometimes the next guy has. But if you look in the newspapers, you'll see the same picture with a variety of different photographers' credits. It's exactly the same principle as sports journalists sharing player and manager quotes or all agreeing to take the same angle with their stories on a particular day. It means everybody has his or her backside covered.

We used to use the term 'gissa neg' for swapping material, but I'm not sure what you'd call it now we're all shooting digitally. It's so much better nowadays because you know exactly what you've got from a game. I had my initial reservations about digital photography because the quality just wasn't there. But it's improved so much over the past ten years that the difference between digital and film is now negligible. Digital photography is also so much more practical. If I was working at a night game, I'd be forced to return to the offices of the *Recorder* to process the film. I'd have to develop the film, using a film-processing unit with a timer switch controlling the heat, hang it up in a drying cabinet and then print up the pictures. But now I just take the memory card out of the camera, put it into the reader and the material is immediately transferred to my PC or laptop. There are even systems that send the images to the laptop without having to take the card out of the camera.

Once the game is over, the only remaining task of the day is to shoot the man-of-the-match presentation, which can involve a bit of hanging around. The players don't generally appear too quickly after the final whistle and if we've had a bad result they're often not particularly desperate to show their faces. But it's something they have to do – even if it means somebody at the club cajoling them into it. I sometimes find the man-of-the-match verdict is based less on performance and more on who the sponsors want to meet. I remember when Kevin Nolan was announced as the winner towards the end of our home game against Barnsley in December 2011 and half the crowd booed the decision. When I went up to the executive box after the game I discovered it was full of his mates and they obviously wanted Kevin to join them for a beer. Maybe they should rename it 'the player that the sponsors would most like to share a can of lager with' award. I've been in boxes when people have voted for somebody who hasn't even played!

The corporate side of things at West Ham has grown spectacularly over the years, particularly after the club redeveloped the West Stand and built lots of executive boxes. It reflects how much the game has changed since the advent of the Premier League and clubs are now so dependent on their commercial revenue.

It probably goes without saying that I gain most job satisfaction from shooting the games, but I'm perfectly happy to cover all the other requirements of the club on match day. When I first got involved in this line of work, Arthur Edwards, the man who passed over his agency work to me in the early 1970s, told me, 'Five per cent of being a good photographer is pressing the shutter, the other ninety-five per cent is dealing with people.' The quality of the shot often depends on how well you handle people and I've been told on various occasions that it's one of my best attributes. It's about talking to people in the right way so that they're comfortable and will give you what you want.

It obviously helps that people often feel as if they know me, and the fact that I'm such a recognisable face at West Ham can only be an advantage, even if it does sometimes lead to a little embarrassment when David Gold is around. Believe it or not, however, there are more famous faces around at the club than mine – and I'm not talking about the players.

Ray Winstone would be a good example of a celebrity who genuinely supports West Ham and tries to get to Upton Park for games as often as possible. I first met Ray when he was competing for Repton Amateur Boxing Club and I was covering a variety of sports for the local press. A lot of people don't realise he was a very good boxer and won eighty out of his eighty-eight fights. I took pictures of him in those days and have followed his acting career with great interest.

Years later, Ray started coming back to West Ham now and again and we'd say hello to each other. 'Oh yeah, I remember you,' he'd say. 'They were good old days down at Repton, weren't they?' Then he acquired the use of an executive box at Upton Park and became more involved with the club. I thought it was very unfair that he got a bit of stick for being given a good deal on a box in return for undertaking promotional work for the club. He commands huge figures for advertising and to hire him would cost a fortune, so I didn't think a contra deal was a bad arrangement. Yet he got some undeserved criticism when it became public knowledge because some people thought that he was freeloading.

Ray was always very friendly and would tell me to pop into his box any time to have a drink. I went up there one day after a game when I had some time to kill and fancied a beer. 'Stevie, come in, come in,' he said when he saw my face appear around the door. He put his arm around me, turned to his mates and said, 'Right you lot, all you Johnny-come-latelies. Me and Stevie go back thirty years. He's a real mate, not like you lot!' I was chuffed and I've been quite pally with him ever since. He'd come to various functions at the club and would sometimes say, 'Are you coming for a beer afterwards?' We'd go to a place in Woodford run by the guy who used to be the landlord of a pub in his village. Ray was never flash, but he just had a way of never letting you pay for anything. Halfway through the evening his mate would turn up with a load of shellfish and tell you to tuck in. Ray is just a nice guy and is great company.

One celebrity who did surprise me when I first met him at Upton Park was comedian Russell Brand. Personally, I've always thought he needed a good wash and could never work out why women seem to find him so fascinating. Russell was at a game one day and a few females in the corporate department were rather keen on me taking a picture of them with him. He came into the lounge and I was amazed when he walked over to me and said, 'Hello, Steve, how are you? You've been here for a long while, haven't you?' It was nice to be recognised by him, but he had the most limp-wristed handshake I've ever experienced. I still can't understand what girls see in him – but maybe I'm just jealous!

Len Goodman, who's the head judge on *Strictly Come Dancing*, is a staunch Hammers fan and I got to meet him through Caron Pettit, who is a match-day hostess at West Ham and knew James Goodman, Len's son. It was coming up to Christmas and Caron asked if I could supply a copy of my photographic book and get some pictures signed for him. I said it was no problem and James subsequently gave them to Len as a gift. A couple of months later, the *Strictly Come Dancing* tour was at the O2 in Greenwich and, as a thank you, Len arranged for Caron and me to have a couple of tickets. We even went backstage to meet him and have a chat. He then came to a West Ham game as a guest in one of the lounges.

We've seen comedian James Corden over at Upton Park and singer David Essex is another face that pops up now and again and generally says hello; Tommy Walsh, the celebrity builder, has been over for several games; and, perhaps inevitably, we've had various members of the *EastEnders* cast at the ground, including Todd Carty and Perry Fenwick. Somebody I didn't expect to see at a West Ham game many years ago was comedian Frank Carson, who sadly passed away in February 2012. That man could certainly talk! He never stopped coming out with one-liners and when he was being introduced to the players and manager, John Lyall was forced to say, 'For Christ's sake, get him out of the dressing room!' I took a picture of Frank being dragged away by the police, which we set up before his jokes got any more criminal.

With the greatest of respect to all the above names, however, they all pale into insignificance compared to one distinguished visitor to the Boleyn Ground in May 2002. I'm talking, of course, about Her Majesty the Queen, who paid a unique visit to Upton Park – no, not to see a game – as part of her Golden Jubilee celebrations and to officially open the new West Stand. The amount of organisation and planning for the big event was unbelievable, especially in terms of learning about protocol and what one should or should not do, if one was lucky enough to be present.

A few days beforehand, we had a big rehearsal at the club of what was set to take place. I think one of the office girls played the Queen – I can only assume that Helen Mirren was unavailable, though admittedly it was a few years before she portrayed Elizabeth II – and somebody stood in for the Duke of Edinburgh, who would be accompanying her. We had to run through everything and we were told in no uncertain terms exactly where we should stand and that we mustn't – under any circumstances – break from the line.

On the day itself, we all had to arrive at the ground very early in order to gain access before the immediate area was sealed off. One of the club's security guys mentioned something about opening the car door but he was quickly told that the Queen's security personnel would take that responsibility, and only when they were convinced that the area was safe. I'd been given strict instructions about where I should stand but thankfully my old friend Arthur Edwards, who by that stage was well established and highly respected as the royal photographer for *The Sun* and good friends with Prince Charles, was also on the visit and he said, 'Just follow me. If you stick with me you'll be all right.' All the private bodyguards knew him so he had the licence to move around.

When the Queen arrived, she stepped out of the vehicle and as Arthur walked forwards, I went with him. I half expected to be wrestled to the ground by the security services, but the fact that I was with Arthur seemed to buy me some freedom. The Queen was set to meet some of the West Ham players and nobody else had been allowed to use the elevator. In fact, we even had an engineer from the lift company on standby just in case anything went wrong and she ended up getting stuck. That might have seemed rather unlikely but you just never know with West Ham.

As it happened, Joe Cole had that very morning been named as part of the England squad for the forthcoming World Cup finals in South Korea and Japan, so that was the picture we believed we needed – the Queen with the West Ham midfielder. But Joe hadn't been scheduled to meet the Queen and we were told that it was totally out of the question. However, I mentioned the idea to Arthur and he thought it might be possible. 'Leave it to me,' he said. He had a few words in somebody's ear and returned to say he'd fixed it. So we got Joe down to the ground floor and we took a nice picture of him in front of a plaque with the Queen. They seemed to get on very well with each other.

The royal parties went upstairs to have lunch with chairman Terence Brown and a select group of people. I later asked Terry what the Queen was like and he told me that she was really good company. She had chosen the menu and decided to have crème brûlée for desert. Everybody on the table was waiting for her to take the lead and she picked up the spoon and said, 'Oh well, here goes.' Bang, bang, bang, right through the layer of hard caramel on the top. And everybody followed suit. Then the Queen and the Duke came back downstairs, signed the special book and off they went. It was a big day for me, even though I wasn't formally introduced to the Queen. Not that I think that was really necessary, given that she probably knew who I was anyway...!

My mother Eileen was a very big fan of the royal family and she loved Arthur because he was always very nice to her. Arthur is very old school and a real charmer. He phoned me up one day and said, 'The Captain of the Queen's Flight is in town for the weekend and he's a big Manchester United fan. He'd love to see them play at West Ham. Any chance of a couple of tickets?' I thought, 'You do pick the big ones, Arthur!'

I said I'd see what I could do and made a call to the club while laying it on thick about how important this guy was, being the Captain of the Queen's Flight. I managed to secure a pair of tickets and Arthur said he'd come round to pick them up. We were sitting and chatting and Mum was telling Arthur what a fantastic job he had. He asked Mum if she had his book and he promised to send a signed copy to her. After he'd left, my mum said, 'What an important man he is.' I said, 'Yeah, I suppose so, but what about when he wants tickets for West Ham?' She said, 'What do you mean?' And I said, 'When he wants tickets for West Ham, who does he need to come to?' And she said, 'Well, you.' I said, 'Exactly! He might be a very important man, but he can't get West Ham tickets, can he?' And she was like, 'Yes, I see what you mean.'

Okay, I was having a little joke there, but I can't help thinking I've been extremely fortunate as I reflect back over the past forty years. I've had a great life and things could easily have been so different had manager John Lyall not embraced me into the West Ham fold in the way that he did. So many things in my life would not have happened if it hadn't been for my role with the club and I'd have missed out on so many great experiences. People have asked me if I've ever wanted to do anything else apart from take photographs of West Ham, or why I've not worked for the national media, and I can honestly say that I've always been totally happy working for the club and the local press.

I always considered it an immense privilege to travel with the management and players to games and stay overnight with the squad in hotels around the country and on our rare trips abroad. I loved the camaraderie with the players

– especially during the 1980s when there was a tremendous bond between everybody – and developed an emotional attachment to the club that will never go away. I was made to feel a part of the team in a way that was totally unique for a photographer and that says everything about the kind of people who have been involved with the club over the years.

I feel indebted to managers John Lyall, Lou Macari, Billy Bonds and Harry Redknapp, in particular, and I have enjoyed some great friendships with former players such as Sir Trevor Brooking, Tony Gale, Ray Stewart, Frank Lampard, Paul Brush, Phil Parkes and Alan Devonshire, to name but a few. And there are so many other people in the game who I've got to know over the years and who continue to say hello when visiting Upton Park in whatever capacity. That means such a lot to me and I consider that to be one of the perks of the job.

I love bumping into people like Liam Brady and having a chat. Former Liverpool star Sammy Lee always finds time to shake my hand and asks how I am. I didn't have many dealings with defender Malky Mackay when he played for West Ham, but as a manager he made a special effort to approach me when he brought Cardiff City to Upton Park in 2011/12. The football is one thing but it's the people in the game who have provided so many great memories – well, most of the time. And I must say a special thank you to the Hammers fans, who have always made me feel at home with their support and sense of humour.

West Ham have had plenty of peaks and troughs over the last forty years and I've inevitably had my ups and downs during that period as well. I will never remember Alan Pardew's arrival at the club with any affection and I had some dark days with my health at that time too. I was also disappointed to miss the climax of our recent promotion campaign. But overall I've had a fantastic time and like to think I've not done too badly for a regular lad from Manor Park. Over the years, people have told me that they really envy me for being so closely involved with a football club as nice as West Ham.

There was certainly something very special about the club. I can't deny that it has changed somewhat in recent years – as indeed has the game as a whole – but it was one of the last clubs to do so and it deserves much credit for that. I was lucky to be involved in what was a special club. I've somehow survived at Upton Park while everything else has moved on – including the owners, directors, managers and players, not to mention the shape of the Boleyn Ground itself.

I suppose you can reach a point where you're considered a valuable part of the furniture that should remain in place. I can remember former managing director Paul Aldridge once saying that he wasn't going to be 'the man who got rid of Stevie Bacon'. The club might want to move certain players out when their time is up, but nobody wants to be the one who points me towards the exit gates.

There are times when I wonder what my contribution has really been, but I like to think I've done a good job of capturing many great moments in West Ham's history in photographs that will live on long after I've shuffled off this mortal coil. One supporter recently told me that if he died there would be nobody at his funeral but that when I pop my clogs there would be hundreds of people there. I guess that could be one way of looking at things, but at this point I'd just like to say that there is only one Stevie Bacon – and he's got no plans to say goodbye to life at West Ham United just yet.

Also available from Biteback

AN IRRATIONAL HATRED OF LUTON

ROBERT BANKS

"A rattling good read" John Inverdale

Laugh-out-loud funny, and devastatingly poignant,
An Irrational Hatred of Luton is an odyssey through the
world of a committed West Ham supporter. A real-life *Fever
Pitch*, and with a Hornby-esque deftness of tone, Banks's
book shows how intricately football interconnects with the
everyday for the most committed of fans. Banks's friendships,
relationships, work, joy and despair all take place against a
backdrop of claret and blue. Then Saturday comes and he
watches his team get thumped again. A compelling and hilarious journey into the nature of obsession.

336pp paperback, £9.99
Available from all good bookshops or order from
www.bitebackpublishing.com

Also available from Biteback

MR MOON HAS LEFT THE STADIUM

JEREMY NICHOLAS

"Laugh-out-loud funny" Simon Walters, *Mail on Sunday*

Jeremy Nicholas is West Ham United's stadium announcer.
A supporter since the age of six, Jeremy's blood runs claret
and blue. In the summer of 1998, after decades in the stands,
he became the voice of his club – announcing the players, the
substitutions, the trials and tribulations, and best of all the
goals. *Mr Moon Has Left the Stadium* is the hilarious tale of
one man's obsession with football and doing things the right
way. Part love story, part autobiography, part nostalgia, it will
make you laugh and cry.

320pp paperback, £12.99
Available from all good bookshops or order from
www.bitebackpublishing.com